THE
SECRET
SHARERS

STUDIES IN CONTEMPORARY FICTIONS

Bruce Bassoff

AMS PRESS
New York

Library of Congress Cataloging in Publication Data

Bassoff, Bruce, 1941–
   The secret sharers.

   (AMS ars poetica, ISSN 0734-7618; 1)
   Includes bibliographical references.
   1. Fiction —20th century—History and criticism—
Addresses, essays, lectures.   I. Title.   II. Series.
PN3503.B34   1983   809.3'04   82-20766
ISBN 0-404-62501-0

   Permission to reprint, with varying degrees of change, previously published material has been graciously granted for "Mythic Truth and Deception in *Second Skin*," *Études Anglaises*, July–September, 1977, pp. 337–342;
"Royalty in a Rainy Country: Two Novels by Paula Fox," *Critique*, December,
1978, pp. 33–48; "Freedom and Fatality in Robbe-Grillet's *Les Gommes*,"
Contemporary Literature, XX (©1979 by the Board of Regents of the University
of Wisconsin System), pp. 452-470.
   Publication of this volume has been aided by the Institute for Advanced
Study of the Euryalus Foundation of Syracuse, Sicily.

MANUFACTURED IN THE UNITED STATES OF AMERICA

To those closest to me: my parents,
Leah, Jonathan, and Evi

Contents

AMS ARS POETICA, No. 1

THE SECRET SHARERS

Preface

René Girard

The one principle about which all avant-garde writers agree is that they do not resemble each other or anyone else, not even themselves. Whatever they write should be entirely novel, innovative and original. It should be a pure experiment in writing, or rather *écriture*, or better still, "unmotivated freeplay." The lack of motivation is essential; it guarantees your originality; it protects you from *imitation*, the one unforgivable sin of our world, and not without a cause.

"Freeplay," we are told, is becoming so unmotivated at long last that henceforth all attempts at "bourgeois recuperation" must fail. We are being really liberated this time, not from superficial conventions only but from the "shackles of Western representation."

Western representation used to be called perception. It means the world as you and I see it. There have been plenty of liberators before but not radical enough. "Always already" they had sold out to the enemy. Only now we are about to get the genuine article.

What do you think of this jargon? It has proved amazingly durable. After a century and more, new variations of it are invented almost daily. Can you still muster the proper enthusiasm or do you regard, or rather disregard, the whole thing as an old record that always gets stuck in the same groove? Whichever course you follow, you probably feel vaguely discontented with it. It seems that real works of art are still being written in this "critical" climate. How must they be read? What is their true relationship to the literary conventions they always so conventionally reject?

If you feel dissatisfied with both the modernistic and the anti-modernistic ideologies, the present book is for you. Behind the consistently bad theory and sometimes good practice of contemporary writing, Bruce Bassoff reveals the presence of the one thing everybody is desperately trying to avoid: *imitation*.

To keep re-generating the rhetoric I have just outlined, it must take an ever-renewed critical mass of frantically imitative people, mimetically united in their hatred of imitation or, in Greek, *mimesis*. This is what we

ix

now have, of course, and Bruce Bassoff shows it. His book is so true to the
realities of contemporary life, especially literary life, that it cannot fail to
appear outlandish and unreal to the people who sincerely believe and
practice one or the other of the standard reactions to the ritualistically
"outrageous" literature of the present: unconditional ecstasy or unconditional rejection.

Bruce Bassoff shows that contemporary fiction makes more sense than
its detractors and even now many of its admirers would like us to
believe. He has not abdicated the major function of the interpreter, which
is to interpret. There is an element of demystification here, but it is
sympathetic and literary demystification. It does not suggest literature
should be promptly replaced by some more prestigious science or philosophy.

How does Bruce Bassoff do it? He tells us himself in the very first pages
of this book; he does not play hide and seek with his readers. Modern
fiction, he believes, is both permeated by and illustrative of mimetic, or
mediated, desire. If this desire is not immediately recognizable, the
reason is that, beyond a certain stage of its evolution, it does not acknowledge its own presence, it resorts to dissimulation. In order to
analyze these works, you must first understand the ways and masks of
mimetic desire.

As soon as mimetic desire is mentioned, the danger of misunderstanding is great. There is a large potential audience for this book, and it may
be deterred not by the reality of mimetic desire but by the sound of its
name. In a world surfeited with unworkable theories of all kinds, mimetic desire sounds like another cheap theory, derived from earlier
theories, a post-Freudian, perhaps, or a post-Marxian simplification of
Freud or Marx, another critical "gimmick" in other words.

The one good thing about critical gimmicks is that their life span is
brief. They thrive only on one kind of food, not eucalyptus leaves like
koala bears but abstract controversy, and if you do not bother with them
they will not bother you for very long; they will quickly vanish. Some
thoughtful people may feel that Bruce Bassoff and "mimetic desire"
belong to the type of criticism that is not worth bothering with. It would
be a mistake.

Mimetic desire has a lot to say about the recent theoretical craze, but it
is not part of it. Its real discoverers are the Dante of Paolo and Francesca,
the Cervantes of *Don Quixote*, the Shakespeare of *Troilus and Cressida*.
The last named writer even gives definitions of it that have never been
surpassed for elegance and accuracy. The mimetic desire of a lover is *to
choose love by another's eyes*. More generally, mimetic desire is the
vastly misunderstood and underestimated propensity of all men to practice "second hand desire," so to speak, and to unconsciously select, as
their objects, the objects already selected or about to be selected by one,

some, more or even all the other men in the vicinity.

If men desire mimetically, they must oppose as rivals the same individuals they venerate as models; and an ambivalence cannot fail to result, similar, yet very different from psychoanalytical ambivalence. Psychoanalysis tells us the real and present rival in our adult lives does not count; he is only a surrogate for dead or aged parents, and this type of message we all like to hear; whereas mimetic desire and literature place the emphasis on the truly obsessional *others* in our lives, not only our erotic, but our professional, our intellectual and our spiritual rivals.

Mimetic desire is not a philosophy or a view of the world, but a tool for the analysis of human relations in and out of texts. It is not a single static configuration but a dynamic principle of complexity. Actions and reactions on all sides of the mimetic partnership are based not on the truth of this relationship but on the misunderstanding it keeps generating.

This process has a life and a logic of its own that can be unravelled for its own sake, independently from any specific human situation. A few researchers are now discovering that this logic is useful to the study of extremely varied phenomena, ranging from ritual behavior in primitive societies to economic and social crises in our society or psychopathological symptoms. And there can be no doubt that literary works, most explicitly the greatest ones, tend to describe human relations according to this mimetic pattern.

If mimetic desire is a gimmick, it is certainly the literary gimmick par excellence. Even though literary criticism, until recently, has never perceived its interest or even identified it conceptually, its entire history indirectly testifies to its relevance. The two components of mimetic desire, *mimesis*, or imitation, and *desire*, have always dominated the literary discourse on literature but always separately. From Plato and Aristotle, down until a few years ago, *mimesis* has been the imperial concept of literary criticism. Now there is a great rebellion against it, and it is rejected with horror, in favor of desire, the Freudian conception of desire generally.

We never speak of literature therefore except in terms of *mimesis* or in terms of desire, but never the two together; it is always a *mimesis* without desire or a desire without *mimesis*, as if the critics did not dare put these two together, but always had to have at least one, knowing fully well it is impossible to say anything even remotely relevant to their subject if you eliminate both.

Thus, mimetic desire is quintessentially literary as well as more "scientific" than the Oedipus complex, and the critics who refuse to see it are moving away both from the truth and from the substance of the literary work. They always want to substitute some non-literary scheme for it, like the Freudian Oedipus, of course, or the old "character study," or the philosophic consciousness, or the monotonous tick tack of the structuralists, or the four elements of Gaston Bachelard, or the *différance* with an *a* . . . . Tomorrow it will be something else again. The more inimical to literature those non-literary ideas really are, the more they are prized by the critics, always in the name of keeping all literature pure and unadulterated.

Another disaster of twentieth-century criticism is the general consensus around Valéry's mistaken definition of literature as "le royaume des choses vagues." Many writers, no doubt, have emphasized the impressionistic and the vague, especially after the rise of science, as if to assert proprietary rights on a domain not yet claimed by this powerful rival. But, taken as an absolute, as it always is, the opposition is misleading. It partakes of an outmoded positivism. Science, too, has affinities for the vague, and literature has always cultivated certain forms of ballet-like, almost mathematical precision.

Literature alone has faithfully described the deluded and mechanical aspects of human relations, a certain geometry of desire and misunderstanding that is always identical to itself and that reappears *as such* only in the greatest writers, reproduced with clockwork accuracy. The idea that geniuses differ more from each other and everybody else in these matters than the lesser breed of less original writers is universally accepted now, but it is pure nonsense nevertheless, the typical contemporary nonsense of frantically imitative would-be originals.

It is always the same force, mimetic desire, that turns human beings into puppets in the erotic and political domains. When its manifestations become collective, it often results in arbitrary victimization. These patterns of delusion reigned supreme in comedy at first and the theater in general, then have shifted to the novel.

Philosophers and thinkers have disdained literature as pure entertainment and they have remained blind. So have literary critics under their influence. Like Polonius they want to be profound, and they always miss the real point, especially when they concern themselves with those aspects of the works they believe to be specific to literature.

How could the same mimetic principle illuminate recent fiction as well as an earlier literature? Bruce Bassoff shows us. The principle is the same, but it does not always operate in the same fashion. There is a historical dimension to the dynamics of mimetic desire. The works analyzed in the present volume, including some by Edgar Allan Poe, the great American forerunner of modernism, belong to a very advanced or, as Lucien Goldmann would have said, a most "degraded" form of mimetic desire. The discontinuities of contemporary fiction, its fragmentations, the proliferation of new narrative techniques become highly significant in this critical light. All this is not as unmotivated and gratuitously experimental as the critics and even the writers themselves profess. New techniques are needed to simultaneously hide and reveal more extreme modalities of the mimetic relationship.

The mimetic perspective combines rigor with "literariness," an unexpected combination to be sure but one that should be welcomed by literary critics uncertain about the specificity of their studies. And yet, mimetic desire is often felt to be hostile to literature, somewhat "reductive." Why is it so?

Many lovers of literature feel that "mimetic desire" is incompatible with the dignity of the art they love. It "reduces," they feel, the noblest works of the human imagination to the proportions of a bedroom farce. Does not Shakespeare himself, in *Troilus and Cressida*, reduce Homer in this fashion? Perhaps, but the reality of that Shakespeare is not yet fully acknowledged by Shakespearians in authority. Only a Frenchman perhaps. . . . Is not mimetic desire the ultimate debasement of literature, its assimilation to . . . a French triangle?

A French triangle. . . . The expression rings more than one literary bell. It rings a Joycean bell. The French triangle is mentioned in *Ulysses* at the end of the talk given by Stephen Dedalus about Shakespeare. The listeners are some Irish intellectuals who become irate under the provocations of the lecturer. One of them, John Eglinton, finally interrupts Stephen with these words: *You are a delusion. . . . You have brought us all this way to show us a French triangle.*

The observation would not sound so insulting if it were less accurate. Stephen's Shakespeare is careless, reckless, even deliberately misleading in its displacement of textual insight onto an imaginary "life" of Shakespeare, and yet, at the time of its writing, it was the most powerful revelation of mimetic desire ever achieved anywhere and in any language, regarding any literary work. It is a crucial event in the history of modern criticism, more important by far than the Freudian reading of Oedipus which is pointedly rejected in the course of that very lecture by a Joyce undoubtedly eager to prevent any confusion between what "a certain Viennese school" was doing and what he himself was doing. This lecture and *Ulysses* as a whole are unique as the birthplace of mimetic criticism, the only place where mimetic desire can be seen emerging out of the literary text into the light of its own concept. Eglinton and his cohort remain totally impervious to the genius of the presentation, completely blind to the truth that is staring them in the eyes. Eglinton correctly identifies the triangle as the configuration that keeps recurring throughout the lecture; he can formulate the secret, yet he does not see it. They have eyes and yet they do not see; they have ears and yet they do not understand.

Joyce was subject to fits of extreme mimetic jealousy. The prominent role played by mimetic desire in his work was certainly rooted in this fascination; he felt that the same must have been true of Shakespeare. He obviously feels that only the creators themselves can be Secret Sharers in the full sense, fully aware of the mimetic desire; they capture it in their own words as they are captured by it in their own lives. Mimetic desire is universal but it is more extreme in a great writer like Joyce, or Shakespeare, than in most people; it is radical to the point of ridicule, and that is why it forces itself upon this writer's consciousness.

Joyce first intended to have Stephen present an interpretation not of Shakespeare but of Ibsen. It would take zero insight into Ibsen and an ineptitude on the scale of Eglinton's to believe that, had the author of Ulysses pursued his original idea and interpreted Ibsen, he would have found in it something completely different from what he found in Shakespeare. In order to justify its presence amidst the triangular and trinitarian configurations of the novel as a whole, any analysis of the type Joyce finally included in the book would have had to emphasize the same mimetic and triangular aspects that the Shakespeare lecture emphasizes, regardless of the author selected. Stephen would have shown us a French triangle in Ibsen as he did in Shakespeare, not only because Joyce needed one but because the triangle is really there, too, and plays the same crucial role in both writers. The detail would have been different but the total thrust would have remained the same and the plunge into the innermost recesses of Ibsen's creative process would have been just as vertiginous as in the case of Shakespeare.

Joyce minutely reproduced the erudite philistinism and insensitivity of Eglinton and his like in order to avenge himself of past indignities and to document his belief that writers like himself are forever separated from ordinary men by the whole breadth of an experience that is fully communicable only to the other great creators because it is shared by them, secretly shared. Second-rate intellectuals like Eglinton must go on mouthing their empty solemnities about the works they worship from afar because they simply cannot understand what Stephen is talking about. Even with their finger on the crux of the matter, they do not see the interest it could hold for a man "interested in literature."

Joyce is the patron saint of the criticism Bruce Bassoff practices, and he really presents himself as its first martyr. He anticipated the resistance it would encounter, the sensitivities it would offend, the irrelevant objections, the general incomprehension. The critics in Ulysses already encouraged each other to regard the sacred works of a writer as totally divorced from his profane life. The critical dogmas they espouse are all secretly destined to consolidate the barriers between themselves and the disquieting Joycean message. Twentieth-century critical schools have worked very hard to make these barriers even higher. No wonder the Shakespeare lecture of Ulysses is still almost universally dismissed as an inconsequential joke. Its detractors are not even bothered at the thought that a writer who is supposed to be a great wit as well as a genius, would waste more than a hundred pages of his major masterpiece stretching a pointless joke beyond all measure. Joyce was a pessimist regarding the possibilities of communication in general and of triangular criticism in particular. But he mischievously planted the wrong signals at every turn and deliberately tempted his readers into following the bad example of Eglinton. Like much of *Ulysses*, the whole episode is a magnificent posthumous joke that depends for its success on the failure of the writer as writer, on his being consistently misread as he, indeed, always was, and still is.

Bruce Bassoff behaves quite differently from his illustrious but diabolical predecessor. He does not play games with his readers. He believes that the secret of mimetic desire can be shared by all. I hope that his honesty and talent will be rewarded. We, the readers, must feel challenged to appreciate the present book as much as it deserves, both to justify the author's confidence in us and to disprove the proud cynicism of Joyce. After reading *The Secret Sharers*, we, too, will repeat the words of Eglinton: *You have brought us all this way to show us a French triangle*, but we will repeat these words in a spirit of gratitude and understanding.

This is a prediction and I hope that it will come true. But, if it did not, it would mean that Joyce was right and the secret of mimetic desire, even half a century after *Ulysses*, is not yet ready for general divulgation. In that case, let Bruce Bassoff take heart at the thought that, for some time at least, he will still be unable to share the fulness of his writers' secret except with such people as Joyce, Ibsen, Shakespeare, and a few others. For a literary critic, this is not the worst possible fate.

CHAPTER 1

After the Law

"Admit that I please you, that it is me you want
through the couples who worship me."
Edmond Jabès, "The Dialogue
of the Two Roses"

This book probably began five years ago when I taught a course on *The
Brothers Karamazov* with a colleague, Edgar Whan. Edgar was a kind of
father figure to me—a role that, despite his kindness and forbearance,
made me somewhat ambivalent toward him. Consequently, his religious
sensibility pushed me more and more toward the kind of ideological
stridency characteristic of figures like Raskolnikov and Ivan Karamazov—particularly since this stridency allowed me some impressive his-
trionics in front of our class. For the first time in my young career as a
teacher, however, reading a book with others made a difference to
me: my own efforts to vindicate myself, to make Edgar's ideas seem
quaint and old-fashioned, eventually enabled me to understand Ivan's
efforts in *The Brothers Karamazov* to claim for himself the higher law of
the higher man. Like Alyosha, whose refusal to *compete* with Ivan
allows Ivan occasionally to drop his guard, Edgar's continuing benevo-
lence toward me enabled me bit by bit to discover what I really felt and
thought. I began to see how much Ivan loathed in particular the human
beings he loved in general; how much his indignation on behalf of the
children—however deeply felt—was also a denial of any complicity in
the base impulses of his own and of his society's fathers; how much his
grand inquisitor, taking on himself all the burdens of mankind, and his
Christ, refusing all judgment and demand, were the complementary
means of freeing him from the common lot of humanity.

It was not until long afterwards that I discovered the work of René
Girard, whose book *Deceit, Desire and the Novel* had an enormous
impact on me. In that book Girard, examining the development of the
novel from Cervantes to Proust, claims that it reveals a profound transformation of human relations. As religious beliefs become less compelling and as hierarchical differences between men are gradually effaced,

1

men begin to look elsewhere for the models of behavior that they once derived from social and religious "differences." Unlike Don Quixote, who chooses a model for himself from among the ranks of legendary knights—figures who abide in a realm qualitatively different from his own—the romantic characters of Stendhal, Dostoevsky, and Proust tend to deny that they are imitating anyone but also tend to imitate (sometimes obsessively) those who differ not at all from themselves. To these others—the mediators of desire—is secretly attributed some essential differences that the desiring person can aspire to; but since these others are men like themselves—not legendary knights—they also become rivals for the objects they valorize. In other words, bemused by the freedom and autonomy that are supposed to be theirs in an enlightened world, the romantic heroes seek to relinquish this burden by scrupulously imitating others while maintaining to themselves that they have preceded these rivals. Moreover, when Dostoevsky's underground man says, "I did not believe it was the same with other people, and all my life I hid this fact about myself as a secret," he is pointing to an important difference between the curse with which he feels burdened (and which is indistinguishable from his subjectivity) and the traditional notion of original sin. Original sin was once the sanctioned, explicit truth about all men, so that no one need face the fear of being inadequate alone, whereas the inability to fulfill the modern promise of freedom has no explicit, general sanction in our culture. Modern inability is experienced instead by the individual as a personal and unique weakness, which he attempts to evade by imitating others who seem to possess the secret of success. "Denial of God," Girard points out, "does not eliminate transcendency but diverts it from the *au-delà* to the *en-deçà*. The imitation of Christ becomes the imitation of one's neighbor. The surge of pride breaks against the humanity of the mediator, and the result of this conflict is hatred."[1] Even erotic relationships are tainted by this hatred since the beloved himself or herself becomes a rival who can defeat us by withholding himself or herself from us—often in imitation of our own manifested desire. For Girard, these dizzying exchanges of desire and the traps they generate pervade all aspects of our culture and are revealed most radically in our great literature.

In later books[2] Girard shows why this rivalry—however deleterious its effects—can be better tolerated in our society than in primitive ones, which do everything they can to mitigate it. For him the basis of all social cohesion and of all cultural acquisition is imitation, but it is also the cause of the violence that threatens those goods. Since the most fundamental form of imitation is acquisitive—both animals and humans tend to reach out for what others reach out for—the conflicts implicit in such behavior may become dangerous. In human societies, where such conflicts snowball until they result in what Hobbes calls "the war of all against all," a scapegoat mechanism is released by which everyone turns spontaneously against an arbitrary victim, whose murder brings about the miracle of peace. In the eyes of the community, the victim is transformed into a god who has sowed violence in order to reap peace; and the crisis of reciprocal violence is perceived as the god's anger at those who have not showed him proper obeisances or followed the rules laid down by him. This "profound deception" frees men from the knowledge of their own violence—knowledge which is itself potentially violent since it encourages men to prepare for the probable aggression of their neighbors or to retaliate against it. It also generates rites that commemorate the community's return to peace and that continue to deflect violence outside it by means of sacrificial victims—offered up to the god whose very substance is the expelled violence. And it generates rules that prevent men's desires from converging again on the same objects—rules of exogamy, for example. At times of "sacrificial" or cultural crisis, however, when the differentiations thus established break down, everything which normally prevents violence contributes to releasing it. In one of Euripides' plays, for example, Heracles, returning from his labors, kills a usurper, Lycus, and prepares to purify himself through sacrifice. He is seized, however, by a homicidal fit of madness and murders his family, whom he mistakes for enemies. What the play brings out is that when sacrificial rites no longer accomplish their task, they swell the tide of "impure" violence that they are supposed to channel. Similarly, in *Oedipus the King* the differences that exist in the community have become sources of strife, and Oedipus attempts to debunk his political rivals: "Tell me, where have you seen clear, Tiresias, with your prophetic eyes?" They, of course, reciprocate. When order breaks down, men become doubles of one another or "enemy brothers"—like Polynices and Eteocles—and each man's attempt to thwart the violence of others only duplicates that violence. A "monstrous double," finally, a scapegoat, must substitute for all of them and restore peace. Then the cycles of ritual may begin again.

In post-primitive societies these periodic purgings have become less necessary since we have rationalized violence in the form of an independent judiciary, which is entitled to commit violence without fear of retaliation. Our society, therefore, can afford to tolerate the kinds of competition outlawed in primitive societies because we need not fear the "China syndrome" of endless reaction. For Girard the history of the modern world is marked by the gradual dissolution of what Shakespeare calls "degree"—those cultural differences that prevent things from meeting "in mere oppugnancy." It is kind of prolonged "sacrificial crisis," which allows great advancement in certain areas because of competition but which also takes its toll on personal relationships. As we shall see over and over again in this book, resentment of various kinds tends to color them all. Girard's hope for this long crisis of "degree" is that it will give birth to the first global society—a society in which there is no inside or outside, no cold wars of symmetrical opposition and mutual escalation. Given the power of our technology, however, we must be vigilant not to fall into the kind of mimetic hysteria characteristic of Jonestown since our present capacity to end violence without committing further violence is also our capacity to end the world altogether. As Girard says in a recent interview, "Only in a sacrificial crisis, which threatens all men with universal violence, is violence itself really threatened."[3]

As the holocaust has shown, we can no longer draw on the resources of sacrifice. On the one hand, our increased understanding of the victimary mechanism makes it less able to polarize violence and to reconcile the community. On the other hand, the danger shown by the holocaust is that men may attempt to revive the power of this mechanism by increasing the dosages of violence—by increasing the numbers of victims. There is much evidence in modern and contemporary literature of the imagination's attempt to come to terms with the loss of sacrificial resources. Raymond Olderman's fine book, for example, *Beyond the Waste Land*, is almost a casebook for this problem. Using Eliot's poem as a means of exploring the mythical structure of various American novels of the nineteen-sixties, Olderman reveals over and over the tendency—if not always realized—to create a sacrificial resolution of the anomie or confusion that pervades these works. Of John Hawkes's *The Lime Twig*, for example, he speaks of "exorcism" as perhaps the only possible act of love in the waste land the author has created. Of *One Flew Over the Cuckoo's Nest*, he writes that McMurphy's sacrifice "gives us, through our recognition of a difference between good and evil, a renewed belief that there is something recognizable about reality, something ordinary which will help us recover a sense that fact and fiction are distinguishable."[4] The danger of this "renewed belief," however, is that it is dependent upon the blatant villainy of Big Nurse—a figure of smothering authority and castrating momism. When I saw the film made from the book, the audience cheered wildly McMurphy's attempt to murder her. This tendency to resolve our sense of indeterminacy by means of scapegoating is the subject of Norbert Wiener's highly influential book on cybernetics, *The Human Use of Human Beings*. Wiener remarks,

> The scientist is always working to discover the order and organization of the universe, and is thus playing a game against the arch enemy, disorganization. Is this devil Manichaean or Augustinian? Is it a contrary force opposed to order or is it the very absence of order itself? The difference between these two sorts of demons will make itself apparent in the tactics

to be used against them. The Manichaean devil is an opponent, like any other opponent, who is determined on victory and will use any trick of craftiness or dissimulation to obtain this victory . . . on the other hand, the Augustinian devil, which is not a power in itself, but the measure of our own weakness, may require our full resources to uncover, but when we have uncovered it, we have in a certain sense exorcised it.

Exorcism comes of itself, so to speak; no rite of exorcism is needed.[5] The Augustinian view is difficult to maintain, however; it tends to yield before the clarity and the simplicity of the Manichaean view.

In exposing the sacrificial victim as the source of our progressive cultural differentiations, Girard finds precedents in the Bible, which both reveal and rehabilitate the victim: "From the earlier stages of the Bible down to the most recent texts, there is a process that moves in the reverse direction of myth: the rehabilitation of the victim, not as a god or a demon, but as a man."[6] When John Gardner, for example, decides to rewrite the Beowulf legend, he does so from the point of view of the victim, whose monstrousness is a function of his cultural role *vis à vis* the Scyldings: "You drive them to poetry, science, religion, all that makes them what they are for as long as they last. You are, so to speak, the brute existence by which they learn to define themselves."[7] Beowulf, like Oedipus, comes from the outside to be a monster killer. Oedipus, however, is really a double of the monster he slays the monster of social undifferentiation. The sphinx is a mixture of differences (woman's head, lion's body, serpent's tail, and eagle's wings), and Oedipus is also: son and husband, brother and father mixed together. That Tiresias also is a monster—a hermaphrodite who mixes together the two sexes—shows that all of the superficial differences in the play conceal the fundamental sameness of mutual imitation and rivalry. The crimes attributed to Oedipus alone—crimes that suggest the dissolution of the *polis*—are alibis for his expulsion. Beowulf is also a double of the monster he slays. Both of them are identified with the nihilistic dragon whose "wrath" is the chaos and meaninglessness that underlie the universe. Grendel describes himself as "like a dragon burning his way through vines and fog," and Beowulf later appears to Grendel with the "terrible fiery wings" of the dragon. That the victim is chosen arbitrarily to bear the blame for the community's malaise (like the brother whose body is exposed to the dogs in *Antigone*) is indicated by the "lie" purveyed by the "Shaper" (the Bard) in *Grendel*:

It was a coldblooded lie that a god had lovingly made the world and set out the sun and moon as lights to land-dwellers, that brothers had fought, that one of the races was saved, the other cursed. Yet he, the old Shaper, might make it true, by the sweetness of his harp, his cunning trickery. It came to me with a fierce jolt that I wanted it. As they did too, though vicious animals, cunning, cracked with theories. I wanted it, yes! Even if I must be the outcast, cursed by the rules of his hideous fable.

Grendel is a monster only insofar as he is the double of all the others— the conduit for their violence or objective guilt. His mother, he says, imagines that she is guilty "of some unremembered, perhaps ancestral crime. (She must have some human in her.)" But he is one with the community in his need for some order and meaning to his existence. As the victim of this deconstructed myth, he reveals to us how arbitrary is the mechanism that generates such meaning: "I'd meant them no harm, but they'd attacked me again, as always . . . I was transformed. I was a new focus for the clutter of space I stood in: if the world had once imploded on the tree where I waited, trapped and full of pain, it now blasted outward, away from me, screeching terror." Similarly, both Beowulf, whose "madman's single-mindedness" makes him "useful in a monster fight," and Grendel are described as insane. It is an infectious violence or insanity that passes from person to person and discharges itself by and against the monster who represents it. (Similarly, a king's bear is described as being "like the young king's anger removed to the end of a chain.")

That Grendel is the point of view of the story indicates an awareness in the world of the book that mitigates the sacralization of the victim—his transformation into a god. He says at one point, "I create the whole universe, blink by blink.—An ugly god pitifully dying in a tree!" But the old gods of violence have already lost their reconciling power. They are revealed as "lifeless sticks," "dry sticks" that the Shaper has turned into gold. But the Shaper is about to die. Grendel describes himself, the Scyldings, and Beowulf as machines, grinding away in their "bloodlust and rage" like a millwheel. A sense of deadness is everywhere: in the eyes of the universal dragon; in the gray eyes of the Shaper; and in the "large, dead eyes" of the ring of gods, whose king is revealed as "the ultimate limitation . . . and His existence is the ultimate irrationality." This continuing inertia of a system that is ceasing to function is represented most dramatically by the goat that repeatedly tries to climb a hill while Grendel pelts it with rocks: "I smile, threatened by an animal already dead, still climbing." Even the sun now climbs "mechanical as a goat," and the coming of the Geats is described in the same terms: "I awaken with a start and imagine I hear the goat still picking at the cliff wall, climbing to the mere. Something groans, far out at sea." Already the state has replaced the tribe, and already men are debunking the arbitrary separation of "legitimate" from "illegitimate" violence: "The state is an organization of violence, a monopoly of what it is pleased to call *legitimate* violence."

"Grendel's law," which sets limits to the amount of violence he can commit if he is to maintain "the gold-egg-laying goose," is that no limit exists for desire but "desire's needs." And desire needs limits. That these limits may now be the fads of popular culture makes them no less binding (though much more ephemeral) than the mores and institutions that men have traditionally taken for granted. The great change in our civilization is that we have come to regard with suspicion all demands made on us from the "outside"—from "society." In the wake of Freud and of "the triumph of the therapeutic," we know that we sublimate— that we sacrifice certain satisfactions of impulse in the hope that we will get back something better; but that awareness makes it difficult to sublimate since we now also wonder whether what we get back is really worth the sacrifice. To relinquish old controls, however, is not to be "abandoned" for long but to assume new ones. As Philip Rieff points out, consumption has become our popular discipline. Our means of release have become means of control.

For Rieff modern man, or "psychological man," emphasizes means rather than ends and is careful not in invest his energy in unprofitable commitments. Freud's is

> a startling inversion of the traditional concern: moral ideas are named as the *problem* in life rather than as the basis for a solution to the problem. The Freudian dislike of social idealism, as a way of symbolizing and masking power, emerges as a powerful suspicion of self-sacrifice as sickness. Placing satisfaction even before achievement, Freudian doctrine questions all achievements by asking first of all what sort of satisfactions they permit.[8]

For Freud, moreover, "human nature is not so much a hierarchy of high-low, and good-bad, as his predecessors believed, but rather a jostling democracy of contending predispositions, deposited in every nature in roughly equal intensities."[9] This kind of leveling is reflected perhaps in the anti-representational aesthetic of certain writers and painters. Gertrude Stein, for example, claims that her experience of Flaubert and Cézanne gave her a new sense of composition: "Up to that time composition had consisted of a central idea, to which everything else was an accompaniment and separate but was not an end in itself, and Cézanne conceived the idea that in composition one thing was as important as another thing. Each part is as important as the whole, and that impressed me enormously."[10] This claim is referred to approvingly by William Gass:

> She realized that the reality of the model had been superseded by the reality of the composition. Everything in the painting was related to everything else in the painting, and to everything else equally (there were no

lesser marks or moments), while the relation of any line or area of color in the painting to anything outside the painting . . . was accidental, superfluous, illusory . . . In any real whole or self-ordered system [like biology, art or mathematics] . . . there was a wonderful and democratic equality of value and function.[11]

Perhaps the most wonderful of these systems, however, is advertising, which makes use of the fact that virtually anything can be made to signify anything else. Cigarette smoke, for example, can be made to signify "spring-time freshness" because images can be combined in a variety of ways. One might object that advertisements, unlike the compositions of Stein, are tendentious, that they have central ideas around which everything else is arranged. But are Stein's compositions really free of central ideas? Are they a perfect democracy of elements? Taking as a touchstone her famous emphasis on repetition, is everything in her work repeated? or does she repeat selectively? If everything is equally important, one thing should not be repeated more than another. Stein's view of composition is really a defense of subjective freedom, but if art disavows its critical function—its need to reveal even as it reflects the relations of order, disorder, and desire—then the only real difference between it and advertising is the greater degree of concealment it entails: "In *Tender Buttons*," Gass says, "the conflict between concealment and expression is especially intense. This kind of contest can sometimes lead to the most beautiful and powerful of consequences, so long as the victory of concealment remains incomplete, so long as the drapery leads us to dream and desire and demand the body we know it covers, so long as passions speak through rectitude, so long as impulse laughs with the lips of duty."[12] That there is something to reveal, though Gass is somewhat prudish about playing the critic, shows that these compositions have *meaning*—that their openness has limits. Writers like Gass and Stein, however, share with the Freudian interpreter a distrust of plot, which Freudians call "secondary revision" when dealing with dreams. The function of secondary revision is to give a false sense of unity and coherence to the dream in order to make it more acceptable. Similarly, Stein and Gass want to free fiction from the forms of history and to allow it the freedom of spontaneous combination of word and image. For this kind of fiction, as for psychoanalysis, the main thing is not to lie, and the social and psychological *topoi* that determine the movement of plot and the development of character are seen as lies. For this kind of suspicion, two kinds of solution have been common in modern aesthetics: silence and pastiche. The aesthetic of silence tries to make a virtue out of a necessity—our embarrassed relation to our cultural patrimony. Similarly, pastiche puts everything one writes into quotation marks so that our stories become accounts of how others tell stories. If the psychological motivation of nineteenth-century fiction indicates a loss of faith in the controlling motifs of Western tradition, pastiche and silence are the wisdom that shows itself by sarcasm.

Modern fiction may be full of gratuitous acts and arbitrary motives—of Lafcadio's and Meursault's—but these figures are not persuasive. The "stranger's" wish, at the end of Camus's novel, is for reconciliation with others though he disguises this fact by calling for their curses. In truth, personal autonomy is always elsewhere—available in principle through all the commodities symbolic of the assurance one lacks, but unavailable in fact since these commodities lose their mystique once possessed. When he puts them on, the emperor needs no boy to tell him about his new clothes. To raise the bugbear of paternalistic repression is to avoid the real issue of contemporary life: how can we find release from the crosshatchings of suggestion that exacerbate our need? How can we relinquish the struggle for prestige that makes everything in our world symbolic of success or failure—from ring around the collar to ring around the moon? René Girard is much more sanguine than Philip Rieff about our ability to live without the Law—the demands and interdictions of previous cultures—but his hope seems to be guaranteed by belief in the divinity of Christ: "The emergence of such a being in a world entirely ruled by violence and by the myths of violence is impossible. To understand that one can see and make seen the truth only if one takes the place of the victims, one would already have to occupy that place oneself, and to assume that place under the required conditions, one would already have to possess the truth."[13] If this proof is unconvincing and if faith is lacking, what can one do to protect oneself against the competing immediacies of everyday life?

"Achilles never would have sulked in Chelm / for we have never had an Agamemnon."[14] Is study, perhaps, the way of justice and modesty? Chelm, the Diaspora, is a meandering world of talk and text, of repetitive interpretation. Its destruction in World War II "seals a sense of absence into the Hebrew month of Heshvan, the autumnal month called 'mar' Heshvan, 'bitter' Heshvan, because no feast days fall within its span. But even the Heshvan of deprivation, the void in the calendar, cannot obliterate the plenitude of that Exile, the seldom silenced talk that lies behind these maxioms: cantilena, lied, song, sonatina, chant."[15] My own childhood was spent in an apartment house in New York City—on a courtyard that amplified all the sounds from the apartments abutting onto it. Many of the families in the house were refugees from Hitler's violence—former inmates of concentration camps. They were noisy in their observance of Jewish ritual and observant of laws that struck me as being gratuitous. My own parents, second generation Americans, were modern, nonobservant, and my own religious training was perfunctory. Mixed with annoyance with my neighbors, who often disturbed the peace of my own place on the courtyard, was a constant sense of exclusion and of looking

in. I had always felt uncomfortable in temple and had no belief in laws
that separated me from other groups. The suffering and exile of my
neighbors, moreover, made any Jewish identification I could achieve
seem paltry and insignificant. It was not until later that I could claim my
own legacy from Jewish tradition—the sense, as Edmond Jabès puts it,
that "man is a written bond and place."[16] As I came to see it, to participate, by study, in Jewish tradition was to explore the nature of freedom,
which cannot exist without a developed sense of responsibility: "You
try to be free through writing. How wrong. Every word unveils another
tie . . . I went to the word / to make it my gesture. / I went. / And I am
going . . . Freedom awakens gradually as we become conscious of our
ties, like the sleeper of his senses. Then, finally, our actions have a
name."[17] The triumph of the therapeutic has brought about an impoverishment of our symbolic capital, which we can renew and make our own
only through study: "The men of Chelm do not despair: / they lift their
lances in the air / and leave them there."[18] We need not despair if continuing interpretation of texts—of the Torah or of other books of wisdom—
is all the Revelation to which we are entitled. Naming our actions, after
all, is our first ethical responsibility, and accepting our lot—opening the
book—enables us to do so: "In order to be heard, I ventured into the
room where the rabbis confronted one another. I have not left since."[19]
Those who cannot name their own actions tend to accept the ready-made
names of others—the clichés and slogans that are current in the world.

The hermeneutic circle, in other words, need not be a trap—particularly now that we can free ourselves from the vestiges of totemic thinking.
"No maxim, axiom, maxiom, no law / must stand as if it were a gateless
wall." Nor is interpretation wasted ingenuity: "And some have said his
logogriphs / were often too elusive. / But others have contended: If /
they veiled the sign, they let it live."[20] Kabbalistic tradition has it that the
written Torah—a kind of mystical organism—is glimpsed only occasionally by master prophets like Moses: "What we call the written
Torah had itself passed through the medium of the oral Torah, it is no
longer a form concealed in white light; rather, it has emerged from the
black light, which determines and limits and so denotes the attribute of
divine severity and judgment. Everything that we perceive in the fixed
form of the Torah, written in ink on parchment, consists in the last
analysis, of interpretation or definition of what is hidden."[21] All hope for
certainty has disappeared with the sacrificial victim, who once drained
off doubt and uncertainty; but the counter-hope of antinomianism is
equally elusive—a kind of gate without walls. Grendel, the monster, is a
"rock broken free of the wall"; like Christ he reveals the role of this stone,
which, rejected by the builders in Psalm 118, becomes the cornerstone of
human society. Unlike Christ, however, he is devastated by this knowledge and can see no alternative to mindlessly filling his part. Defeated by

the equally inhuman Beowulf, whose enemy brother he is, he talks of his death as an "accident": "Blind, mindless, mechanical. Mere logic of chance." As opposed to the treasure hoard of the dragon, however—the accumulated riches of repeated sacrifice—is the sister of a defeated king, whose gentle calm nourishes and quiets the warring men: "Let her name from now on be Wealtheow, or holy servant of the common good." Like the Shaper, whose myths attract Grendel because they make the world meaningful, Wealtheow attracts the Grendel who was once sickened by the world of slaughter and who cried "Mercy! Peace!" as he bore one of the victims in his arms. Grendel's knowledge at the end, however, is indignant and cynical, without the love that is the evangel of a new world. "Loving God," says one of the rabbis in Jabès' The Book of Questions, "means making your own His love of men."[22] The Kabbalah tells us that when creation took place, the vessels designed to receive God's light were shattered under its impact. As a result of this flaw, the powers of evil are cast out but not totally eliminated. As emanations of God's own power of judgment, they assume a kind of perverse independence in the world. Until they are eliminated or transformed into the powers of love and mercy, our spiritual exile will continue.

The following studies show the way in which contemporary writers deal with these powers of judgment. Because some of the books seem to invite Freudian readings, I decided to analyze these potential readings and to determine what they conceal. The second chapter, consequently, was to treat Jacques Lacan's famous Seminar on "The Purloined Letter" as a work of fiction in itself and to reveal its strategy. Poe's stories, however, which I read only to prepare for this task, proved so fruitful for an inquiry into imitation, desire, and rivalry that the chapter became the most extensive of the book. Particularly in the early chapters, I will try, at the risk of redundancy, to state and restate the thesis of this book: that desire is imitative and that the violence (or indifference) it encounters tends to become a sign of its end.

My thanks to the University of Colorado for the grant that made this book possible. My thanks also to Paul Levitt, my department chairman, who has enhanced the work of many of us; to my colleagues Bruce Kawin, Martin Bickman, Richard Schoeck, and Laurie Magnus, whose remarks were tactfully chastening; to my students Michael Gilbert, Elizabeth Fox, John Billingsley, and Constance Studer, who helped me along the way; to my typists Colleen Anderson and Carolyn Dameron, who were patient with me; and to René Girard, Allen Mandelbaum, and Edgar Whan, who have been the most benevolent of models. "Gentlemen," as Dimitri said, "I have had a wonderful dream."

CHAPTER 2

Robbe-Grillet's Café des Alliés

In *Les Gommes* a secret agent named Wallas comes to a northern European city from the "capital" in order to investigate a murder that may have been politically motivated. This murder, however, one of a series that have taken place at exactly seven-thirty p.m., has not really occurred. The murderer, Garinati, has not followed instructions to the letter and has only wounded his victim, Daniel Dupont, who then arranges with his doctor to make it appear that he has died. When Wallas, however, pursues certain clues to this aborted murder, he himself ends up shooting Daniel Dupont. This intrigue is complicated by the narrative, which often gives alternative versions of events, which suggests various kinds of doublings among the characters, and which includes allusions to the myth of Oedipus. Interpreting the novel is complicated by the fact that Robbe-Grillet is an extraordinary instance of a writer bedazzled by one of his critics, Roland Barthes, so that his own programmatic statements about his work have vacillated between the extreme objectivity posited by Barthes as distinctive of Robbe-Grillet's work and the lyricism that is the real quality of that work. As we shall see, things in Robbe-Grillet's novels are indices of human struggle; they are not alien to human concerns, as Robbe-Grillet sometimes claims.[1]

The "Prologue" to the novel, which is quite surrealistic in effect, compresses some of its salient motifs. Wallas, the secret agent, is staying at the Café des Alliés, which is very close to the Boulevard Circulaire, and this location suggests the ambivalent alliances and the circularity that will pervade the book. The *patron* is said to anticipate "les meurtriers et leurs victimes" sitting together while communion is served to them. Here arrives Garinati, in search of Wallas, who is supposed to be in search of him; and Garinati, the assigned murderer, is described by the *patron* as a victim: "Bonne victime décidément, petite figure d'araignée triste, perpétuellement en train de reconstituer les lambeaux de son intelligence fripée."[2] Consistent with these motifs of doubling, inversion, and fragmentation are "l'inscription mutilée" of the café sign, "les spectres familiers" who imitate the *patron*, and the "masque de gargouille" that contemplates itself in the mirror. The *patron*, having decomposed into a "kyrielle indéfinie des ombres," asserts himself here and at the end of the book as "le patron, le patron, le patron," but he is described as a "nébuleuse triste, noyé dans son halo." The problem suggested by this *mise en scène* is: what happens to power (*Kuros*: from which *kyrielle* is derived) when the *patron* no longer transcends the world of men? What happens to men when religion no longer dehumanizes their violence and directs it outward in the form of a transcendent being? What happens when that transcendent being no longer demands certain renunciations and obeisances from men and when his own prestige becomes the stake for their competition?[3]

One way in which Robbe-Grillet indicates this process of secularization is through the story of Oedipus that he embeds in his narrative.[4] The Oedipal myth involves a profound deception: for the violence of all against all represented by the plague in Thebes, the myth substitutes the one transgressor—guilty of those crimes, incest and patricide, that are most subversive of the social order. In the play by Sophocles, however, the mutual violence underlying this scapegoat mechanism is restored in the play's stichomythic exchanges. The relations between Oedipus and Tiresias and between Oedipus and Creon are ones of mutual recrimination. Oedipus' apotheosis in *Oedipus at Colonus*, moreover, reveals how the victim in earlier societies is, once expelled, transformed into a divinity because the peace brought about by the unanimous violence against him is attributed to his person. By the time Freud takes up the myth of Oedipus, however, Western society has undergone a progressive elimination of what Shakespeare's Ulysses calls "degree," which is no longer restored by periodic crises and their sacrificial resolutions. Things meet "in mere oppugnancy" because the arbitrary cultural differences that once controlled rivalry have now become the stake of that rivalry. Since the models for our desire no longer transcend our own sphere of existence (as Amadis of Gaul, for example, does for Don Quixote), they become rivals for the objects they valorize. Consequently, our fathers, the less they represent the Law, the more they become the rivals of Freud's schema. By the time Robbe-Grillet takes up the Oedipal myth, he sees it as a cliché: At one point Wallas sees "un sujet allégorique de grande série: bergers recueillant un enfant abandonné, ou quelque chose dans ce genre-là."[5] At another point he encounters a "cliché pâli" (187)—a snapshot in which a little boy looks up to his mother while the "figure sévère" of a possible father looks on. In other words, the Oedipal plot has to do with those aspects of our behavior that are more imposed upon us than decided by us. In primitive societies they derive from the rules and rituals that protect men from their own violence, and from the scapegoat mechanism that resolves their periodic crises. In Freud's society they derive from the residual authority of the father, which is still significant but which has been eroded enough for the father to be considered a rival for the son. In our society, where that repressive authority has become a cliché of radical politics and aesthetics, they derive from mutual imitation and rivalry.

To explore this change in the nature of social constraints, let us consider the objects that furnish the title of the book. Wallas's investigation of Dupont's murder is punctuated by his attempts to buy "une gomme douce, légère, friable, que l'écrasement ne déforme pas mais réduit en poussiàre." This "cube jaunâtre, de deux à trois centimètres de côté, avec les angles légèrement arrondis—peut-être par l'usure"[6] bears a manufacturer's brand that contains the letters "di" (which suggest "Oedipus"). This self-erasing eraser is related, however, to other cubes, one of which seems quite hard: On Dupont's desk "une sorte de cube, mais légèrement déformé, un bloc luisant de lave grise, aux faces polies comme par l'usure, aux arêtes effacées, compact, dur d'aspect, pesant comme l'or, sensiblement de la grosseur du poing; un presse-papier? C'est le seul bibelot de la pièce." This cube is described again as a "cube de pierre vitrifiée, aux arêtes vives, aux coins meurtriers," which lies harmlessly between an inkwell and a memo pad.[7] Other cubes occur in the automat to which Wallas repairs for lunch. Having selected his plate from "six exemplaires" of the same composition of food, he cuts his food into little cubes—as do three other men in the restaurant. These cubes are associated with disaster. Their geometric regularity reminds one of the quincunxes that will appear in La Jalousie—the cultivations of banana trees that obsess the eye of the book's narrator. In La Jalousie Blacks are perceived as a "shapeless darkness" threatening to engulf the articulated culture of the Whites. In Les Gommes the chief of conspirators, Bonaventure or "Bona," observes a landscape that seems to lose "son naturel" and to assume the overexactitude of a painting. Like the Whites in La Jalousie, petrified by the centipede that forebodes historical change, the geometry of this landscape suggests "cités perdues, pétrifiées pour des siècles par quelque cataclysme—ou seulement pour quelques secondes avant l'écroulement, un clignement comme d'hésitation entre la vie et ce qui déjà porte un autre nom: après, avant, l'éternité." That the cube on Dupont's desk is made of gray lava portends the fantasy Wallas will have of a "cité de style pompéien" in which he is talking to "des personnages qu'il n'arrive plus à séparer les uns des autres, mais qui étaient à l'origine nettement caractérisés et distincts. Lui-même a un rôle précis, probablement de premier plan, officiel peut-être."[8] This Pompeian disaster, then, is a crisis of undifferentiation (Dupont himself has written a book on the phenomenology of a crisis). Like all the participants in such a crisis, Wallas thinks of himself as distinct from the uniformity to which violence has consigned the others.

Similarly, in the main narrative the more Wallas, like Oedipus, tries to maintain his official role as outside investigator, the more complicit he becomes in the violent intrigue. As in Wallas's Pompeian fantasy, all the characters in Les Gommes become doubles of one another. To give just a few examples, a man who is apparently Wallas leans over a parapet and watches the slow progress of a cable connected on one end to some barges that have not yet appeared and on the other end to a tug that is lowering its smokestack in order to pass under a footbridge. After a long interval of text, we read, "Et d'un seul coup, précédée par un flot d'écume, surgit de dessous l'arche du pont l'étrave obtuse de la péniche—qui s'éloigne lentement vers la passerelle suivante.

"Le petit homme en long manteau verdâtre, penché sur le parapet, se redresse."[9]

That man turns out to be Garinati. Earlier, one of the other characters thinks about "cette étrange conjoncture où le coupable prend lui-même la direction de l'enquête." When Wallas decides to take the place of Marchat, a businessman who is himself taking the place of Dupont, we read that Wallas wants to see if by some "miracle" someone will come to murder him. Elsewhere, Dupont turns around to face the doctor, who is helping him maintain the deception that he is dead. After a typographic interval, the next sentence reads, "Il aperçoit son visage dans la glace" —a face we infer to be that of Garinati [10]

A memory Wallas has of being in this city as a boy evokes the impasse posed by a major cultural crisis: "Une image lui est restée d'un bout de canal en cul-de-sac; contre un des quais est amarré un vieux bateau hors d'usage—une carcasse de voilier? Un pont de pierre très bas ferme l'entrée. Sans doute n'était-ce pas exactement cela: la bateau n'aurait pas pu passer sous ce pont."[11] Wallas's vision of the tug lowering its smokestack in order to go under the bridge provides a solution to the aporia. As his name indicates, Dupont, in his role as scapegoat, will bridge the dangerous gap, the unbounded waters feared by Ulysses in his speech on degree. Since the scapegoat mechanism, to be effective, must be misunderstood, the cube associated with the crisis of undifferentiation is also associated with effacing the traces of this process. Laurent, the commissioner of police, covers up a little piece of eraser on his desk. Wallas's eraser will be friable enough to efface itself as well as the traces. Laurent says of the conspiracy, "Nous n'arrivons pas toujours à empêcher le crime, quelquefois même le criminel parvient à s'enfuir, mais sans exception nous trouvons au moins sa trace, alors que cette fois nous sommes au milieu d'empreintes sans nom et de courants d'air qui poussent les portes. Nos agents de reseignements ne sont ici d'aucun secours. S'il s'agit, comme vous l'assurez, d'une organization de terroristes, il faut croire qu'ils se sont préservés des contaminations; dans ce sens ils ont les mains pures, plus pures que celles d'une police qui entretient des

rapports si intimes avec ceux qu'elle surveille."[12] Because the murderer
seems to have "tombé du ciel," it is as if the crime never happened. In
any event, the violence has come from *outside* and does not threaten
contamination—like the blow of Apollo that lays Oedipus low. In Dr.
Juard's office, on the other hand, a whole bookshelf is devoted to the
plague, the real nature of which is revealed by his nurse's cryptic remark
that the people who come to the office are "tous les mêmes." As we have
seen, the substitution of Wallas for Marchat and Dupont is described in
religious terms. The "miracle" is the sudden transition from internecine
violence to peace that the scapegoat, doubling for all doubles, brings
about. Similarly, the effacing of the traces, the necessary deception that
allows the scapegoat to function, is also described in religious terms:
"Ses pas sont silencieux comme ceux du prêtre . . . des pas si légers
qu'ils ne laissent aucune ride à la surface des océans."[13]

   In *La Jalousie* the rationality that has made the White colonists masters over the Blacks has been pathologically exacerbated by the threat
posed by this adverse universe. At the moment of intense crisis, when
everything seems paralyzed by the "shapeless darkness," the narrator
relieves his anguish temporarily by creating "a regular rhythm capable
of measuring something, if something remains to measure, to limit, to
describe in the total darkness, until the day breaks now."[14] What is
interesting about his language, which is that of a regressive colonial
group trying to stave off the threat of its own destruction, is that it occurs
almost verbatim in an essay written about a year before and included in
Robbe-Grillet's collection *For a New Novel*: "The visual or descriptive
adjective, the word that contents itself with measuring, locating, limit-
ing, defining, indicates a difficult but most likely direction for a new art
of the novel."[15] In this quote also these activities seem to counteract the
threat of domination which is associated with "words of a visceral,
analogical, or incantatory character" (although Robbe-Grillet's own
writing often has great incantatory power). In a later essay Robbe-Grillet
notes, "We see at once why the Balzacian objects were so reassuring:
they belonged to a world of which man was the master; such objects were
chattels, properties, which it was merely a question of possessing, or
retaining, or acquiring. There was a constant identity between these
objects and their owner."[16] After saying that our novelists must restore
the "presence" of the world, he makes a statement reminiscent of the
description of the vitrified cube in *Les Gommes*: The surfaces of things
"are distinct and smooth, *intact*, neither suspiciously brilliant nor transparent. All our literature has not succeeded in eroding their smallest
corner, in flattening their slightest curve."[17] Before we return to *Les
Gommes*, perhaps we should analyze the struggle that is being waged on
these surfaces.

   Robbe-Grillet never distinguishes between "natural" objects like mountains and lakes and man-made objects like those he is presumably alluding to in his remarks on Balzac. Can man-made objects be treated with such *askesis* that they no longer convey any sign of their use or their value? That it is not man's spurious mastery over the world that Robbe-Grillet is objecting to is indicated by the fact that his "new kind of narrator" is a man who does not describe "the things he sees" but who "invents the things around him and who sees the things he invents."[18] Robbe-Grillet's meanings are *competitive* with the social and psychological *topoi* of Balzac's novels, and Robbe-Grillet asks his reader to be an *ally* in this struggle. When Roland Barthes, in his influential essay on Robbe-Grillet's "objective literature," says that "the whole purpose of the author's work . . . is to confer upon an object its 'being there,' to keep it from being something,"[19] he is only partially right: Robbe-Grillet does want to force the object out of the sphere of influence that Barthes calls "myth," but only to have it signify Robbe-Grillet's own heroic lucidity. Whether the voyeurism of Robbe-Grillet's work suggests the regressive colonialism of *La Jalousie* or the heroic lucidity of "A Future for the Novel," objects are no more "present" in this work than in the novels of Balzac. When, for example, the notorious tomato of *Les Gommes* appears, it articulates the dialectic of stability and disaster that we have already adumbrated: It is "un fruit d'une symmétrie parfaite" with homogeneous flesh, but "un accident à peine visible" has slightly stripped a corner of the skin.

Robbe-Grillet is aware that men's desires are mediated by others although he seems to think, like the outside investigator of *Les Gommes*, that he can resist this contagion: "What constitutes the novelist's strength is precisely that he invents, that he invents quite freely, without a model."[20] Having observed the "bridge of souls thrown between man and things" by the "humanist outlook," the "pledge of solidarity" that makes it difficult to discern "the origin of anything," Robbe-Grillet concludes, "Man looks at the world, and the world does not look back at him,"[21] a statement consistent with the voyeurism that characterizes much of his work. To see without being seen is to be master; the "world" here is really the mediator, whose mastery is a function of his apparent imperturbability. What separates us from earthly goods is, in fact, the sacred—violence that becomes immanent again in human societies when sacrificial resources become ineffective. In a world where "degree" breaks down and we are supposed to be on our own ("abandoned," as Sartre would say), the autonomy that we never experience always seems to be the possession of another, who now mediates our desire. That is, the Other represents fullness of being, access to which can be achieved through imitation. Because pride, however, dictates that we not imitate (if anything, others must imitate *us*), we indulge in the illusion that our desire is spontaneous and that the mediator is only a rival for the desired object. Since the mediator's prestige, however, is a function of his inaccessibility, it increases with each obstacle that he can place in the path of our desire. The violence (which can take the form of indifference) with which he defeats or repudiates us becomes a sign of his mastery, which we wish to overcome under the very circumstances that make it impervious to us. Objects, then, become, only a pretext for this rivalry, and both the "wear" of Dupont's vitrified cube and the "accidental" tear of Wallas's tomato are signs of this violence. The problem of "origin," then, does not concern the relation between man and the "world" but between man and man since value is conferred on things not so much by their quality of use as by their role in exchange: like the newspaper in Kafka's "The Judgment" and "Metamorphosis," they are talismans of prestige. When Robbe-Grillet debunks the idea of human nature and the anthropocentric analogies that make certain objects partake of it, he is really assaulting the transcendence of the Other: "The idea of an interiority always leads to the idea of transcendence," which is why the Other must be flattened by the sense of sight. Tragedy, in attempting to recover the distance between men and things, establishes a "painful" communion, in which evil must triumph: "Unhappiness, failure, solitude, guilt, madness—such are the accidents of our existence which we are asked to entertain as the best pledge of our salvation. To entertain, not to accept: it is a matter of feeding them at our expense while continuing to struggle against them. For tragedy involves neither a true acceptance nor a true rejection. It is the sublimation of a difference."[22] This statement is exactly right except that the difference that is sublimated is the difference between men. Since the mediator maintains his prestige by his indifference to us (or sometimes by more violent repudiation), he is Evil, but although we represent the Good in our own eyes, it is really the persecuting Evil that we worship. We attempt to destroy this Evil (or debunk it) because the God within remains inaccessible to us, but that Evil is destined to triumph. Robbe-Grillet himself, in his critique of socialist realism, is aware of the dangers of Manicheism, but he does not see that his own remedies tend to mimic the disease. To counteract the prolonged indecision of the tragic attitude, he suggests a conflation of the real and the imaginary so that description keeps us from "seeing" what it is "showing."[23] If the kinds of myths analyzed by Roland Barthes, in essays written about the same time as *Les Gommes* and some of the essays in *For a New Novel*, deprive their objects of their accumulated meaning—that is, their history—in order to produce an "inverted image of an unchanging humanity, characterized by an indefinite repetition of its identity," Robbe-Grillet advocates not letting anything in his writing accumulate a past, writes a collection of "snapshots" in which various kinds of inversion and displacement substitute for time, and often plays with freezing the action of his novels (or with animating his images).[24] In addition, his vacillation in critical statements between total objectivism and total subjectivism ("The new novel aims only at a total subjectivity") is in truth a change of tactics like that of Dostoevsky's underground man, who embraces the good and the beautiful and boasts of his aesthetic fantasies in order to justify his isolation and mediocrity and then invokes "contact with real life" in order to justify pursuing the Other. Robbe-Grillet analyzes this problem in his statements about history and also understands how "realism" is often an ideological weapon that one "brandishes" against one's neighbor, but he does not see that, despite the protestations of "new" novelists, "realism" always belongs to the Other—to his "false nature," to his myths that become "the very presence" of his concepts and which consign a mythologist like Roland Barthes to the "theoretical sociality" of sarcasm.[25]

If we return from this long detour to *Les Gommes*, we can see how objects focus the mimetic conflicts that provide the real intrigue of the book. As the *patron* emerges "painfully" from his own dissolution, he notices a spot that looks like blood: "Un coup de chiffon distrait, comme alibi, sur la drôle de tache. Entre deux eaux des masses incertaines passent, hors d'atteinte; où bien ce sont des trous tout simplement." These waters, like the Biblical element of chaos, contain monsters against which "se dresse la ligne de défense des pignons, où les ouvertures se font plus myopes—instinctivement—et les remparts plus épais."[26] For those on land, we are told, "les sirènes depuis longtemps appellent sans espoir"—"sirènes" that are both whistles and those mythical sirens who fall silent in Kafka's parable. In that parable silence is more powerful than song because it forces the Other to interpret it—inevitably to his own disadvantage: "But Ulysses, if one may so express it, did not hear their silence. He thought they were singing and that he alone did not hear them." Ulysses, however, is blissfully absorbed in his wax and chains, which free him from the effect of this silence and endow him with a "radiance" in the sirens' eyes.[27] Similar to this equivocation between song and silence is the equivocation above between "des masses incertaines" and "des trous tout simplement." Black holes, one recalls, are stars that have collapsed at the speed of light and that exert an irresistible attraction over anything that crosses their "event" threshold. These astronomical monsters can be seen as analogous to the mediators of our exacerbated desire, whom we take to be qualitatively different from ourselves. In order to maintain this illusion—which gives us hope of partaking of their transcendence—we seek out those whose inhuman qualities seem to deny us, who seem to approach the imperturbable condition of the inorganic. Like Stavrogin, whose *acedia* draws everyone around the black hole that he makes at the center of *The Possessed*, "Bona" sits motionless "au milieu d'une pièce vide" and contemplates his work.

That the citizens keep, in their own eyes, "la tête solide" in not heeding the call of the sirens is evoked ironically by the jester's head that forms the finial of Dupont's staircase. Just as the twenty-one steps of this staircase suggest the twenty-one numbered cards of the Tarot deck, a painting above the sixteenth step is reminiscent of the sixteenth Tarot card: "Au-dessus de la seizième marche, un petit tableau est accroché au mur, à hauteur du regard. C'est un paysage romantique représentant une nuit d'orage: un éclair illumine les ruines d'une tour; à son pied on distingue deux hommes couchés, endormis malgré le vacarme; ou bien foudroyés? Peut-être tombés du haut de la tour." Later, the painting appears as follows: "C'est une nuit de cauchemar. Au pied d'une tour démantelée, que l'orage illumine d'un éclat sinistre, gisent deux hommes. L'un porte des habits royaux, sa couronne d'or brille dans l'herbe à côté de lui; l'autre est un simple manant. La foudre vient de les frapper de la même mort."[28] This is a marvellously compressed transition that reveals the secret of the Oedipal myth. When Oedipus attacks his father at the crossroads (an attack that has been provoked by the father himself), the relation between father and son is transformed into the relation between enemy brothers, which emerges as such in the subsequent battle between Polynices and Eteocles. One recalls that with the deposition of Oedipus, his two sons are supposed to rule alternately, but one of them refuses to let the other assume rule when his turn comes. In the ensuing battle both brothers die at each other's hands—a conflict described by Euripides in terms of identical gestures, blows, and feints. When Creon assumes office, he sacrifices one brother (leaving him unburied, in disgrace) in order to consolidate the community around his expulsion. It is then Antigone who opposes this mythological lie, who says that the doubles are identical and that both must be treated in the same way. Similarly, in the later occurrence of the painting, the earlier "two men" are differentiated arbitrarily into a king and a peasant. The secret of this differentiation is the jester, who corresponds to the unnumbered Tarot card, which J.E. Cirlot analyzes as follows: "The Fool is to be found on the fringe of all orders and systems in the same way as the Centre of the Wheel of Transformation is 'outside' movement, becoming and change." As far as the Fool's role in inverting the prevailing social order is concerned, Cirlot remarks, "When the normal or conscious appears to become infirm or perverted, in order to regain health and goodness it becomes necessary to turn to the dangerous, the unconscious and the abnormal. Further, the Fool and the clown, as Frazer has pointed out, play the part of 'scapegoats' in the ritual sacrifice of humans."[29]

Daniel Dupont writes works on the organization of production, and he has friends in high places—including the Minister of the Interior, whose name, Roy-Dauzet, suggests the *roi* whose prestige is up for grabs in our middle-class court, and the verb *doser*: to give doses of medicine (or poison). At stake in all cultures has been the separation between legitimate and illegitimate violence—like the two drops of Gorgon's blood in Euripides' *Ion*, one drop of which is a deadly poison, the other drop a remedy. Despite the judiciary systems of modern societies, this distinction is never absolute—as the various rivalries and collusions in our society indicate. Can it be that Robbe-Grillet has imagined a prolonged catharsis for the prolonged crisis of degree in modern society? The fact that Roy-Dauzet has an intense dislike of theosophical societies, which Wallas has hitherto investigated, parodies the animosities of the cold war, as does the fact that one street in the book is named "Rue de Berlin." To reinforce the legitimacy of governmental power, what better way than manufacture a conspiracy against that power? At one point Wallas encounters a man who looks like Fabius, the legendary head of the Bureau of Investigation, for which Wallas works. Because of his glorious years of struggle against the enemy agents during the war, Fabius is the object of much "vénération aveugle." The role of his "police en marge de la vraie" is no longer counter-espionage, as it was during the war, but supervision of the cartels. The man who looks like Fabius wears black and is going to send off a telegram announcing someone's death. Just as the relation between this marginal police and the cartels is really a complicity, like the relation between local police and smugglers, the name "Fabius" suggests the fictive role conspiracy plays in legitimating power. In other words, the battle against the enemy has been "imported" by Fabius's organization to help reinforce society: Sometimes, Wallas thinks, "on s'archarne à découvrir le meurtrier, et le crime n'a pas été commis."[30] That crime is, in fact, brought about by Wallas's investigation of it, which leads him to a place between two glass doors, where he feels caught in a trap. Amidst this "piège" of echoing impressions, amidst the "mythomanie" of the Minister of the Interior and the "folie collective" that seems to make each man as mad as the minister, amidst the delirious suppositions of Wallas and his conjecture that he himself may be "une pure création d'un ministre à l'esprit trop fertile"—amidst all the doublings and revolving oppositions of the book, Dupont, as his wife indicates, provides a saving lack of imagination that temporarily resolves this mimetic hysteria. Through the scapegoat mechanism, these oscillations are resolved into a melodrama: Dupont "a même accepté des lunettes noires, afin que personne ne puisse le reconnaître; on n'a trouvé à la clinique qu'une paire de lunettes médicales, dont un des verres est très foncé et l'autre beaucoup plus clair—ce qui donne au professeur l'aspect comique d'un traître de mélodrame."[31] The next victim, by the way, will be Albert Dupont—head of one of the "export" houses that seem to constitute the chief business of the city. The gratuitous quality of this "exportation" is indicated by the fact that the employees of these houses are imagined as entering the first house they come to, "pour exporter au hasard les bois de Louis Schwab ou de Mark et Langler."

The relative anomy of modern society means that desire is free to float haphazardly and to fix itself where it will. Amidst the "cheminements courbes, hésitants, discontinus, aléatoires" of a railroad station, "des courants notables" occasionally appear. In this setting a crisis of information occurs which translates what we said earlier about cultural crisis into terms reminiscent of information theory: "Une immense voix remplit le hall. Tombée de haut-parleurs invisibles, elle vient frapper de tous les côtés contre les murs chargés d'avis et de placards publicitaires, qui l'amplifient encore, la répercutent, la multiplient, la parent de tout un cortège d'échos plus ou moins décalés et de résonances, où le message primitif se perd—transformé en un gigantesque oracle, magnifique, indéchiffrable et terrifiant."[32] Without the "negative feedback" of norms and rituals, the signs and gestures of one person produce corresponding signs and gestures in another that amplify the original movements (which are themselves amplifications of other movements), and a kind of "runaway" results. The voice in the hall is both "monstrous" and "divine" because it is both the collective interference of all these "conflicting echoes and resonances" and the oracular solution to them: When Dr. Juard says that he has given Wallas the "clef de l'énigme," that key is the secret of cultural negentropy: the scapegoat mechanism. The signals that he gives the detective are signals of complicity, which Wallas, "enfermé dans leurs conventions primitives," ignores.

Now that the secret is revealed to us, however, we are forced to ask with Dr. Juard whether "il est bien nécessaire de poursuivre la comédie." One possibility that the history of the twentieth century suggests to us is that the more our understanding of violence diminishes its power to reconcile and renew, the more we may multiply violence in an effort to restore its efficacy: the crime in Les Gommes takes place "n'importe où, chaque jour, une fois ici, une fois là. Que s'est-il passé dans l'hôtel particulier du professeur Dupont, le soir du vingt-six octobre? Un double, une copie, un simple exemplaire d'un événement dont l'original et la clef sont ailleurs."[33] The other possibility is to create a society that can eschew this mechanism of sacrifice and exclusion. When Garinati leaves his boss, "Bona," who has assured him that the murder has taken place (one repeated refrain in the book is "vous ne lisez pas les journaux?"), he hears a faint whistle, an irritating noise, the source of which remains unknown to him. That noise, like the prolonged orchestral note following Marie's death in Berg's Wozzek, is the sound of fatality: "Au bout de quelques pas il se trouve à nouveau devant l'immeuble d'où il vient de sortir. Il porte la main à son oreille avec agacement: cette machine d'enfer ne s'arrêtera donc jamais?"[34] But if "le parcours immuable se poursuit. A mouvements comptés," if Wallas seems to be walking "volontairement" toward "un avenir inévitable et parfait," we know that these impressions of continuity (durée) are illusory. After Wallas is said to "rentrer en scène . . . ," presumably the scene of the murder, a typographical break ensues, after which Wallas is said to be walking toward the bridge, which is the real meaning of that scene. Dupont, as we have said, is a bridge between one moment of equilibrium and the next, but this scapegoat mechanism does not really function "sans un à-coup, sans une erreur": "Mais, de l'autre côté de la barrière, on pouvait constater que tout n'était pas encore terminé: par suite d'une certaine élasticité de la masse, la descente du tablier n'avait pas pris fin avec l'arrêt du mécanisme; elle s'était poursuivie pendant quelques secondes, sur un centimètre peut-être, créant un léger décalage dans la continuité de la chaussée, une remontée infime s'effectuait qui amenait à son tour la bordure métallique à quelques millimètres au-dessus de sa position d'équilibre; et les oscillations, de plus en plus amorties, de moins en moins discernables—mais dont il était difficile de préciser le terme— frangeaient ainsi, par une série de prolongements et de régressions successifs de part et d'autre d'une fixité tout illusoire, un phénomène achevé, cependant, depuis un temps notable."[35] The various flaws in Robbe-Grillet's work— the spot of blood that the *patron* tries to wipe away, the "accident" undergone by the otherwise "homogeneous" tomato, the continuing oscillations of the bridge—are threatening because they forebode a greater evil, a more pervasive destruction than the murder committed at 7:30 each night by "Bona's" organization. But these flaws also suggest a way out of the hermeneutic circles in which man has moved throughout his history:[36] a society in which sacrifice and exclusion are eschewed. If the waters in *Les Gommes* seem full of invisible monsters, they also represent "l'espace, la temptation, la consolation du possible." If the vitrified cube is associated with the "geometry" of disaster, it can also be used to stop the whole system, "avec un grincement de mécanique détraquée." If the whistling noise heard by Garinati seems to forebode a necessary collapse into indistinction, the *sirènes* still represent the lure of something else. We can say, then, of the wink of hesitation contemplated by Bona that *Les Gommes* keeps open a crucial interval in which man can, if he chooses, exercise his freedom and responsibility: the interval between Dupont's abortive murder and its realization, the interval between Wallas's bending over the parapet and Garinati's bending over the same parapet—where, as in *La Jalousie*, the debris of an old order can be seen.

CHAPTER 3

Dupin Meets the Sandman

The flaws in Robbe-Grillet's world also pervade the world investigated by Edgar Allan Poe's detective, Auguste Dupin. While Dupin himself is, as he says, "not . . . once 'at fault,' " he discovers an invisible "fissure" that allows him to solve the case of the Rue Morgue.[1] Similarly, in "The Purloined Letter" the police fail to detect any flaw (which "would have sufficed to insure detection") in the Minister's chambers, but later Dupin is made suspicious by a letter "torn nearly in two across the middle," as if by "design." These fissures recur in "The Man of the Crowd," where the narrator perceives both a diamond and a dagger through "a rent" in the pedestrian's cloak; in "The Assignation," where a "cracked and blackened goblet" reveals the "terrible truth" of the suicide of the story's Byronic poet; in "The Pit and the Pendulum," where the narrator discovers a "sulphurous light" proceeding from a "fissure" that extends around the walls of his cell; and in "The Fall of the House of Usher," where a "barely perceptible fissure" runs zigzag down the wall of the house. The inside of that house, moreover, is described in terms of the "ebon blackness" of its floors, the "phantasmagoric armorial trophies," the windows at "so vast a distance" from the floor as to be "altogether inaccessible from within," and the "feeble gleams of encrimsoned light" from those windows. These details recur in "A Descent into the Maelström," where the fissure becomes apocalyptic: "The boat appeared to be hanging, as if by magic, midway down, upon the interior surface of a funnel vast in circumference, prodigious in depth, and whose perfectly smooth sides might have been mistaken for *ebony*, but for the bewildering rapidity with which they spun around, and for the *gleaming and ghastly radiance* they shot forth, as the rays of the full moon, from that circular *rift* amid the clouds which I have already described, streamed in a flood of golden glory along the *black walls*, and *far away down into the inmost recesses of the abyss*" (emphases mine). It is as if the scene in "Usher" has been set spinning to create the scene in "Maelström."

Is Poe's detective really unflawed? Is he really different from Poe's dreamers and neurasthenics? When we first encounter Dupin in "The

Purloined Letter," he sits "amid a perfect whirlwind of smoke"—like a still point within the various whirlwinds, maelströms, and collapses that occur in Poe's work. In "The Murders in the Rue Morgue," this privileged position is derived from Dupin's method, which the narrator introduces by discussing chess and checkers. He says that the "different and bizarre motions" of chess demand of a good player primarily "attention" and "concentration" whereas the "unique" moves in checkers demand "superior acumen": "It is obvious that here the victory can be decided (the players being at all equal) only by some *recherché* movement, the result of some strong exertion of intellect. Deprived of ordinary resources, the analyst throws himself into the spirit of his opponent, identifies himself therewith, and not infrequently sees thus, at a glance, the sole methods (sometimes indeed absurdly simple ones) by which he may seduce into error or hurry into miscalculation." Dupin's "acumen" resembles the knowledge gained by the mariner in "Maelström," who, having committed "invariable" miscalculations concerning the welter of objects in the maelström, learns that cylinders sink slowly whereas spheres sink quickly. This knowledge enables him to make the sudden leap that causes him to survive. It is also like the physiological clairvoyance shown by the narrator of "The Man of the Crowd," who, at the beginning, reduces the "tumultuous sea" of "human heads" to various types. But, as we shall see, identifying with one's opponent is not always the calm and lucid strategy that Dupin's friend makes out. Sometimes, as all the doubling in Poe reveals, it is involuntary and, in fact, obsessive.

What are the "ordinary resources" of which the "analyst" is deprived? Dupin has lost his "patrimony"—only a "small remnant" of which he is allowed to keep by his creditors. What remains is "a time-eaten and grotesque mansion, long deserted through superstitions into which we did not inquire; and tottering to its fall in a retired and desolate portion of the Faubourg St. Germain"—a mansion, in fact, like that of Usher, whose patrimony is also exhausted. Usher presents an interesting comparison and contrast to Dupin. Although Dupin has withdrawn from the world ("We existed within ourselves alone") he and his confidant, unlike Usher and his sister, sally out at night "amid the wild lights and shadows of the populous city," seeking the kind of mental excitement that Usher's nerves cannot tolerate. Similarly, Dupin's rival, the Minister, pretends to be "in the last extremity of *ennui*," although he is really the most "energetic human being now alive." Usher's *ennui*, on the other hand, is genuine: he is "enchained by certain superstitious impressions in regard to the dwelling which he tenanted, and whence, for many years, he had never ventured forth—in regard to an influence whose suppositious force was conveyed in terms too shadowy here to be re-stated."

If we conflate the two stories, we get the following situation: a figure of "illustrious family" has exhausted his patrimony. Unable to face a world in which his aristocratic qualities do not demand esteem, he withdraws into the "fantastic gloom" of the past. The image of that past, its "still perfect adaptation of parts," is wildly inconsistent with "the crumbling condition of the individual stones." Aided by the "ghastliest and feeblest of rays," he and a fascinated companion busy their souls, "in dreams." His feigned ennui (Dupin's, as we shall see, is as feigned as the Minister's), which is a strategy to gain the world's attention, becomes—by dint of habitual exertion—real. That is, ennui in Poe's stories tends to develop into the kind of morbid sensitivity shown by Usher or into the actual paralysis experienced by many of Poe's characters. The "superstition" that torments Usher is a "suppositious force"—in fact, it is the force of supposition. The Romantic withdraws into himself in order to disguise his dependence on Others, but his every gesture depends on what he supposes the Others to think and to feel. Dupin, we are told, takes great delight in the "exercise" of his analytic ability but not in its "display," yet Poe writes in one of his letters, "You are right about the hair-splitting of my French friend:—that is all done for effect"[2]—the kind of effect Poe talks about elsewhere as his primary consideration in writing poetry. Consider, in this respect, another aristocratic figure whose world-weariness seems extreme. The Byronic poet of "The Assignation" has the face of a deity, the strength of Hercules, and the kind of intense passion that expands his whole figure. Although the "glare" and the various improprieties of his furnishings defy Poe's own strictures on fashion, the poet claims that he is doing nothing for effect: "This is better than fashion—is it not? Yet this has but to be seen to become the rage—that is, with those who could afford it at the cost of their patrimony. I have guarded, however, against any such profanation." The important thing, he says à propos of this display manqué, is "to die laughing." He seems not to notice that the narrator has read his agonized poetry (which includes lines like "Now all my hours are trances"), but he does make sure that the narrator witnesses the finale of his death, just as he has exposed "the mysteries" of his "imperial precincts" to him.

It is the struggle for prestige (prestigiae="juggler's tricks," illusions) that generates all of the phantasmagoria in Poe's work. Alexis de Tocqueville, writing shortly before Poe, noted that "in democracies, where the members of the community never differ much from each other, and naturally stand so near that they may all at any time be confounded in one general mass, numerous artificial and arbitrary distinctions spring up, by means of which every man hopes to keep himself aloof, lest he should be carried away against his will in the crowd. . . . In aristocracies, men are separated from each other by lofty stationary barriers: in democracies, they are divided by many small and almost invisible threads, which are constantly broken or moved from place to place."[3] If we keep in mind Poe's own aristocratic pretensions and his hatred of the "mob," we can appreciate some of the details of his stories. Tocqueville's image of "invisible threads," for example, occurs in Poe's "The Tell-Tale Heart," where the "dim ray" of the narrator's lantern (a metonomy for his obsessed eye) falls like "the thread of the spider" upon "the vulture eye" of his antagonist. Similarly, the narrator of "The Black Cat" sees a "solitary eye of fire" at the end of the story—the eye of an antagonist who has "seduced" him into murder. The theme of enemy brothers (or doubles) is present in both these stories: In "The Tell-Tale Heart" the narrator chuckles because he has forced his antagonist to experience the terrors that have previously beset him. When he writes, "It was the mournful influence of the unperceived shadow [death] that caused him to feel—although he neither saw nor heard—to *feel* the presence of my head within the room," one is reminded of D. H. Lawrence's observation that "the more mental and ideal men are, the more they seem to feel the bodily pressure of other men as a menace, a menace, as it were, to their very being."[4] In "The Black Cat" the antagonist bears a kind of mark of Cain: a "mark of white hair" that is the "sole visible difference between the strange beast and the one I have destroyed" and that comes to represent something the narrator shudders to name. What Poe reveals in these situations—like the "concealed spring" in "The Murders in the Rue Morgue"—is the effect of violence on human societies that can no longer periodically expel it. In primitive societies the evil eye is the mythic accusation *par excellence*: it is mysteriously responsible for their crises, and the intentions of the culprit are irrelevant to the effects of his eye. Like Oedipus, whose eyes are put out after he is discovered to be responsible for the plague, the man with the evil eye is the ideal scapegoat. In our world, however, where imitation and rivalry tend to dominate individual relations without exploding into periodic and collective crises, they tend to assume forms of such permanence that we call them "character" or "symptom." It is these forms that Poe's Monos, whose "deceased understanding" has allowed him to become clairvoyant, perceives as exacerbated moments of the mimetic process: "As these crossed the direct line of my vision they affected me as *forms*; but upon passing to my side their images impressed me with the idea of shrieks, groans, and other dismal expressions of terror, or horror, or of woe." Una alone, representing his hope for the good reciprocity of love, "habited in a white robe, passed in all directions musically about [him]."

In "The Silence" the "solitary eye of fire"—that Cyclopean eye that tends to reduce others to "Noman"—appears as the "red eye of the sun" presiding over the "tumultuous and convulsive motion" of waters that have no outlet into the sea. Within a desolate landscape, a man wearing "the toga of old Rome" and having "the features of a deity" sits on a rock

and, disgusted with mankind, longs for solitude. The Demon who nar-
rates this tale to the primary narrator convulses the landscape with
violence, but the man remains relatively unmoved. Then he curses the
landscape with silence, and the man flees in terror. When the Demon
concludes this tale, we have an ending not unlike the ending of "The
Assignation": "He fell back within the cavity of the tomb and laughed.
And I could not laugh with the Demon, and he cursed me because I could
not laugh. And the lynx which dwelleth forever in the tomb, came out
therefrom, and lay down at the feet of the Demon, and looked at him
steadily in the face." What is the function of laughter here and in "The
Assignation," and what is the curse with which the narrator is stricken?
Laughter is a kind of catharsis. The one who laughs expels a threat to his
autonomy, but he demands at the same time the complicity of others. In
"The Assignation" all the characters are made alike by *ennui*. Like "the
imp of the perverse," which makes all men alike by making them act in
the same gratuitous way, the "Genius of Romance" stalks the canals of
Venice and infects men with the fashion of *ennui*. As the narrator
encounters the "Satyr-like figure" of the implied villain, the husband of
the Byronic poet's mistress, he seems "*ennuyé* to the very death." The
narrator himself parodies this *ennui* by his own, involuntary paralysis:
"Stupefied and aghast, I had myself no power to move from the upright
position." Both the poet and his mistress are also "*ennuyé* to the very
death" since they engage in a suicide pact, which is what causes "a tide
of ungovernable crimson" to suffuse the body of the woman who agrees
to it. Death has become for them the true aphrodisiac. But this death—
apparently preferable to the impotence expressed by the poet's lines—
must be properly witnessed to be effective. It is here that the Byronic
poet uses laughter as a strategy. Having impressed the narrator with the
"unparalleled splendor" of his apartment, he laughs at the narrator's
astonishment and implies by scholarly allusions that the narrator ought
to join in this laughter. While the poet's laughter implies a superiority to
his fate (and to the narrator) not unlike his asserted superiority to
fashion, the narrator's induced laughter *with* him would validate this
superiority. In "The Silence" the god-like figure wants solitude but is
appalled by silence. The Demon who has watched him attentively and
has found him out, now assumes his relinquished superiority; but when
he cannot induce the narrator to laugh with him, he curses him with the
same impotence that besets himself. At the end a lynx, watching the
Demon attentively, seems to await his turn.

This structure is not unlike the structure of "The Purloined Letter,"
where an "illustrious personnage" thinks that the letter she has left open
before her (in order to conceal it from another "exalted personnage") has
escaped notice. The "lynx eye" of the Minister, however, "fathoms her
secret." Later, it is the Minister who leaves a letter open in order to

conceal it, and it is Dupin who fathoms the Minister's secret. This trick of open concealment is compounded by the Minister's show of *ennui*, which Dupin also sees through because his own *ennui* disguises his rivalry with the Minister and the Prefect. Moreover, the fact that Dupin and his confidant seek out "the wild lights and shadows of the populous city" aligns them with the unnamed and compulsive narrator of "The Man of the Crowd." Just as the content of "the purloined letter" is never read, the narrator of "The Man of the Crowd" alludes to a book that "does not permit itself to be read." In fact, "the essence of all crime is undivulged"—except to those who, like Dupin, know how to read. Dupin's own facsimile of the purloined letter contains the following words from Crébillon's "Atrée":

> —Un dessein si funeste,
> S'il n'est digne d'Atrée, est digne de Thyeste.

Enemy brothers of this sort appear everywhere in Poe—most explicitly in "William Wilson." In "The Purloined Letter" the Minister is one of two brothers who are confused with one another. Similarly, Dupin and the Minister are both mathematicians and poets; each is a match for the other's intelligence. What differentiates them is not some melodramatic essence (although names like "Lebon" and "Legrand" in Poe's work suggest such an interpretation) but the fortunes of strategy—the "*recherché* movement" that differentiates the players of checkers. Previously, the Minister has defeated Dupin, and now Dupin has turned the tables. That is the real meaning of the game of "even and odd" Dupin refers to in order to illustrate the way imaginative identification can give one person an advantage over another.[5] It is to be "even" with the Minister that Dupin disguises his watchful eyes in green spectacles, just as the Minister has disguised his watchfulness by means of *ennui*. The Minister, significantly enough, "has written learnedly on the Differential Calculus"—on the variations undergone by a function in accordance with changes in independent variables. Such a function in this story is the law which, no longer controlling rivalries created by mimetic desire, is now (as the "letter" of legality) simply the stake of those rivalries. In "William Wilson," letters and copies also occur. The narrator says of his rival: "That the school, indeed, did not feel his design, perceive its accomplishment, and participate in his sneer, was, for many anxious months, a riddle I could not resolve. Perhaps the *gradation* of his copy rendered it not readily perceptible; or, more possibly, I owed my security to the masterly air of the copyist, who, disdaining the letter (which in a painting is all the obtuse can see), gave but the full spirit of his original for my individual contemplation and chagrin." The "design" of this "copyist" reminds one of the "*dessein si funeste*" that Dupin quotes in "The Purloined Letter," but it also recalls the "design" to depict Dupin's character in "The Murders in the Rue Morgue." Character, as we have said, is a design to hypostatize the play of mimetic desire. What the quote from "William Wilson" shows, moreover, is that no "origin" can be assigned to this play. The copy (now also the "spirit") becomes an "original" for the narrator's "individual contemplation and chagrin," as this play of mirrors undermines all notions of propriety.

The Queen's ownership of "the purloined letter," consequently, is really illusory since her ownership of a letter that threatens the prerogatives of the King is no more proper than the Minister's ownership of a letter that threatens the whole political order. In "The Man of the Crowd," the references to a book that does not permit itself to be read and to the undivulged essence of all crime are followed by the following account of the narrator's mood: "For some months I had been ill in health, but was now convalescent, and, with returning strength, found myself in one of those happy moods which are so precisely the converse of ennui—moods of the keenest appetency, when the film from the mental vision departs. . . . Merely to breathe was enjoyment, and I derived positive pleasure even from many of the legitimate sources of pain." The cyclothymia suggested by this passage has to do with the relations between men whose places in society are not determined in advance, and whose advantages over each other are subject to sudden reversals. Objects, to be valued, must be valorized by men whom we take to be our models (note how the narrator pores over advertisements in the coffee house), but these models, since no qualitative differences separate them from us, are also our rivals for the desired objects. In these competitions our experience of success is always more disappointing, ultimately, than our experience of failure. Since the model over whom we triumph loses his prestige and since the object that we gain is devalued, we tend more and more, as our desire is disappointed by success, to seek out rivals who will maintain their prestige by defeating us. Without the illusion of plenitude and autonomy that such defeat sustains, our world becomes as desolate as the world of Poe's "The Silence."

In "The Fall of the House of Usher" the manic state of "The Man of the Crowd" has been succeeded by depression, and the removal of the film (or "veil," in this case) from one's mental vision is compared to the aftermath of an opium high. This cyclothymia seems to generate the very pulse of Poe's universe: "And now, from the wreck and the chaos of the usual senses, there appeared to have arisen within me a sixth, all perfect . . . Let me term it a mental pendulous pulsation. It was the moral embodiment of man's abstract idea of time." Although Poe criticizes man in this story, "The Colloquy of Monos and Una," for his "dominion" over nature and for his stalking "a God in his own fancy," he indicates in "Eureka" that man can become God. Man, he says, would have to be God to know something about His nature or essence, but man is not everlastingly consigned to ignorance on this point.[6] This ambivalence toward the Godhead is also Poe's ambivalence toward his detective and toward the Byronic gestures of some of his work. What Poe does resent unequivocally is the kind of "abstraction" that results in "odd ideas" like "universal equality": "In the face of analogy and of God—in despite of the loud warning voice of the laws of *gradation* [as opposed to facsimile] so visibly pervading all things in Earth and Heaven—wild attempts at an omniprevalent Democracy were made. Yet this evil sprang necessarily from the leading evil—Knowledge. Man could not both know and succumb" ("The Colloquy of Monos and Una"). Poe seems to both know and not know that it is man's pride—his desire to achieve the knowledge, power, and autonomy that were once God's only—that violates "the law of gradation" and results in the doubles or facsimiles that pervade Poe's work. That is, the more men try to differ in essential ways from one another, the more they seem to mime each other's efforts.

In "Eureka," where Poe posits the principles of attraction and repulsion as fundamental to the universe, he writes a passage that conveys this uncanny process:

> Any principle which will explain why the atoms should tend, according to any law, to the general centre, must be admitted as satisfactorily explaining, at the same time, why, according to the same law, they should tend to each. For, in fact, the tendency to the general centre is not to a centre as such, but because of its being a point in tendency toward which each atom tends most directly to its real and essential centre, unity—the absolute and fundamental union of all.

On a cosmic level, of course, this final attraction of all to all is as much a part of the cosmic process as the "continual differences at all points from the uniquity and simplicity of the origin." But we also read that the "Heart Divine" that beats in the continuous systole and diastole of attraction and repulsion is also "our own."[7] This tell-tale heart recalls the process by which man had, through his long history, been diverted from the violence (and the fatal knowledge thereof) that threatens to destroy him. The scapegoat mechanism, by investing all of the community's internecine violence in one person, expels that violence in the form of a Deity who has, by a kind of retrospective loop, sowed violence in order to reap the peace that has resulted from it. Because the violence of all against all that threatened to destroy the community is now attributed to the Deity—angry with men for the improper obeisances they have shown him—each member of the community is now diverted from the knowledge he has of the others' violence. What results from these sacrificial rituals are the cultural prescriptions and interdictions that prevent men's desires from converging on the same object.

Poe's account of "Union" is this process in reverse. The "centre" is the

Godhead, which, no longer keeping men apart in awe of its interdictions, draws them together in competition for its power or *kudos*. On the social level Poe's passage is highly reminiscent of a passage in which Tocqueville describes "how the aspect of society in the United States is at once excited and monotonous": "Like travellers scattered about some large wood, intersected by paths converging to one point, if all of them keep their eyes fixed upon that point, and advance towards it, they insensibly draw nearer together,—tho they seek not, tho they see not and know not each other; and they will be surprised at length to find themselves all collected on the same spot."[8] It is interesting, by the way, that when the Minister resorts to "simplicity" in "The Purloined Letter," he encounters Dupin, who defeats him by repeating his own gestures.

Perhaps now he can appreciate Dupin's discussion of algebra. In "The Mystery of Marie Rogêt," Dupin notes, "The mass of people regard as profound only him who suggests *pungent contradictions* of the general idea. [But Dupin himself quotes with approval Chamfort's *bon mot* concerning the stupidity of all general ideas.] In ratiocination, not less than in literature, it is the *epigram* which is the most immediately and the most universally appreciated. In both, it is of the lowest order of merit." Epigram is then associated with the "melodrama" of an idea about the missing girl. This structure of opposition occurs in Poe's critical writing as well. In his "Letter to B—," for example, he says that Coleridge "has imprisoned his own conceptions by the barrier he has erected against those of others." Later, he writes, "You are aware of the great barrier in the path of an American writer. He is read, if at all, in preference to the combined and established wit of the world. I say established, for it is with literature as with law or empire—an established name is an estate in tenure, or a throne in possession."[9] In "The Purloined Letter" meaningless epigrams ("All fools are poets" and "All poets are fools") are followed by a reference to the two brothers who are difficult to differentiate. These epigrams are algebraic in the sense that they have the structure $x = y$, and that, despite Dupin's preference for one of them, each epigram fills this structure equally well and equally badly. One is reminded of Dostoevsky's underground man, whose motto "I am alone, and they are all" begins as an assertion of unique individuality but turns into a statement of algebraic anonymity. The "algebraists," Dupin tells us, believe in "pagan fables": they believe that these equations are "absolutely and unconditionally" true whereas they have no real content. In the same way an *assertion* of individuality over and against others does not achieve anything except an obsessive concern with those others. As we have seen, however, Dupin's lucidity about the "algebraists" only exacerbates his own efforts to differentiate *himself* from the "mass of the people."

In "The Man of the Crowd," the narrator says of the old man he has been following, "This old man . . . is the type and the genius of deep crime. He refuses to be alone. *He is the Man of the Crowd.*" As in Pascal, then, the essence of all crime is man's inability to be alone (and in this respect the "man of the crowd" differs not one whit from the Byronic poet of "The Assignation," who only wants to *appear* alone). But how is the narrator's obsessive pursuit of the old man any different from the old man's pursuit of the crowd? As in all doublings, a reversal of position is always imminent: "Still more was I astonished to see him repeat the same walk several times—*once nearly detecting me as he came round with a sudden movement*" (emphasis mine). The old man is character- ized by "the absolute idiosyncrasy" of his facial expression, and various ideas about him (all of which suggest the devil) arise "confusedly and paradoxically" within the narrator's mind. Within the disorder (the "continuous tides of population") that the narrator tries to reduce to physiologies, the old man becomes "the type and the genius" of victim- age: as the "man of the crowd," he is both a double for this "promiscu- ous company" and an anomaly, a "singular being," who absorbs and isolates the evil "genius" of the crowd. The Minister, one recalls, is also a "*monstrum horrendum*, an unprincipled man of genius," who fasci- nates and exasperates Dupin—however insouciant the latter tries to appear. Similarly, in "William Wilson" the image of authority is that of a "gigantic paradox, too utterly monstrous for solution." In "The Murders of the Rue Morgue," which begins with the romantic gesture of repudiat- ing society (which seems to consist of creditors and debtors), mimetic desire again appears in exaggerated form: the "wild ferocity" and "imi- tative propensities" of an Ourang-Outang. The purposes of this creature are "probably pacific," but his propensity to imitate results in violent repudiations. First, the animal's master comes home to find him shaving, in imitation of what he has seen his master do. The master, afraid of the possible weapon in his hand, resorts to the whip, which causes the beast to escape. Second, the Ourang-Outang tries to display this new-found skill to the women whose apartment he enters, but the screams that thwart his purposes turn them "into those of wrath." The real "re- pressed" that returns in the form of this creature is the violence latent in the double bind.

In our society rules and rituals no longer channel our energies and prevent desire from floating where it will. In Poe's work one image for this prolonged crisis is the maelström: "Here the vast bed of the waters, seamed and scarred into a thousand conflicting channels, burst sud- denly into phrensied convulsion." Other images occur in the verses composed by Ligeia: "Mimes, in the form of God on high," and "mimic rout," into which a "crawling shape" intrudes to destroy it. A "troop of echoes" occurs in "The Fall of the House of Usher," and a troop of Ourang-Outangs in "Hop Frog"—whose "contrast" with the ordinary company of the court is, of course, illusory. Since the models of our desire no longer transcend our own sphere of existence, they become the rivals of their own disciples. The double-bind is that these models say to their disciples, "Imitate me," but they repudiate this imitation when their prerogatives are threatened. For the disciple, then, violence itself becomes the sign of that fullness of being that is always eluding him, and objects become only a pretext for rivalry. In "William Wilson," for example, where the protagonist's common name belies the "noble descent" that he claims for himself, the enemy brother represents the "intolerable spirit of contradiction." What else does the "nevermore" of the Raven represent, which gives the narrator the same paradoxical pleasure referred to in "The Man of the Crowd"—that pleasure from "the legitimate sources of pain." As his double tells William Wilson, "In me didst thou exist," and in conquering him, the protagonist is now lost to Hope. In another story the movement of a pendulum punctuates the alternations of hope and despair experienced by the narrator, who discovers that a "unique" bandage or surcingle attaches him to his tormentors. This algebra of persecution is described as follows by René Girard: "Instead of that inert, passive, benevolent obstacle, which is identical for everyone and which is never truly humiliating or traumatizing, that religious interdictions opposed to them, men more and more have to do with the active, mobile, and ferocious obstacle of the model metamorphosed into rival, an obstacle actively interested in thwarting them personally and marvellously equipped to succeed in it."[10]

As was common among the Romantic poets—recall the agreement between Wordsworth and Coleridge regarding the *Lyrical Ballads*—Poe plays on the distinction between the *outré* and the ordinary. Like the odd impression given by Roderick Usher, which is only an "exaggeration of the prevailing character" of his features, one is an exaggeration of the other. The crime against Marie Rogêt is not *outré*, but that fact makes the mystery more difficult of solution. The crime of the Rue Morgue is "*excessively outré*"—a "grotesquerie in horror absolutely alien from humanity"—but that fact makes it more easy of solution. In effect, the very problem of man's own mimetic propensities disappears when projected onto the outrageous figure of the Ourang-Outang. As we shall see when we come to the themes of light and perspective in Poe, the ordinary and the *outré* are matters of perspective. What is unintelligible and mysterious, for example, to the romantic temperament presiding over "The Spectacles" is obvious to everyone else. In "The Purloined Letter" what the Queen believes to be concealed is obvious to the Minister, and what the Minister believes to be concealed is obvious to Dupin. In "William Wilson" it is the "dismal monotony" of his childhood that seems full of the *outré*. Impressions of that childhood are stamped upon the protagonist's memory "in lines as vivid, as deep, and as durable as the exergues of the Carthaginian medals"—or as the imprint, perhaps, of the Minister's cipher in "The Purloined Letter."

An anomaly that has gone virtually unnoticed in the criticism of Poe is the fact that the Minister, in disguising the purloined letter so that it now appears addressed to himself in a feminine handwriting, places his own cipher on that letter "very conspicuously." Although discussions of verisimilitude often sound like the fruitless debate on psychology carried out by the lawyers in *The Brothers Karamazov*, it seems clear that in realistic terms this "disguise" is a blunder. Dupin, surveying the room under the protection of dark glasses, sees both the address and the cipher; surely the police, going over every inch of the Minister's apartments, would notice the incongruity. What is more interesting, however, is that Dupin never comments on the incongruity, but only on the Minister's use of simplicity. Perhaps we can approach this anomaly by observing that a "cipher" is not only a seal; it is also a cryptographic system by which units of text are arbitrarily transposed or substituted according to a predetermined key, which is also called a "cipher." The ingenuity necessary to construct or decipher such a system would seem to correspond to the Romantics' notion of "fancy," a notion treated rather severely in "The Murders in the Rue Morgue": "The constructive or combining power, by which ingenuity is usually manifested, and to which the phrenologists (I believe erroneously) have assigned a separate organ . . . has been so frequently seen in those whose intellect bordered on idiocy, as to have attracted general observation among writers on morals. . . . It will be found . . . that the ingenious are always fanciful, and the *truly* imaginative never otherwise that analytic." Although Poe, as we have seen, takes Coleridge to task for his competitiveness, his own notion of imagination is often less of an esemplastic power than the power of one-upmanship. Fancy lacks the power of imagination to identify with one's opponent so completely that one can anticipate his every move: in cards it is "as if the rest of the party had turned outward the faces" of their cards while the "analyst" keeps his own secret. He may, of course, deliberately turn a letter inside out in order to deceive the acumen of others. In Poe's work fancy tends to take over when the initiative of imagination is lacking, and it tends to be associated with "impressions." In "The Fall of the House of Usher," the narrator's imagination is impotent, but "shadowy fancies" crowd in upon him: "It was possible, I reflected, that a mere different arrangement of the particulars of the scene [like the rearrangements of particulars brought about by the Minister] . . . would be sufficient to *modify*, or perhaps to *annihilate* its capacity for sorrowful impressions" (emphasis mine). That rearrangement, however, is already accomplished in the "black and lurid tarn that lay in unruffled lustre by the dwelling," and this preemption exacerbates the narrator's sense of impotence (he has already suffered from the "vacant eye-like windows" of the house). In "The Mystery of Marie Rogêt," on the other hand, Dupin is never anticipated: it is he who rearranges the details of the newspaper accounts in order to compose a more powerful picture of the crime. That Dupin's priority (the priority of imagination) is no trivial matter is shown in "The Murders in the Rue Morgue," where the "impressions" associated with fancy are made by the Ourang-Outang on the murdered woman's throat. Before Dupin displays to his friend the facsimile he has made of these impressions, he asks, "What impression have I made on your fancy?"

Dupin's rivalry, past and present, with the Minister suggests a process by which one man proposes and the other man disposes, a process that can reverse itself with such rapidity that it becomes difficult to establish priorities. Whatever "wild improvisations" take place on Usher's "speaking guitar," the theme itself is set by the "sympathies of a scarcely intelligible nature" that exist between himself and his twin. One man's imagination becomes another man's fancy through the permutation of certain fixed elements, but that imagination, in turn, is a fancy relative to someone else's imagination. The "design" of Dupin's character is the imprint of a cipher that really belongs to no one—like the exergue in "William Wilson," which signifies a value of exchange. The cipher represents the "intolerable spirit of contradiction" embodied in the Other—whose apparent insolence makes him both hateful and fascinating. He puts his stamp on everything, and he holds the key to life's mystery, but his "identity" is only positional: "There were many points of strong congeniality in our tempers, operating to awake in me a sentiment which our position alone, perhaps, prevented from ripening into friendship," William Wilson writes about himself and his double. As Monos develops a sixth sense that allows him to discern the pulsating, pendulating rhythm of a universe of doubles, he says, "The consciousness of being had grown hourly more indistinct, and that of mere locality had, in great measure, usurped its position. The idea of entity was becoming merged in that of place."

Usher's "speaking guitar" brings up another important topic of investigation: the theme of breath and voice. Whatever the etiology of Poe's obsession with being buried alive, that theme tends to focus his concern with the "promiscuous company" that one of his narrators sees through a glass darkly. At the beginning of "The Man of the Crowd," he illustrates his manic state by his delight in breathing. As his compulsion to follow the old man, however, draws him into the street, where he becomes "wearied unto death," he sees his double "gasp as if for breath" as he throws himself into the crowd. Illness and cure seem one since the Others are what make Poe's characters suffocate, yet they are turned to for relief. In "The Imp of the Perverse" breathing is associated with perverseness: "I am not more certain that I breathe, than that the assurance of the wrong or error of any action is often the one unconquerable force which impels us, and alone impels us to its prosecution." In order to differentiate himself from the mob, the narrator commits an apparently gratuitous crime, but he begins to suffocate in the unwelcome security of remaining unknown. That need to be recognized by the disdained mob drives him to confess: "I turned—I gasped for breath. For a moment I experienced all the pangs of suffocation . . . and then some invisible fiend . . . struck me with his broad palm upon the back. The long-imprisoned secret burst forth from my soul." The narrator of "Berenice" is "breathless and motionless" before the revelation of Berenice's being: the teeth that, as D. H. Lawrence brilliantly points out, are the dragon's teeth of myth: "The teeth are the instruments of biting, of resistance, of antagonism. They often become symbols of opposition, little instruments or entities of crushing and destroying. . . . Hence the man in "Berenice" must take possession of the irreducible part of his mistress. '*Toutes ses dents étaient des idées*,' he says. Then they are little fixed ideas of mordant hate, of which he possesses himself."[11] As Lawrence's own work shows, erotic relations are the most intense examples of the rivalry that underlies all relations in a competitive universe.[12] In both "William Wilson" and "The Tell-Tale Heart," fascinated figures approach their doubles with lanterns at night in an attempt to see without being seen. In "William Wilson," where metaphysical doubling is dramatized further by physical doubling, the narrator gasps for breath when he sees the Other and experiences an "objectless yet intolerable horror," not unlike the "objectless curiosity" in "The Murders in the Rue Morgue" which indicates the irrelevance of all objects when rivalry reaches a certain pathological pitch. In "Loss of Breath" the narrator is berating his wife at the beginning of the story in order "to convince her of her insignificance." Losing his breath, however, he cannot sully "even the delicacy of a mirror"—an interesting periphrasis for a double. Trying to elude his "wife's penetration" and the "well-merited indignation" of the "multitude," he develops his voice in a compensatory, theatrical way. The sense of persecution continues, however, as the narrator is continually anatomized (like his wife, who appears at one point as "a set of false teeth, two pair of hips, an eye, and a bundle of *billets doux* from Mr. Windenough"—the narrator's rival). Having been expelled from a coach replete with passengers whose features are undistinguished, he is mistaken for a mail-robber and executed like "Marsyas"—a "consummation" of fate also undergone by the narrator of "The Imp of the Perverse," who is also a scapegoat for the undifferentiated violence that pervades Poe's world. In the tomb, moreover, this "Lack'breath" encounters his double (both of them have had bandages around their jaws), whose insolent rivalry is signified by the fact that the narrator's loss of breath has resulted in his rival's double-windedness. At the end the narrator berates his rival, as he berates his wife, and then regains his breath from him by feigning indifference to it. Sacrifice "to the proper God" ends this story in a gesture that seems strangely superfluous.

This suffocation (represented, perhaps, by the Ourang-Outang's hand upon the windpipes of his victim) results in strange alterations of voice. In "Loss of Breath" the narrator's voice becomes a "singularly deep guttural" that he attempts to make theatrically effective by "a certain spasmodic action of the muscles of the throat." In "The Murders in the Rue Morgue," two voices are heard in loud contention. One is "gruff" and says repeatedly "sacré," "diable," and "mon Dieu"—words that reject the violence that it is witnessing. The other is that of a "foreigner": its words are indistinct, but they are "loud and quick—unequal—spoken apparently in fear as well as anger." This unevenness, which reminds one of the "spasmodic action" in "Loss of Breath," occurs also in "Fall of the House of Usher," where Usher's steps are "unequal" and "object-less." Usher's voice, moreover, seems to combine the two voices heard in contention: its occasional "huskiness of tone" (like the "gruff" voice) is replaced by a "tremulous quaver, as if of extreme terror." The anger present in the Ourang-Outang's voice but absent (suppressed?) in Ush-er's occurs as "petulance" in Dupin's voice, but it is disguised by Du-pin's "deliberateness and entire distinction of . . . enunciation." Final-ly, in "William Wilson" the double's "singular whisper" grows to be "the very echo" of the narrator's: the "key" of both voices (like the "cipher" in "The Purloined Letter") is "identical." The fact that the narrator's voice was a "household law" in his childhood, by the way, suggests the debacle of authority that generates this doubling. The play of voices in Poe's work also indicates the deception involved in sacrifi-cial expulsion: the words of the Ourang-Outang are indistinct because the Ourang-Outang represents the very threat of indistinction, the col-lapse of all cultural differences. The passage from this state (much feared by the anti-democratic Poe) to the articulated culture represented by Dupin is suggested by the recapture of the Ourang-Outang (a kind of scape-ape, to anticipate the reader's jape). But this mechanism is only residual in the modern world. In "The Purloined Letter" Dupin himself assumes, for the sake of argument, the victim's role: "Had I made the wild attempt you suggest [seizing the letter openly], I might never have left the Ministerial presence alive. The good people of Paris might have heard of me no more." Dupin's calling card, however, indicates that the struggle between enemy brothers will continue unabated.

Not only voice but also vision is affected by mimetic desire. Dupin, we are told, is "enamored of the night for her own sake." Just as he later counterfeits the purloined letter in order to defeat the Minister (who must also be made to know about his defeat), he "counterfeits" night in his apartment in order to impress the world. The narrator hastens to assure us that Dupin is *himself* no counterfeit: "There was not a particle of *charlatânerie* about Dupin," but we have already seen that the narrator's claim that Dupin enjoys the "exercise" of his method rather than its "display" is as suspect as the Byronic poet's disavowal of ostentation. It is clear, for example, that Dupin likes to get a rise out of pedestrian souls like the Prefect, who finds it "odd" that Dupin turns out the light in order to reflect.[13] Dupin, like the Byronic poet, is characterized by "wild fervor" and "wild whims" in a room lit by "the ghastliest and feeblest of rays," by a "rich ideality" that seems to be the "treasure beyond price" that the narrator finds in him. In the same way, the hero of "The Gold Bug," Legrand, who is suspected of being a madman, located a treasure that becomes equivalent to his new-found prestige. As Dupin solves "The Murders in the Rue Morgue," the narrator's first response to his reconstruction of the crime is that "a madman" has done the deed (perhaps also the deed of reconstruction, since he is answering the question, "What impression have I made upon your fancy?"). Dupin's "rich ideality" becomes the "excited and highly distempered ideality" of Usher that throws a "sulphureous lustre over all." Conversely, if Usher plays "wild improvisations" on his guitar, Dupin's own improvising on the course of his comrade's meditations is pretty wild, and his own mind seems a bit "distempered." In assuring us that Dupin has no "mystery" or "romance" about him, the narrator says, "What I have described in the Frenchman was merely the result of an excited or perhaps of a diseased, intelligence." The lucidity shown by the narrator does not, however, dispel his fascination, just as the underground man's awareness of his comrades' mediocrity does not dispel their prestige in his eyes. Dupin and Usher are both figures of the *poète maudit*, and Dupin's mansion, like Usher's, is "tottering to its fall." The strategy of the *poète maudit* is to make his sense of exclusion by society (perhaps because of his mediocrity) into a willed fate: the essence of his poetic calling. Like Dostoevsky's underground man, who parades back and forth before his insolent and mediocre rivals in order to display his contempt for them, the *poète maudit* wants to *appear* alone to those whose attention he craves.

Besides the vacillation *within* each figure, Dupin and Usher represent different poles of that cyclothymia we have discussed. Dupin, we learn, is successful in drawing to himself the attention of the world: "He found himself the cynosure of the political eyes." That Dupin's singularity results from a strategy rather than from some essence is revealed in many subtle ways by Poe. For example, the *grisette*, Marie Rogêt, is described as accepting eagerly the "liberal proposals" of a man who will arrange for her traffic with men; shortly afterwards Dupin receives a "liberal proposal" from the Prefect, who is similarly drawn to his coquettishness, to the air of *ennui* that he shares with the Minister. Usher, on the other hand, represents the strategy that has failed. To his "disordered fancy" the whole world of matter has become sentient because he is the center of all contemning eyes. Having tried to bury his twin alive (in order to avoid being buried himself), he is borne to his death by her "emaciated" figure, which bears all the signs of her struggle with him. In "The Murders in the Rue Morgue," the "fissure" discovered by Dupin remains "invisible" to others; in "The Fall of the House of Usher," it becomes visible to everyone.

Since they like to believe that their desires are spontaneous, Poe's characters often have trouble discerning the source of the light by which they see. In "The Fall of the House of Usher," the rapid oscillation of desire between Usher and his twin results in a "whirlwind" that has "apparently collected its force" in their "vicinity." Although clouds are dense and although no moon, stars, or lightning is visible, everything "glows" in the "unnatural light of a faintly luminous and distinctly visible gaseous exhalation" that hangs around and enshrouds the mansion. In the crypt where Usher's sister has been buried alive are signs of a "highly combustible substance"—the desire that is ignited hither and thither in Poe's work. This mimetic combustion (or infection, as other images in Poe suggest) is made explicit by the relation between the main story and the recessed story of Sir Launcelot Canning, who, like the narrator, seeks entrance to the house of a hermit (whose obstinacy and malice are variations of Usher's *ennui*). Each scene in that tale now reverberates in the story of Usher. Since Poe, moreover, may have coined the name "Sir Launcelot Canning" from a name in the works of Thomas Chatterton, the writer of pseudo-archaic poems, we can see an infinite regress of mimesis in this story. In "The Masque of the Red Death," as in "The Sphinx," "The Fall of the House of Usher," and "William Wilson," this contagion is represented by pestilence.

As we have seen, identity in Poe's work is a function of place—one's position in a circuit of desire—so the "dreams" in "The Masque of the Red Death" take their "hue" from particular chambers. In the rooms of the Duke's labyrinthine mansion, there is no direct source of light, which is projected through the tinted windows of each room, producing a "multitude of gaudy and fantastic appearances." Similarly, in "The Pit and the Pendulum" a "wild, sulphurous lustre," the origin of which he cannot discern, enables the narrator to determine "the extent and aspect of the prison," although those qualities change with the changing tactics of his tormentors. Shortly afterwards, he is surrounded by "demon eyes" that gleam "with the lurid lustre of a fire" that he cannot force his "imagination to regard as unreal." Finally, in "Ligeia" the heroine renders "vividly luminous the many mysteries of the transcendentalism" in which she and the narrator are immersed. If "glare" is, as Poe says in his essay on furniture, the major error of American taste in furnishings, his own interiors—avatars of Plato's cave—are always full of "glare": the divine and demonic aura of his mediators. When Poe's protagonists are themselves bearers of light—as when William Wilson and the narrator of "The Tell-Tale Heart" approach their antagonists with lanterns—the effect of that focusing of light is simply to darken the scene of the confrontation. Obsessive concern with the Other, that is, is often exacerbated by one's awareness of it. This is the "*primum mobile*" of perverseness.

Poe's protagonists, as D. H. Lawrence points out, long for knowledge. They all want to be the transcendent subjects of classical philosophy, who perceive the world solely by means of their own power, but they find their perceptions of even ordinary objects affected by a more transcendent Other. They sometimes find a cloud appearing between themselves and the world, as in "William Wilson" and "The Imp of the Perverse"; and they sometimes locate that cloud in the eye of their hated antagonist, as in "The Tell-Tale Heart" and in "The Cask of Amontillado." Vision itself becomes a strategy for them because it reveals the concern that they often want to hide. In "The Purloined Letter" Dupin hides his intense concern under green glasses that make him look indifferent. In "The Mystery of Marie Rogêt" this same strategy is inverted: Dupin, while the Prefect analyzes the case, remains "the embodiment of respectful attention" although he sleeps under the guise of his dark glasses (we know how indifferent he is). In "The Murders in the Rue Morgue," Dupin claims that people are led astray by their desire for profundity; truth, he says, is "invariably superficial." To appreciate a star, for example, one should not look at it directly because that will reduce its "lustre": "By undue profundity we perplex and enfeeble thought; and it is possible to make even Venus herself vanish from the firmament by a scrutiny too sustained, too concentrated, or too direct." The way to sustain the "lustre" of Venus is to look askance—to look without appearing to look. In "Ligeia" profundity appears again in the well of Democritus to which her eyes are compared. When the narrator, however, attributes to Ligeia a "passionate devotion" to himself amounting to "idolatry," one wonders about a passion that consists of "tumultuous vultures." Her own implacable will implies *contempt* for the feckless narrator, who may be one of the "mimes, in the form of God on high," who partake of the "motley drama" of her poem. The ending of the story, in which Ligeia takes possession of the narrator's second wife, strikes one more as a persecution for this mediocre remarriage than as a devotion that transcends the grave. The vulture, by the way, appears again in "The Tell-Tale Heart," where it is the persecuting eye of the old man. The well of Democritus appears again in the epigraph to "A Descent into the Maelström," where it is equivalent to the funnel formed by the conflicting channels of the sea. It is these conflicting channels that create "profundity"—the deadly mirage so irresistible to those seeking the elusive mastery of Others. It is, like identity itself, a function of position, an accident of mutual interferences.

One interesting contrast in vision is between the pedestrians in "The Man of the Crowd" and the dead man in "The Colloquy of Monos and Una." Concerned with "making their way through the press," the pedestrians have eyes that roll quickly—like the mechanical reflexes of dolls. Monos, on the other hand, describes his experiences as follows: "The eyelids, transparent and bloodless, offered no complete impediment to vision. As volition was in abeyance, the balls could not roll in their sockets—but all objects within the range of the visual hemisphere were seen with more or less distinctness; the rays which fell upon the external retina, or into the corner of the eye, producing a more vivid effect than those which struck the front or anterior surface." Since volition is in abeyance, nothing mediates Monos' vision except his own eyelids, which have become transparent. Undistracted by Others, his vision is still, receptive, and able, as Dupin recommends, to see things more vividly than by a concentrated look. Whereas Dupin, who only feigns a lack of volition, has a "diseased" intelligence, Monos, who no longer strives to strive for such things, has a "deceased [passive] understanding."

This problem of perspective pervades Poe's stories. In "Berenice" the narrator's monomania, which exaggerates the interest of ordinary objects, bids "defiance to any thing like analysis or explanation." The counterpart to this intensity of interest is Berenice's "epilepsy," which, resulting in trances "very nearly resembling positive dissolution," make her something not "to admire, but to analyze." Similarly, in "Ligeia" the narrator finds "in the commonest of objects of the universe" a "circle of analogies" to the expression in Ligeia's eyes. Those eyes are also associated with the constellation of "Lyra," which the narrator perceives with "telescopic scrutiny," and with certain sounds from stringed instruments, which are also the only sounds that Usher's morbid sensitivity can tolerate. In contrast to the monstrous assertion of will also associated with Ligeia's eyes, which remind the narrator of Joseph Glanville's statements regarding the pervasive will of God and the inexorable will of man, is the epigraph to "The Fall of the House of Usher": "Son coeur est un luth suspendu; / Sitôt qu'on le touche il résonne." Like the systole and diastole of the tell-tale heart, aggressiveness and passivity alternate in Poe, and in "Usher" it is Lady Madeline, buried alive, who returns from the tomb to suffocate her brother. The unnamed "sentiment" in "Ligeia," like the "suppositious force" in "The Fall of the House of Usher," is envy, resentment. The death of a beautiful woman (or of an insolent man) is indeed the only fit subject for Poe's writing. This fact is writ as large in Poe's work as the place name hidden upon "the motley and perplexed surface of the chart" in "The Purloined Letter"—a name that may escape notice because it is "excessively obvious." It is as obvious as the "arabesque" in "Ligeia," which takes form only when seen "from a single point of view." When the "telescopic scrutiny" of "Ligeia" recurs in "The Sphinx," "superstition" and "suppositious force" assume the proportions of a plague. Looking through the window at the devastated landscape, the narrator sees a "monster," just as his counterpart in "The Man of the Crowd," his "brow to the glass," sees an anomalous figure amid the "tumultuous sea" outside. About this "monster," which is really a small insect, the narrator's host insists "that the principal source of error in all human investigations lay in the liability of the understanding to underrate or to overvalue the importance of an object, through mere misadmeasurement of its propinquity." Dupin's investigations also uncover monsters: a ferocious Ourang-Outang and a "*monstrum horrendum*." He does not see himself in them, nor does he recognize how they magnify or diminish the objects associated with them. The idealized figure of the schoolboy in "The Purloined Letter" manifests the real astuteness demanded of us in a competitive universe: "Of course he had some principle of guessing; and this lay in mere observation and admeasurement of the astuteness of his opponents."[14]

At this point, perhaps, we should consider why Poe's stories have been purloined for a book on contemporary fiction. The plot of this critical process may sound familiar to readers of "The Purloined Letter." Some years ago the French psychoanalyst Jacques Lacan substituted for this story a reading of Freud's *Beyond the Pleasure Principle*—a reading that, unlike the letter "of no importance" left by the Minister, is of considerable interest. Lacan's reading, in turn, became one of the originals for Jeffrey Mehlman's "Poe Pourri: Lacan's Purloined Letter," which is even more interesting. Mehlman, however, warns us against the process of substitution. "One begins wondering to what extent the French, in idealizing Poe, have not quite simply fallen for Poe's deluded idealization of Gallic genius. . . . In taking Lacan's text seriously, our task in this essay, might we not *at best* be lapsing into Poe's delusion?"[15] The guardians of *intentio* might want to replace Mehlman's theoretical candenzas with Poe's "original," but a text never exists in-itself, and interpretation always originates elsewhere. That is, because each critic tends to pursue certain ongoing inquiries by means of certain texts, interpretation tends to become circular: "That which must be understood becomes that which permits understanding; that which permits interpretation becomes that which must be interpreted."[16] Having begun with an inquiry into mimetic desire, I became interested in the contemporary texts of Lacan and Mehlman, which both reveal and conceal it. How these texts transformed Poe's "The Purloined Letter" became part of my own interpretation of them, so I read that story and many others.

But Poe's stories became particularly interesting for a diagnosis of those commentaries because Poe himself is so revealing about his own Romantic delusions. These complex actions and counteractions resulted in the proportions of this chapter.

The emphasis of Mehlman's essay is on the self-delusion that he calls "narcissism." Both the Queen and the Minister delude themselves into believing that they possess the letter, which is the "text" of the unconscious, but that pretension to master the free-play of the unconscious is always undermined by one's relations to others. Since Freud attributes narcissism particularly to women, Lacan and Mehlman want to see both the Minister and Dupin as "feminized" by their possession of the letter. Although Dupin relinquishes it finally, his vengefulness is the "rage of a manifestly feminine nature." The Minister, who does not relinquish the letter, assumes the role of the Queen. Since his power, moreover, depends on not using the letter, he becomes passive and is eventually ruined by his own success. Mehlman writes about this process of substitution: "Is not the structure of the Minister's predicament, in its play of specular reflection, precisely that which we posited in our introduction? Between, on the one hand, the French idealizing an American's (Poe's) idealization of the French (Dupin) and, on the other, the Minister, addressing the disguised letter to himself and placing his own seal upon it, a common narcissism may be intuited."[17]

Before we continue with Mehlman's observations, perhaps we should indicate our differences so far with this stimulating essay. First of all, one is disturbed by the arbitrary identification of narcissism with women. If women have traditionally manifested the kind of coquettish behavior that Freud associated with narcissism, perhaps it is because their socially weak position necessitated their using this kind of behavior as a *strategy*. In that sense it is no different from the ennui manifested by Dupin, the Minister, the Romantic figures like Usher—a strategy that may, through persistent use, become *wholly* involuntary. The description of Dupin's vengefulness as "the rage of a manifestly feminine nature" is equally arbitrary since Poe associates it with the deadly antagonism of Atreus and Thyestes. In this context, the continually displaced letter is the letter of the law, of legitimacy, that each person assumes in order to frustrate the "illegitimate" pretensions of everyone else. At no time are the rights of the King, the traditional source of all legitimacy, vindicated. The Minister, far from being debilitated by his possession of the letter, is quite *active* in its use: "The power thus attained has, for some months past, been wielded, for political purposes, to a very dangerous extent." It is the Queen and her supporters who are paralyzed by the Minister's machinations, whose true nature they are powerless to point out without exposing their own subterfuge. As to Mehlman's account of the Minister's seal, everyone attempts to place his own stamp of legitimacy upon that letter. The Minister's feminine handwriting, like his *ennui*, is only a strategy to throw people off the track of his real purposes. Dupin, having used the letter to ruthlessly defeat his most prestigious rival can now deal with the Prefects of the world by another, less hazardous tactic: he remains the "cynosure" of political eyes through the same kind of coquettish withdrawal that characterizes the Byronic poet. The poetry of his "method" is displayed with the same air of distraction as the theatrical anguish of the poet, who, in criticizing the "coquetry" and the "affectation" of the "Venus of the Medici" is inadvertently alluding to himself.

Mehlman then goes on in dazzling fashion to relate Lacan's analysis of "The Purloined Letter" to Freud's analysis of E.T.A. Hoffman's "The Sandman." Having asserted that the doll Olympia is a double for Hoffman's protagonist, Nathanael, Mehlman observes that this kind of doubling becomes for Freud "a permanent function of the ego" rather than a genetic phase. Since "it is the essence of the 'double' to be an instrument of self-defeat for the subject, an illusory defence for fending off 'the power of death,'" narcissistic doubling is a kind of vicious circle in which to win is to lose. In "The Sandman" the manic phase of this cycle is the idealization of Olympia, and the depressive phrase is the dismemberment of her lifeless body. The resulting paralysis of Nathanael, like that of the Minister, is related to the effect Socrates was supposed to have had on his interlocutors: to reduce them to immobility. After discussing the relation between repetition and the uncanny, Mehlman goes on to posit a conflict in Freud's writing between a conceptual scheme "teleologically oriented toward a fusion—or successful integration of subject and object," and one that "articulates the bizarre rhetoric of a structure of exchange in which subject and object are together alienated." This exchange is "the total evacuation of affect from representation to representation in symptoms and dreams: i.e., the fact of unconscious displacement and condensation of primary process thinking." If the fragmentation of Olympia is a psychotic attack on the Other with whom one has identified, the fragmentation of Nathanael is the castration, the loss of one's imaginary integrity, that one must accept in order to escape the vicious circle of narcissism.[18]

If mimetic desire, however, is a function of historical conditions, then genesis is indeed important in doubling: historical genesis rather than psycho-biological genesis. The double, far from being a dissociated part of the individual's psyche, is the real person whom we perceive as a rival—often after we deny our imitation of him. We have already discussed manic-depression as the shifting tides of will between rivals. No one can know what it would be like to experience the fullness of being that is supposed to be our individual lot in the modern world, so it always exists elsewhere. Poe writes in "Eureka": "The universe of space is 'a sphere of which the centre is everywhere, the circumference nowhere'. In fact, while we find it impossible to fancy an end to space, we have no difficulty in picturing to ourselves any one of an infinity of beginnings." The starting point, Poe goes on to say, is the "Godhead," with which man does not now coincide but may in the future.[19] As for the two conceptual schemes in Freud, could we not say that the choice is between the idea of positive reciprocity between men and the "scandalous" displacement of violence from one object to another? Although we cannot return to the religious interdictions that prevented men's desires from converging on the same objects, we must not confuse those external obstacles with the internal obstacle of the mimetic partner. Mehlman's reference to Socrates is especially revealing. In The Symposium, Socrates is crowned by Dionysus (in the person of Alcibiades) as the best poet. Having played a little comedy of love with Alcibiades (whose beauty and force of personality seem to make him ascendant in this relationship), Socrates turns the tables on him by showing absolute indifference to his charms. This reversal brings about a tragic recognition on Alcibiades' part of the futility of his life, but he is unable to act on that recognition in order to change his life. Socrates' indifference derives from his disinterested love of the truth and from his devotion to teaching, but Alcibiades interprets this indifference as a strategy to gain the affection of others.

To complete our permutations of Mehlman's text, let us bring together Dupin and the Sandman.[20] The Sandman who terrorizes Nathanael, the poète maudit of Hoffman's story, is one aspect of the paternal figure: the malevolent, punitive aspect. The name "Coppelius" suggests coppo, which is Italian for "eye socket," and coppelare, which means "to test metals." The father's role as model is indicated by the fact that he bequeaths to Nathanael the same "higher external principle" that inspired his own alchemical experiments. His role as obstacle is indicated by his constant threats to Nathanael's bodily integrity: he threatens to take Nathanael's eyes and, in competition with God, tries to rearrange Nathanael's body (in almost a parody of what Poe calls "imagination"). Like the old man in "The Tell-Tale Heart" whose evil eye haunts the narrator, Coppelius seems to contaminate everything he touches. As a consequence, Nathanael, like many of Poe's figures, finds that a "somber destiny" hangs "a murky veil" over his life. That Nathanael never succeeds in understanding the relation between these two aspects of his father is indicated by his blaming one for the death of the other.

Klara, Nathanael's fiancée, wants to convince him that he alone gives the Sandman the power to haunt him, but Nathanael cannot relinquish this dreadful figure without also relinquishing his inspiration. It will be a new avatar of this figure who will give Nathanael the spy glass that will transform the world in such a way that Nathanael also will feel transformed. For example, the flaming glances of the lifeless doll, Olympia, are kindled by Nathanael's own Romantic ardor; and her mechanical refrain "Ah, ah!" like the Raven's mechanical "nevermore," enables Nathanael to provide his own content to the algebraic formula of his own uniqueness. Ironically, it is Klara whom he regards as an "automaton" because she fails to acknowledge his lugubrious and "shapeless" writings.

Nathanael's madness comes about when "Spalanzani" (whose name suggests *spalancare*—"to open wide," "throw open") reveals the secret of the automaton to him: "The eyes—the eyes stolen from you." His vision of whirling fire recalls the poem that he earlier reads to Klara, in which Klara's eyes spring into his breast, where they burn—like Coppelius' own "fiery eyes" or like the prosthetic eyes that surround Nathanael with "flaming glances" that shoot their "blood-red rays" into his breast. These criss-crossing rays become a "whirlwind" in Nathanael's poem, a "blazing circle of fire." The paradoxes of winning and losing are shown in the contrasts between Olympia, whose lifeless eyes reveal a "loving glance" that scorches Nathanael "to his very soul" and whose mechanical performances make him feel embraced by "burning arms"; and Klara, whose "kindly eyes" reveal death and whose sanity seems "impervious to any ray of the mysterious which often embraces man with invisible arms."

Nathanael, then, is the Romantic poet whose mediocrity makes the eyes of Others burn into him in judgment. Turning that judgment into a curse, however, Nathanael can make of it his inspiration. In fact, he worries sometimes because Coppelius does not seem sufficiently vivid as a "sinister bogey-man." Coppelius is the father's "repulsive and diabolical mask," which becomes the sign of a superior destiny: the higher, spiritual knowledge gathered from a vision of the world beyond." Like his father, who dies for this higher principle, Nathanael will be cursed by it, excluded by it from the ordinary run of men. His madness is a tragic counterpart of the comic revelation of Poe's "The Spectacles," where the narrator's "romantic temperament" creates a mystery out of what is obvious to everyone else. When the narrator of that story, moreover, says that "the brightest and most enduring of the psychical fetters are those which are riveted by a glance," he is rewriting as farce the deadly configuration of "The Tell-Tale Heart." To discover that our own look has been fascinated by the Other's, which has played Midas to the objects of our world, or to discover that the glance that admires us is worthless—these are the nightmares of Poe's and Hoffman's work. Dupin, the successful *poète maudit*, becomes the cynosure of (admiring) political eyes; Nathanael (and Usher), the unsuccessful *poète maudit*, remains the cynosure of persecuting eyes. Dupin claims that most men for him wear "windows in their bosom," whereas Nathanael feels his own bosom penetrated by contemning glances. Like the narrator in "The Imp of the Perverse," who compares the perverseness of the will (which must frustrate the prudent expectations of others) to the fascination of jumping off a tower, Nathanael defies the insolent Coppelius by jumping from a tower.

The kind of figure who almost never appears in the work of Poe (perhaps the narrator's host in "The Sphinx" is an exception; although somewhat depressed himself, he can distinguish between the "substances" and "shadows" of terror) is Klara, whose "spirited imagination" and mature, "sympathetic" feelings make her impervious to "suppositious force(s)." Dupin both discovers and dehumanizes these forces, these "imitative propensities," in "The Murders in the Rue Morgue." He remains, after all, an "excited" or "diseased" intelligence—himself the case he will never solve. In "The Sphinx" the morbid eye of the narrator remains too close to the pane that separates him from the outside world. That eye magnifies a tiny insect (or a grain of sand) into an imposing monster—the Sphinx, whose riddle has to do with the mimetic propensities of man. The Sphinx is eliminated by the common sense of the narrator's host, who is unaffected by "unrealities." To know that the monster is only a grain of sand is to know that the Sandman is only a man like ourselves, and it is to relinquish our own claim to some essential difference. A "cipher," after all, is also a zero.

CHAPTER 4

In Search of Narcissus:
The Crying of Lot 49

As we have seen, the key to the Lacanian approach to "The Purloined Letter" is narcissism—the ego's resistance to anything that threatens its illusion of autonomy. What Lacan and Mehlman do not see, however, is that this experience of mastery is always *copied* from the illusions of others. When we, like Dupin, successfully attract the interest of others, we can then use that interest as an "original" for our own imitation of mastery. This experience, however, is precarious, not because of some free play of the unconscious, as Lacan and Mehlman make out, but because the only recognition that can sustain us in this role is the recognition we can never get. As soon as the Other recognizes us, his recognition becomes insignificant, and so the paradise of narcissism is always lost as soon as we enter it. It always exists elsewhere—where the violence of the Other (if only in the form of indifference) bars the way to those who seek entrance. This is the meaning of N.A.D.A. (National Automobile Dealers' Association) in *The Crying of Lot* 49: A vision of life in which reality always seems to be elsewhere.[1]

The heroine of the book, Oedipa Maas, is made the executor of the will of Pierce Inverarity, who seems to own most of California. Her effort to bring this estate into some kind of order constitutes the plot of the book. Her husband, Mucho Maas, is a used-car-salesman-turned-disc-jockey who has suffered from "the endless rituals of trade-in, week after week," which "never got as far as violence or blood, and so were too plausible for the impressionable Mucho to take for long." He has seen "each owner, each shadow" file in "only to exchange a dented, malfunctioning version of himself for another, just as futureless, automotive projection of somebody else's life. As if it were the most natural thing. To Mucho it was horrible. Endless, convoluted incest." The most conspicuous "rituals" of modern society are those of commerce and advertising—the rituals of personal eclecticism. Products are invested with certain values, often impersonated by figures of enviable self-confidence and success. Consuming these products means the transubstantiation not of some divinity in whom we are all reconciled but of each of us individually. The fashion of advertising is a fashion of life styles and personalities—all of which circulate through us along with the products that are their talismans. The aura of commodities, however, lasts only until they are owned, when they become part of the banality they were supposed to relieve. This spiritual function is then taken up by other commodities (perhaps of the same type) that have already been used to the same depressing effect by others. Mucho's vision of men exchanging their disappointing identities points up the fact that they continue to delude themselves that it was only the particular product that was at fault. "Endless, convoluted incest" suggests that our society, which encourages our competition for prestige, has discarded constraints that traditionally mitigated it. The "plausibility," however, of rituals that never result in "violence or blood" (and which thus appear "natural" to us) torments Mucho, who, under the exacerbating influence of LSD, becomes a "walking assembly of men" and perceives everyone else as the same person because the spectra of their voices are the same: "Then you'd have this big, God, maybe a couple hundred million chorus saying 'rich, chocolaty goodness' together, and it would all be the same voice."

This psychotic awareness takes many forms in *The Crying of Lot 49*. Oedipa's psychiatrist, Dr. Hilarius, moves from "relative paranoia" ("where at least I know who I am and who the others are") to complete paranoia, where dark shapes "replicate" and haunt him. Buchenwald, where he practiced inducing insanity by means of grimaces, is a nightmare version of the national non-consciousness that Pynchon finds in America. Similarly, the doctor's grimaces caricature the grimaces taught by modern success manuals—strategic dissimulations calculated to devastate Others with their own apparent self-assurance. The psychosis of Mucho and Hilarius is an acute awareness of the truth (unlike Oedipa's "tupperwareness" at the beginning): of the sterile rivalry of doubles. In this ritual of exchange, nothing objectively separates people, yet the psychotic (exaggerating the "relative paranoia" of more ordinary people) stakes his whole being on that nothingness. Oedipa seeks redemption from "inertia" and a "vital difference" between "San Narciso" and "the rest of Southern California." Just as Saint Narcissus changed "well-water to oil for Jerusalem's Easter lamps," Narcissus (or so the illusion goes) can transform ordinary existence into supreme self-possession. The mythical Narcissus, one recalls, was loved by the nymph Echo, who, having wooed him with fragments of his own speech, turned into a disembodied voice when rejected by him. In a place called "Echo Courts" Oedipa encounters an image of herself: "a nymph holding a white blossom" (the narcissus). This blossom occurs later in the "languid, sinister blooming" of the Tristero—Oedipa's antagonist throughout the book. Our Echo-like heroine also dreams of "disembodied voices from whose malignance there was no appeal, the soft dusk of mirrors out of which something was about to walk." The more Oedipa seeks a "vital difference," the more she encounters sameness: "a nightmare about something in the mirror, across from her bed. . . . When she woke in the morning, she was sitting bolt upright, staring into the mirror at her own exhausted face." Having become obsessed with The Tristero and having lost Mucho to psychosis, Oedipa realizes that it is "too late to make any difference." When she seeks redemption from inertia, she encounters two old men "who might have been twins and whose hands, alternately (as if their owners were asleep and the moled freckled hands out roaming dream-landscapes) kept falling onto her thighs." In Metzer, the lawyer who helps Oedipa execute Pierce Inverarity's will, she finds an "aging double of the child star they see on television." Both Oedipa and Tristero are involved in an endless strip tease—their infinite removal of clothes resembling the "receding" doorways in which she pursues her clues and the "endless rooms" into which her husband's identity recedes. This sense of inertia and repetition is present in the relation between Metzer, a child actor turned lawyer, and Manny Di Presso, a lawyer become actor who is playing the role of Metzer in a film. It is present in a rock group called the "Paranoids," who, imitating the Beatles, become themselves a multiple of four: "Oedipa . . . saw in the doorway Miles, the kid with bangs and mohair suit, now multiplied by four." When Metzer runs away with one of their teeny-boppers, they retaliate by seeking out eight-year-olds for themselves. It is this carnivalization of the social order that Oedipa finds in the "dark doubles" that she encounters in San Francisco, which reveal the truth behind the one villain of traditional detective fiction.

As the name "Di Presso" indicates, moreover, the relation between doubles entails the same kind of cyclothymia we saw in Poe's work. "Keep it bouncing" is Pierce Inverarity's motto, and "Yoyodyne" is the company in which he has major shares. (Another version of this motto, "Keep it all cycling," will be discussed later in connection with Pynchon's scientific metaphors.) As in Poe, but somewhat decelerated, these oscillations generate a "whirlwind rotating too slow" for Oedipa to feel it. At the center of one vortex, Mucho gives the illusory appearance of calm and serenity. Similarly, from the "eye" of a whirlwind Oedipa expects a revelation, but that eye is already dead (and associated with God): "Oedipa stood in the living room, stared at by the greenish dead eye of the TV tube, spoke the name of God." Since the center does not hold, nothing stabilizes these oscillations, as one character, speaking of his gambling, indicates: "Always just that little percent on the wrong side of breaking even." Another character, the "ancient driver" of a jitney, ends each day in the red.

Those vortices and whirlwinds are part of the "storm-systems of group suffering and need, prevailing winds of affluence," which suggest conflicts that have little to do with material need and satisfaction. These conflicts occur among people who, having come closer and closer to each other materially, create arbitrary distinctions and exclusions that have incalculable effect. This is the meaning of the diacritical marking that distinguishes Tristero from Thurn and Taxis: the mute added to the latter's post horn. Although at first Tristero seems to be a force of concrete political opposition, its function becomes purely negative. When the Scurvhamites, for example, an extreme Puritan sect, do a version of *The Courier's Tragedy*, a Jacobean drama, they use Tristero to "symbolize the Other" in their Manichaean view of the world: "the brute Other, that kept the non-Scurvhamite universe running like clock work." As in all Manichaean oppositions, the Other is both hateful and fascinating because it represents the void one refuses to recognize in oneself. However much one adheres to the principle of "Good" that one represents, the Other always seems destined to triumph: "Somehow those few saved Scurvhamites found themselves looking out into the gaudy clockwork of the doomed with a certain sick and fascinated horror, and this was to prove fatal. One by one the glamorous prospect of annihilation coaxed them over."[2] The shaking of Degree results in the kind of negative collaboration that Pynchon indicates over and over. Emory Bortz, an expert consulted by Oedipa, holds to a "mirror image theory, by which any period of instability for Thurn and Taxis [the 'legitimate' monopoly of the postal service] must have its reflection in Tristero's shadow state." When Thurn and Taxis is made vulnerable to opposition by changes in political power, one faction of Tristero wants to take over its function by force; another, "conservative" faction wants to remain in opposition; and a third faction, "men above the immediacy of their time who could think historically," propose a *positive* collaboration with their old enemy to "unify the continent." The spokesman of this last group, who foresees "the breakup of the Empire, the coming descent into particularism," notes that "the salvation of Europe . . . depends on communication." With the failure of this scheme and with the end of the Holy Roman Empire, "the fountainhead of Thurn and Taxis legitimacy is lost forever among the other splendid delusions. Possibilities for paranoia became abundant," and the qualities of the Scurvhamites' "blind, automatic anti-God" are transferred to "the secular Tristero." The sense, however, of how these Manichaean poles oscillate makes Oedipa suspicious of the binary and symmetrical choices that seem to offer themselves when she attempts "to project a world." In *The Courier's Tragedy*, which foreshadows the devastations of the English civil war, The Tristero are on the side of the villains. The figure emerging successful, however, from the play's blood and gore is "the colorless administrator, Gennaro," whose subsequent avatars assume the role of villain: as Yoyodyne, the monstrous corporation that grinds its engineers into anonymity; and as another corporation that spawns, by its automated cruelty, "Inamorati Anonymous." Eventually, the members of Tristero "simply stay on . . . in the context of conspiracy. . . Their entire emphasis now toward silence, impersonation, opposition masquerading as allegiance." Tristero becomes, in fact, the unhappy consciousness suggested by its name: the sense, wherever it is found, of being disinherited or excluded.[3]

Like Dupin and his confidant, who close out the daylight of common opinion and become "enamored of the night for her own sake," the founder of Tristero ("The Disinherited") has his followers dress in black "to symbolize the only thing that truly belonged to them in their exile: the night." When Oedipa discovers that this consciousness can be found "anywhere in her Republic," she imagines some railroad tracks as a kind of celestial map: "knowing they laced, deepened, authenticated the great night around her." Elsewhere, however, she wonders if the clues she has been given are only compensation: "to make up for having lost the direct, epileptic Word, the cry that might abolish the night." On the one hand, night is a *part* of the whole: opposed to the "America coded in Inverarity's testament." Authenticating the night, then, is authenticating one's opposition. On the other hand, night is the whole the confusion out of which Oedipa's quest arises. In this book, as in the others we have examined, the imagination tends to abolish confusion through the mechanism of sacrifice—the "epileptic Word" suggesting violent revelation. Elsewhere, Oedipa thinks of "the voice before and after the dead man's that had phoned at random during the darkest, slowest hours, searching ceaseless among the dial's ten million possibilities for that magical Other who would reveal herself out of the roar of relays, monotone litanies of insult, filth, fantasy, love whose brute repetition must someday call into being the trigger for the unnamable act, the recognition, the Word." This imagined Logos relieves men of their own "brute repetition" by assuming responsibility for it: first as a scapegoat, then as a Deity. The deception that obscures men's knowledge of each other's violence (knowledge which perpetuates that violence) is suggested by other passages: "She too might . . . be left with only compiled memories of clues, announcements, intimations, but never the central truth itself, which must somehow each time be too bright for her memory to hold; which must always blaze out, destroying its own message irreversibly, leaving an overexposed blank when the ordinary world came back." In order to be effective, the scapegoat mechanism must efface its own traces. The restored sense of community, which is the goal of this process, is suggested by a scene that follows Oedipa's longing for the "epileptic Word." She comes across a group of children who claim that they are "dreaming the gathering": "The night was empty of all terror for them, they had inside their circle an imaginary fire, and needed nothing but their own unpenetrated sense of community."[4] Elsewhere, this necessary deception, this bridging the gap, is associated with a "time differential" generated by an old man's DT's:

> Behind the initials was a metaphor, a delirium tremens, a trembling unfurrowing of the mind's plowshare. The saint whose water can light lamps [Saint Narcissus], the clairvoyant whose lapse in recall is the breath of God, the true paranoid for whom all is organized in spheres joyful or threatening about the central pulse of himself, the dreamer whose puns probe ancient fetid shafts and tunnels of truth all act in the same special relevance to the word, or whatever it is the word is there, buffering, to protect us from (emphasis mine).

The sacrificial Word protects us from our own violence as long as we are not aware of its workings; but Oedipa's situation, like the situation of modern man generally, is that her awareness undermines the effectiveness of the Word (which becomes suspect as hallucination): "The act of metaphor then was a thrust at truth and a lie, depending where you were: inside, safe, or outside, lost. Oedipa did not know where she was." The "anarchist miracle" of Jesus Arrabal (himself a "competitor" of the bourgeois heroine) is only a comedy acted out by Pierce Inverarity, who, in Mexico, plays the quintessential gringo:

> You know what a miracle is . . . Another world's intrusion into this one. Most of the time we co-exist peacefully, but when we do touch there's cataclysm . . . Like your friend. He is too exactly and without flaw the thing we fight. In Mexico the privilegiado is always, to a finite percentage, redeemed—one of the people. Unmiraculous. But your friend, unless he's joking, is as terrifying to me as a Virgin appearing to an Indian.

More probable in a world of sterile oppositions (the initials of Arrabal's organization are "CIA") is the "dialectical" thinking parodied by the Peter Pinguid Society, which is so far to the right of the John Birch Society that one of its members, Mike Fallopian, ends up wearing a "modified Cuban ensemble." When one character says of the founder, Peter Pinguid, that his protest against "industrial capitalism" would seem to disqualify him as an anti-communist figure, Mike Fallopian replies: "You think like a Bircher . . . Good guys and bad guys. You never get to the underlying truth. Sure he was against industrial capitalism. So are we. Didn't it lead, inevitably, to Marxism? Underneath, both are part of the same creeping horror." Pinguid's protest against industrial capitalism takes the form of becoming rich through speculating in California real estate, just as another founder, Pierce Inverarity, seems to have bought up everything in California. Perhaps we can understand now why "every access route to the Tristero" can be "traced also back to the Inverarity Estate," which is America. The unhappy consciousness of Tristero finds a home in America, which is the Western world at its most antinomian. In a society where, by and large, traditional constraints have been replaced by the various disciplines of consumption, "founding father(s)" like Pierce Inverarity are highly protean. When Pierce telephones Oedipa, he goes through a whole repertoire of stereotypes before settling on "The Shadow"—a role that makes him no less elusive than the "shadow state" of the adversary. The "effeminate" appearance of Tristero in *The Courier's Tragedy*, moreover, suggests the vanity, the mutual emulation, that constitute what most people take to be ambition in our society.

This mutual emulation constitutes the tower in which Oedipa is encapsulated before her quest (one variation of "Thurn and Taxis," by the way, is "Torre and Tassis"—the Italian word "*torre*" both signifying "tower" and being contained in the specular "Tristero"). Even during her affair with Pierce Inverarity, Oedipa feels confined to her tower (having "gently conned herself into the curious, Rapunzel-like role of a pensive girl somehow, magically, prisoner among the pines and salt fogs of Kinneret"). In Mexico City they view a painting by Remedios Varo, which depicts a number of girls,

> prisoners in the top of a circular tower, embroidering a kind of tapestry which spilled out the slit windows and into a void, seeking hopelessly to fill the void: for all the other buildings and creatures, all the waves, ships and forests of the earth were contained in this tapestry, and the tapestry was the world. Oedipa, perverse, had stood in front of the painting and cried. . . She had looked down at her feet and known, then, because of a painting, that what she stood on had only been woven together a couple thousand miles away in her own tower, was only by accident known as Mexico. . . . Such a captive maiden, having plenty of time to think, soon realizes that her tower, its height and architecture, are like her ego only incidental: that what really keeps her where she is is magic, anonymous and malignant, visited on her from outside and for no reason at all. . . . If the tower is everywhere and the knight of deliverance no proof against its magic, what else?

If the "tower" and the "ego" are only "incidental," it is because they are functions of what Henry James calls "the endless expressional question," which needs, as counterbalance, "*some* intensity, some continuity of resistance" to the "assault of experience."[5] Pynchon's concern with "entropy" is a concern with this lack of resistance—the failure of our culture to enjoin the kinds of renunciations that would allow us some fulfillment in communal purposes. The "anonymous and malignant" magic that keeps Oedipa in thrall is the ethos of consumption that encourages infinite availability (of things to oneself and of oneself to things), which encourages hostility to culture of *any* form. The word "malignant" is later applied to the replicating signs of Tristero that immobilize Oedipa. Although these signs seem to come from another world (the mysterious and mobile persecutors who substitute for traditional, passive constraints), they are really signs of withdrawal from "the life of the Republic, from its machinery. . . . Since they [the citizens] could not have withdrawn into a vaccum . . . there had to exist the separate, silent, unsuspected world."

As Mucho's vision of "endless, convoluted incest" reveals, imagery associating Oedipa with her namesake in Greek tragedy has to do with anomy. When Oedipa, leaving a gay bar entitled "The Greek Way," enters an "infected city," she encounters diseased human relations like those of Inamorati Anonymous, who refuse to love as a remedy for not being loved. In Sophocles' play the scapegoat's crime against the *polis* is conveyed by the image of furrows since the furrows he plows are his mother's loins and not the Theban land. In *The Crying of Lot 49*, however, the plowing of land, far from being a symbol of communal achievement, is a symbol of banal routine. About the old man suffering from the DT's, Pynchon writes, "Cammed each night out of that safe furrow the bulk of this city's waking each sunrise again set virtuously to plowing, what rich sails had he turned, what concentric planets uncovered?" Is the delirium associated with dreams, DT's, and paranoia in this book a breakthrough (rather than a breakdown), as it is for certain radical writers? Salvation depends on "communication," but the DT's of the old man give him access to "dt's of spectra beyond the known sun, music made purely of Antarctic loneliness and fright. . . . Nothing she knew of would preserve them, or him." Using W.A.S.T.E., the alternative postal service, he has written a letter to his abandoned wife, but we never know its contents. The one message transmitted through this service that we do know is utterly vacuous: "Dear Mike . . . how are you? Just thought I'd drop you a note. How's your book coming? Guess that's all for now. See you at The Scope." The medium—an unauthorized *kind* of message—is the message.

Much of Oedipa's revelation comes through the stamp collection left by Pierce Inverarity: "his substitute often for her—thousands of little colored windows into deep vistas of space and time: savannas teeming with elands and gazelles, galleons sailing west into the void." Dupin, one recalls, claimed that most men wore for him "windows in their bosoms," but Dupin, through the schoolboy he used as an example of one-upmanship, expressed contempt for what he saw. Oedipa cannot seem to provide these splendid other worlds for Pierce, just as Pierce is no "knight of deliverance" for her. The stamps, moreover, are flawed ("inverse rarities," as Pierce's name suggests)—like the letter addressed to the Minister but bearing the Minister's own seal. They also resemble the purloined letter in that they are always on the way "to any number of new masters." Like the purloined letter, which reveals its truth to those who can see the obvious, seals and rings in this book also reveal the truth. In *The Courier's Tragedy* the letter bearing the villain's seal is "miraculously" transformed from a "lying document" into a confession of crimes. Just as Oedipus, instructed by the oracle at Delphi, enables Thebes to reconstitute itself around his crimes, the villains of *Lot 49* provide the means to "project a world." The ink with which history is written comes from the bones of dead men (the murdered soldiers in the "Lago di Pietà") since history is written by the winners. Elsewhere, a "dull gold signet ring" reveals the truth, which is presided over by a declining "Mr. Thoth," whose name suggests the Egyptian god of wisdom and writing. As the sunlight pours through the windows and the old man recalls an old story of villainy (which, like Oedipus' recollection of the crossroads, involves his [grand]father), Oedipa experiences an epiphany: "She looked around, spooked at the sunlight pouring in all the windows, as if she had been trapped at the centre of some intricate crystal, and said, 'My God.'" Toward the end of the religious tradition (in "Vesperhaven House"), with the scapegoat reduced to an anarchist in a Porky Pig cartoon, Mr. Thoth still experiences God on days of "a certain temperature . . . and barometric pressure."

Although Oedipa claims that she has never "seen the fascination" of the other worlds represented by the stamps—the illusions of others being our common sense—she also becomes fascinated by them. Backstage after *The Courier's Tragedy*, she meets Randolph Driblette, who describes his role as director in terms not unlike those used to describe the tower in Varo's painting: "I'm the projector at the planetarium, all the closed little universe visible in the circle of that stage is coming out of my mouth, eyes, sometimes other orifices also." Around the name of Tristero, however, he creates "the same aura of ritual reluctance" as he created on stage since it is his own unhappy consciousness, his own lack of autonomy that he wants to suppress. The form Driblette gives to Warfinger's text, like the form he gives to himself, "wreathed in steam," is transitory: "If I were to dissolve in here . . . be washed down the drain into the Pacific, what you saw tonight would vanish too. You, that part of you so concerned, God knows how, with that little world, would also vanish." Later, after Driblette has walked into the Pacific, Oedipa tries to communicate with him and fails, "wondering whether . . . some version of herself hadn't vanished with him." Oedipa, co-executor of Inverarity's will (the negative collaboration of rivals), also tries to "project a world," but she is unable to fill the void: "For this, oh God, was the void. There was nobody who would help her. Nobody in the world."

To project a world one has to be outside that world—like the God of Poe's "Eureka." This illusion of superiority is similar to the illusion in

Oedipus the King by which each of the protagonists thinks that he is outside the conflict pursued by the others. This putative role is filled in *Lot 49* by the "sensitive" who makes the "Nefastis machine" (a kind of perpetual motion machine) work. The basis for this apparatus is the theoretical Demon of James Clerk Maxwell, who, by observing the molecules moving in a box and by sorting out the fast ones from the slow ones, creates a difference of temperature that can be used to perform work. Since the sorting itself is not supposed to be work, one is violating the second law of thermodynamics in getting something for nothing. The machine invented by Nefastis works as follows: "All you had to do was stare at the photo of Clerk Maxwell, and concentrate on which cylinder, right or left, you wanted the Demon to raise the temperature in. The air would expand and push a piston. The familiar Society for the Propagation of Christian Knowledge photo, showing Maxwell in right profile, seemed to work best." The Christian knowledge suggested by that photograph, however, seems to have been lost forever: Maxwell is described as gazing "away, into some vista of Victorian England whose light had been lost forever." As in Vesperhaven, "belief" here is associated with TV cartoons. What can be shared, apparently, are hallucinations: "The true sensitive is the one that can share in the man's hallucinations, that's all." We are most of us true sensitives in this sense since our daily fare of advertising and popular entertainment is high powered fantasy—tupperwareness. If Maxwell's Demon doesn't respond immediately to Oedipa, he does later: all that night she is given multiplying signs of Tristero that she is "meant to remember."

The problem with Maxwell's Demon is that perception affects the course of what is perceived:

> Before an intelligent being can use its intelligence, it must perceive its objects, and that requires physical means of perception. Visual perception in particular requires the illumination of the object. Seeing is essentially a nonequilibrium phenomenon. The cylinder in which the demon operates is, optically speaking, a closed black body and, according to the principle enunciated by Gustav Kirchoff in 1859, the radiation inside a black body is homogeneous and nondirectional because for any wavelength and any temperature the emissivity of any surface equals its co-efficient of absorption. Hence, although an observer inside a black body is exposed to quanta of radiation, he can never tell whether a particular photon comes from a molecule or is reflected from a wall. The observer must use a lamp that emits light of a wavelength not well represented in the black-body radiation, and the eventual absorption of this light by the observer or elsewhere increases the entropy of the system.[6]

On the social level each person is at the center of his own system of shuffling and sorting and plays "sensitive" to the systems of others. The right and left cylinders of Nefastis' machine are comparable to the "matrices of a great digital computer"—the binary logic bemoaned by

Oedipa as an impoverishment of real possibility: "How had it ever happened here, with the chances once so good for diversity?"[7] The basis of this logic is the opposition of success and failure, which are measured not by communal norms and designs but by our temporary cathexis of Others. Oedipa's lawyer, for example, nourishes a fierce ambivalence toward Perry Mason, whom he wishes both to emulate and to destroy. Success is never stable since it constantly recedes toward the next horizon established by the next and more prohibitive model, which is why the galleon of Inverarity's stamp will continue to sail on into the void. The "sensitivity" of one person to the next, then, is not a positive sensitivity but a negative one, which Nietzsche called "*ressentiment*." Whenever one person becomes a model for another, his every action becomes suspect—part of a project that excludes or defeats his disciple. This kind of feedback also creates business cycles and armament races since the behavior we anticipate from others (often as that vague statistical entity called "public opinion") causes us to act in ways that actually bring about the anticipated behavior. Oedipus puts out his eyes, whose searching and suspicious look resulted in his own self-righteous *ripostes*. Oedipa tries something similar: "Then she went out and drove on the freeway for a while with her lights out, to see what would happen. But angels were watching." The old blindness and deception no longer work to release us from mimetic conflicts, and Oedipa finds herself calling a member of Inamorati Anonymous as a last resort.

The perpetual motion suggested by this "nefastous" or nefarious machine is the oscillation of mimetic conflict—like the stichomythia of Greek tragedy. Oedipa waits for this "symmetry of choices to break down, to go skew"—like the moment when the Lucretian atoms suddenly swerve. As Pynchon's short story "Entropy" makes programmatically clear, entropy for Pynchon represents a prolonged cultural crisis. One of the characters in that story sees in American consumerism a "tendency from the least to the most probable, from differentiation to sameness, from ordered individuality to a kind of chaos. He found himself, in short, restating Gibbs' prediction in social terms, and envisioned a heat-death for his culture in which ideas, like heat-energy, would no longer be transferred, since each point in it would ultimately have the same quantity of energy; and intellectual motion would, accordingly, cease."[8] The question is whether "ordered individuality" can exist without the unwitting part of culture that Freud called sublimation. Can it exist without the ordered renunciations and remissions that traditional societies imposed on their members? In *The Crying of Lot 49*, most of the people encountered by Oedipa disintegrate or die—as if defenseless against the Augustinian Devil of their own anomy. Unlike the sage in Conrad's *Lord Jim*, Driblette, for example, walks into the destructive element but has no "continuity of resistance" to keep him afloat. A sense of irreversibility, moreover, pervades *Lot 49*. Both Mucho and Metzer seem to tend "ultimately, statistically" toward teen-age girls because they lack some inner resistance. As Oedipa muses over the "massive destruction of information" entailed by Nefastis' perpetual motion machine, she seems to discover "the irreversible process" in the death of an old sailor: "It astonished her to think that so much could be lost, even the quantity of hallucination belonging just to the sailor that the world would bear no further trace of."

The past has little authority for our technetronic society, which is oriented toward exploitation and consumption. Consequently, truth has lost what Walter Benjamin called its "haggadic consistency," which is what people used to call wisdom. In addition, since the modern world can no longer be encompassed by one man's experience, the art of story-telling itself has become problematic and must compete with the dissemination of information.[9] Entropy, then, is the erosion of certain structural constraints, which leads to a more random, homogeneous distribution of elements. The result of this randomness among men, however, is various kinds of obsessiveness: intense mimesis and equally intense denial. The fact that the "central truth itself . . . must always blaze out, destroying its own message irreversibly" indicates how Western society continues to efface the traces of that victimary mechanism that allowed it to evolve in spiraling patterns of order and disorder. Our own misunderstanding of religion repeats religion's own misunderstanding of its generative mechanism, but the growing ineffectiveness of that mechanism makes further demystification inevitable. In this hiatus between the old, sacrificial order and some brave new world, Oedipa shuffles through "a fat deckful of days" searching for clues but miming the principle of thermodynamics itself. Since competing orders contribute to the disorder they are attempting to solve, Oedipa's shuffling conflicts with the unseen shuffling of "clues" going on elsewhere. The structures, codes, and conventions that impose order on equiprobability are parodied in this book by the code of happy endings that Oedipa invokes in order to predict the ending of the film she is watching with Metzer: "This is absurd . . . of course they'll get out." She herself is not convinced, however, since she asks Metzer to give her odds on the film's outcome.

As we have seen, Oedipa continues to await a revelation. At one point, impressed by the "hieroglyphic sense of concealed meaning" that she derives from San Narciso, she feels "parked at the centre of an odd, religious instant." This "promise of hierophany," which pervades the book, seems imminent at the end. The auctioneer, whose name "Passerine" suggests "pass her in," spreads his arms in a gesture that seems to belong "to the priesthood of some remote culture; perhaps to a descending angel." And Oedipa awaits "the crying of lot 49," which is, however, a lot of forgeries. Similarly, the figure of Passerine is not without ambiguities. One of the forged stamps depicts the "capitol dome," at the top of which is "a tiny figure in deep black, with its arms outstretched." The devil, one recalls, tempts Jesus by placing him on the highest point of the temple and by telling him to prove himself God's son by jumping. He also places Jesus on a very high mountain, from which he tempts him with the worldly kingdom before him. Jesus, who resists these temptations in the *Bible*, who repudiates the mechanism by which men have achieved a *modus vivendi* with their own violence,[10] is still indistinguishable from his adversary in *Lot 49*. Just as the "descending angel" recalls the "coming descent into particularism," the "distant figure" is "dressed in deep black" like the Tristero and the "pale, cruel men" who portend death at the end of the book. That Maxwell's Demon does not sort out the elements of the system supports our sense that the old Logos no longer polarizes all that men do not succeed in mastering in their relations with each other, but that a new Logos of love (of good reciprocity) has not yet emerged to command men's allegiance.[11]

If sacrificial resources have become more problematic in the modern world because their significance has become progressively more apparent, what loopholes remain available for the modern imagination? How can it transcend the changing fashions that it reflects? The name "Remedios Varo" suggests "remedy for man," but nothing about his painting suggests how this "remedy" differs from the illness it is supposed to cure. As a matter of fact, a reproduction of one of Varo's paintings is found in a hotel room where Oedipa awakens to her own image in the mirror. Oedipa's own surname means "loophole" in Dutch, but Oedipa's detection, because it is self-justifying, only complicates the mystery. In *Lot 49* the problem of order (or *taxis*) centers around the notion of metaphor: "Entropy is a figure of speech," says Nefastis, who claims that the Demon makes this figure objectively true. The two equations—one for information and the other for thermodynamics—express levels of equiprobability, but between them the Demon (whose own "objective existence" is as fideistic as certain ontological proofs of God's existence) creates the order of a concept. Later, this mediating role is attributed to "Trystero": "Now here was Oedipa, faced with a metaphor of God knows how many parts; more than two, anyway. With coincidences blossoming these days wherever she looked, she had nothing but a sound, a word, Trystero, to hold them together." And then to Pierce: "The dead man, like Maxwell's Demon, was the linking feature in a coincidence. Without him neither she nor Jesús would be exactly here, exactly now. It was enough, a coded warning." Metaphor, as we have seen, is "a thrust at truth and a lie," depending on where you are: "inside, safe, or outside, lost." It is, as one critic says, an "unité polémique du semblable": "It is metaphor which reveals the logical structure of the 'similar' because, in the metaphorical statement, the 'similar' is perceived *in spite of* difference, *despite* contradiction. Resemblance is then the logical category corresponding to the predicative operation in which 'rendering near' encounters the resistance of 'being far away'. . . . By this specific trait, an enigma is retained at the heart of metaphor."[12]

By metaphor, then, we can integrate various phenomena and perspectives while maintaining some sense of their diversity. Throughout human history the basis for this progressive differentiation of culture has been sacrifice and the attempts of human societies to consolidate the gains made by its reconciling power. But sacrifice itself is a kind of metaphorical (or proto-metaphorical) operation: the immanent and internecine violence of a society transferred to one person, who is made responsible for it. Since the unanimous violence against him brings about the sudden and miraculous transformation of war into peace, the victim also becomes a god, whose transcendent goodness ("being far away") will maintain the society he has chastised by having come near. As René Girard points out, it is because of the victim that the very notions of inside and outside, before and after, community and sacredness exist. The victim is the *unité polémique du semblable* because he combines badness and goodness, violence and peace, death and life; and it is the various combinations and permutations that religious cultures make of these functions that constitute their diversity. These founding metaphors reveal "the logical structure of the 'similar' " only when they are no longer effective—only when the "enigma" at their heart, the sacrificial victim, has been solved.

Oedipa's detection brings her backstage of *The Courier's Tragedy* to meet its director. She circles "the annular corridor outside twice before settling on the door in the shadowy interval between two overhead lights." This "shadowy interval" portends the "interregnum" that she discovers later in the "rituals of miscarriage" performed by a Negro woman—one of the many alienated figures she encounters. In a sense all religious rituals are "rituals of miscarriage" since they commemorate a miscarrying of society in order to enact its revival. Backstage Oedipa encounters "soft, elegant chaos, an impression of emanations, mutually interfering, from the stub-antennas of everybody's exposed nerve endings." What exposes these nerve endings is the acute mutual awareness caused by free-floating desire. The kinds of mutual emulation and denial that result from this "primary process" suggest the "region of brightly-lit mirrors" into which she then enters and encounters Driblette, whose eyes are "bright black, surrounded by an incredible network of lines" —like a spider's web or a magnetic field. These lines will later become the "burst veins" of the old sailor's eyes and the furrows of routine. They will become a "net of invisible cracks" between Oedipa and Mike Fallopian, whom she suddenly distrusts, and the broken mirror presiding (with endless bad luck) over Metzer (that "aging double" of himself) and the Paranoids.[13] But they also become lines of communication: railroad tracks and telephone wires. That energy can be converted from deceit and willfulness to love and sympathy remains one of the hopes of this book: "Exhausted, hardly knowing what she was doing, she came the last three steps and sat, took the man in her arms, actually held him, gazing out of her smudged eyes down the stairs, back into the morning."

When Driblette's head emerges from the steam of the shower, its "eerie, balloon-like buoyancy" foreshadows Oedipa's vision of binary thought: the "balanced mobiles" of zeros and ones. Some versions of this paradigm are: "Behind the hieroglyphic streets there would either be a transcendental meaning, or only the earth. . . . Another mode of meaning behind the obvious, or none. Either Oedipa in the orbiting ecstasy of a true paranoia, or a real Tristero. For there either was some Tristero beyond the appearance of the legacy America, or there was just America and if there was just America then it seemed the only way she could continue, and manage to be at all relevant to it, was as an alien, unfurrowed, assumed full circle into some paranoia." But, as Oedipa herself intuits, these static dichotomies are false. The "true paranoia" *entails* a "real Tristero" since what is false in paranoia is not the double—mimetic desire *makes* men doubles of one another—but the difference that they continue to *dispute*. Similarly, Tristero is not an alternative to the legacy of America; it is the legacy of America: the unhappy consciousness of those who cannot fulfill an endless promise. The idea that paranoia can be Oedipa's only "relevance" to America is homeopathic magic of the worst kind: a kind of willful mimesis of social compulsions. Finally, meaning can transcend the earth only in the sense that men can stop making it a stake in their bitter rivalries.

The pathetic thing about Driblette is that although he is only one of the "balanced mobiles" that men are *vis à vis* each other, he thinks that his disinterestedness contains the whole. That lie is part of the "ritual reluctance" that he creates around Tristero. Toward the end of the book, Oedipa, "her isolation complete," tries to face toward the sea, but she is unable to find either the sea or the mountains: "As if there could be no barriers between herself and the rest of land." At that moment San Narciso, no longer unique, becomes part again of America, and Pierce Inverarity seems really dead. To relinquish the illusion of uniqueness is to dispel the fascination of the Other; it is to recognize his humanity and to accept one's own. Although the ending of the book is unmistakably grim, forty-nine days is also the period specified in *The Tibetan Book of the Dead* as the period between death and rebirth. The modern world threatens us with universal violence, but perhaps it is only in such a crisis that violence itself becomes threatened: "Today the problem is how to create the society that will be open, that will not collapse in mimetic hysteria, but save itself through something that will not be sacrifice, exclusion, ostracism; a society that will have no *outside*."[14]

CHAPTER 5

Royalty in a Rainy Country:
Two Novels of Paula Fox

At the end of Plato's *Phaedrus*, the urban man, Socrates, delivers a beautiful pastoral prayer that includes the request: "May the outward and inward man be as one." Having shown that both erotics and rhetoric are arts of acting on somebody when you have full knowledge and the other does not, Socrates asserts a new kind of erotics—of the living word of face to face dialogue—and prays for that word's adherence to what is present and what is personal. In Paula Fox's *Desperate Characters*[1] Sophie Bentwood, whose last name suggests the crookedness against which Socrates is arguing, makes a statement that seems almost parodic of Socrates' prayer: "God, if I am rabid, I am equal to what is outside." Besides sickness, "rabid" also suggests an abusive use of language. In the same book the animadversions against contemporary civilization uttered by one of the characters, a college professor and an erstwhile socialist, are described as "an old habit of words." In *The Widow's Children*[2] Peter, an editor for a publishing company, takes exception to Laura's use of the word "nigger," to which she responds, "All right, my dear Peter. I know your sensibilities. They're all about *language*, aren't they?" If at one point in that novel Fox seems to parody the ambition to have words adhere to what they designate—a group of women have badges "inscribed" with their names pinned to their gowns—in *Desperate Characters* Otto (Sophie's husband) tells of a man who takes apart and reassembles used typewriters so that the keyboards spell out "mystic nonsense words." The idea is an enormous commerical success, which the man justifies by saying that "the destruction of a typewriter and its reconstitution, its humanization, as a kind of oracle, was a direct blow at American Philistinism." He begins to buy things, but, in order not to be corrupted by his success, he deforms these luxurious objects enough to ruin their function. This "revolutionary" aesthetic is, interestingly enough, accompanied by a brutal authoritarianism toward his wife, whose least creative gesture he suppresses.

The deformation talked about here is a theme of both *Desperate Characters* and *The Widow's Children*. In the former novel Sophie buys a radio for her lover, Francis Early, who then seems to replace it with a better, more powerful radio, about which he says: "I can get the world," which allows him to crowd out Sophie. Instead of smashing the new radio, which is what Sophie wants to do, she smiles: "She didn't know how to violate that mutual smile of theirs. It was miasmic. It stayed on her face while she undressed. It would not go away, and she bore it home with her, a disfiguring rictus." Smiles are always disfiguring in Fox's novels because they are masks used to disguise intent, to ward off aggression, or to play at one's own feelings: "At the thought, she felt her mouth contort into what she could only imagine as a hideous smile of malice" (*The Widow's Children*). Sophie also notes of her relation with Francis that it has shoved her violently into herself, a turnabout that relates to both novels' theme of crookedness. In *Desperate Characters*, for example, Charlie Russel talks with Sophie about the break-up of his partnership with Otto. Suddenly he mutters, "Why do I feel like a crook?" One character says of Charlie that he is "a bleeding heart, dying to be loved. He has a face of a handsome baby, doesn't he?" What another character calls Charlie's "impeccable attitudes" stem from his desire, above all, for innocence, a desire that falsifies his "virtuous opinions." Charlie, however, points to the same kind of crookedness in the culture at large. Everything, he says, is a business: "the having children business, the radical business, the culture business, the collapse of old values business, the militant business . . . every aberration becomes a style, a business. There's even a failure business." Francis Early's personality is interesting in this respect:

> He couldn't seem to help himself—even his bitterness was somehow turned to personal profit. It added to his mystery, it gave his smile an elusive sadness, and it was an element in that quality he had of always recognizing the *real* meaning that lay behind people's words, as though his soul attended in the wings of a theater, ready to fly out and embrace them in universal awareness.

Despite her own awareness, however, Sophie is taken in by Francis, whom she sees in the same way as Charlie sees himself. In this society irony becomes a kind of cancer that makes it almost impossible to distinguish between reflecting and reacting against cultural phenomena: "Whether she was celebrating their new affluence, or making an ironic comment, I don't know."[3] When, in *Desperate Characters*, Leon, the erstwhile socialist, says to his former wife, Claire, "I'd take my shopping sack all over the city before I'd settle for sour grapes," he reveals in Aesopian fashion the anxiety with which the middle class tries to certify its experience as genuine. Charlie, talking indignantly about the problems of the poor, says, "You just wait"—as if he identifies with them and against his own class. Immediately, however, he excludes Sophie also from the warning: "I didn't mean you, Sophie. I don't know what I mean." Because he feels "murdered" by Otto's refusal to recognize his virtue, he becomes murderous by class proxy. Similarly, Charlie's letting go of Sophie's arm as she stumbles—"as though by stumbling she'd forfeited her right to his support"—shows how understanding can be a means of evasion, as if virtuous opinions exempted one *a priori* from the judgments they implied.

When Sophie points out that she and Francis Early have "both been crooked," it follows an exchange in which Francis notes that his wife is indifferent to things but wants to know the name of everything and Sophie claims, disingenuously, not to know the names of anything—as if a shell game were being played with reality. One can appreciate why problems of order (like the theme of entropy in Thomas Pynchon's work) are so crucial in contemporary fiction. The art critic Rudolf Arnheim notes that since outer, perceivable order tends to manifest an underlying order, whether physical, social, or cognitive, one must evaluate orderly form in terms of the organization it signifies: "The form may be quite orderly and yet misleading, because its structure does not correspond to the order it stands for."[4] This statement reminds one of the opacity of rhetoric decried by Socrates in *Phaedrus*. At one point in *Desperate Characters* Sophie observes Otto as he sleeps: "Even in sleep he looked reasonable, although the immoderately twisted bedclothes suggested that reason—in sleep—had been attained at a cost." Late in the book Sophie discovers a passage underlined twice by Otto: "To vindicate the law." Having learned that young boys have been hanged for this vindication, Sophie thinks:

> How had Otto felt, reading those lines sometime during the night? Had the hanging of young boys appalled him? But why had he underlined the words? Did he mean that the horror of law is that it must be vindicated? Or had he thought of himself, of his own longing for order? Or was the double line an expression of irony? Or did he think law was only another *form* of that same brute impulse which it was directed toward restraining?

This lucidity concerning the law is fatal in primitive societies, which depend on a scapegoat mechanism to relieve them of their immanent violence and then to confound it with other natural forces. A judiciary system, on the other hand, limits violence by rationalizing it—by investing it in a legitimate authority. Sophie's concern with the legitimacy of the law is part and parcel of the concern Fox's characters express with the validity of values in general. Otto, for example, unlike Charlie, wants to be "left out" because he doesn't want to be "taken in." As Sophie says to him, "You're so full of cunning, catching everyone out . . . the American form of wisdom!" When he looks back at his brownstone house, he wants "to catch the house empty," as if to indicate that he is not duped even by his own sense of security. Otto, in fact, formulates a paradox reciprocal to the one concerning the law when he says of the young, "They are dying from what they are trying to cure themselves with." But Otto does want the security toward which he seems ironical, which is why he expresses such respect for the legal process that Charlie sees as "an ironic joke." Accused of being a "square" and thought of as being "reductive," Otto tells Sophie that she does not "draw enough lines." His desire for rational limits is seen in the following description: "Telephone cables, electric wires, and clothes lines crossed and recrossed, giving the houses, light poles, and leafless trees the quality of a contour drawing, one continuous line." Sophie, who has lost all real interest in work and bemoans her own inertia, seeks an illusory redemption in her relationship with Francis. If Otto tries "to catch the house empty," she tries to force from her consciousness the realization that the room in which she lives with Francis is "except for her own presence . . . empty." When she assures herself, however, that she is "going to get away with everything" (her affair with Francis and her being bitten by a cat), she begins to cry and finds the following sentence in a book: "Illnesses do their work secretly, their ravages are often hidden." During her affair it is "harrowing" to her that she is getting away with it, that such a "violation" of her intimacy with Otto should leave so little evidence. When she looks at Otto, who is unaware of this "violation," his forehead is "furrowed" as he eats some applesauce. This kind of imagery occurs also in *The Widow's Children*, where Peter has "a worrying sense that a day had passed without leaving a mark," and where problems of intimacy tend to be "harrowing." In *The Crying of Lot 49*, as we have seen, Thomas Pynchon uses images like these in a context that recalls the furrows of Sophocles' *Oedipus the King*: "How, how could the father's furrows, alas, bear to keep silence for so long?" (ll. 1210–1212). In an "infected city" Oedipa Maas imagines an "unfurrowing of the mind's plowshare" as a "special relevance to the word" that will liberate man from relations of sterile rivalry. Fox's characters suffer from the same sense that real existence is somehow elsewhere and that their acts have no real consequence.

Otto's drawing of lines (which sometimes result in excluding Sophie also: "He had closed her *out* into the house") is not in itself sufficient: "I wish someone would tell me how I can live," he says at one point. But Charlie's sentimentality is no solution, as one parodic figure in the book indicates: "She was staring down at a copy of *Life* magazine, her mouth open." In a subtle way Fox associates Charlie with the dissolution that contrasts with Otto's fastidiousness. The trigger for the novel's plot is a cat's biting Sophie as she tries to show it affection. The words "edge" and "ledge," repeated frequently throughout the book, help to convey the sense of violation committed by the cat. At first the creature is described rubbing its half-starved body with "soft insistence" against the door of a house that seems "powerfully solid" to Otto, but when it turns against Sophie's insistently friendly hand, it is a "circle of barbed wire."[5] The cat's head, moreover, is described as "massive, a pumpkin, jowled and unprincipled and grotesque." When Charlie knocks on the door early in the morning, Sophie holds her bitten hand "stiffly against the soft folds of her nightgown," and before she recognizes Charlie, she sees a large body swaying on the other side of the door and a "large head" veering toward it. In addition, Charlie turns on Sophie at one point and says, "You don't know what's going on. . . . You are out of the world, tangled in personal life." The cat's attack brings home the same point to her: "Life had been soft for so long a time, edgeless and spongy." This association between Charlie and the cat is compounded by another "beast" in the book. Sophie's friend Claire tells her about Leon's new wife, a "dull girl who's convinced herself she's a creature of unbridled lust." Having deceived Leon by a thesis on Henry James, she now waits for him "behind the door, stark naked, liberated from intellectual concerns, his beast, she calls herself." The mention of Henry James in connection with "beast" reminds one of James's story "The Beast in the Jungle"—about a man who spends his whole life waiting for something extraordinary to happen and then discovers that the extraordinary thing is that nothing has happened in his life. When Sophie is bitten by the cat, she feels shame—as though she has been caught "in some despicable act"; she feels "vitally wounded" though she tries to tell herself that it is only her hand; and when she tells someone that she has been bitten before, she stammers slightly as if she has "tripped over a lie." Her statement "I'd been feeding the damned beast and it turned on me" sounds like a line from Aeschylus' *The Libation Bearers*, but here the "beast" is her own inertia and sloth—the good sentiments that substitute for the half-starved reality of the cat—and the bite is a "small puncture" in her "fatuity."

The beast in the jungle is a deception—like *Le Canard Privé* (the decoy) visited by the restaurant goers in *The Widow's Children*. That book also contains a significant lie. When Laura asks her daughter, Clara, whether her dress is French, Clara replies: "No . . . I got it on sale." Fearing Laura's judgment of her extravagance—and of the self-assertion that it represents—Clara passes her original off as a copy. This problem of personal sovereignty is accompanied in Fox's novels by various kinds of lighting, indications of weather, and vision. In *Desperate Characters* "brilliant wall lights" make it look as if a sale is in progress although there is not "a copy of anything on the premises." In keeping with the theatrical imagery of both books, the host of that house (a psychiatrist) looks like "a man preceded into a room by acrobats," and Sophie holds up a mirror to his face after reciting these verses by Baudelaire:

Je suis comme le roi d'un pays pluvieux,
Riche, mais impuissant, jeune et pourtant très vieux.

In this "rainy country" light has some peculiar qualities. Although Sophie, for example, criticizes Otto for examining everything "in the light of what Charlie would have to say," she admits to having seen her lover, Francis, in the same way Charlie sees himself. In her recollection of being with Francis, "Light seemed everywhere at once" although the room seemed empty of his presence. Light and seeing are deceptive. At first Sophie finds Francis "touching," but he cannot really touch anyone (Otto, with unintentional ambiguity, says that Francis does not take him in). Francis's apparent responsiveness to people is the "only provision" he carries. Similarly, when Mr. Haynes—a factotum used by the Bentwoods for their country house—says of his family, "We're here for all the world to see," he is repudiating the city folks with this exaggerated image of "country folks" who "do love their kitchens." During this episode in the country, Mr. Haynes's truculence is described as "gleaming through his smile like a stone under water." A stone, we recall, has been thrown through the window of a house belonging to friends of the Bentwoods, and Sophie experiences her momentary but powerful detestation of Otto as her having assumed a "Medusa's face," which, of course, turns people to stone. In *The Widow's Children* Peter thinks of "something hopeless . . . embedded like a stone at the heart" of his failed marriage, and shortly afterwards enters a bookstore in which a mirror is being installed to prevent thefts. The proprietor complains, "Who's supposed to watch that mirror all the time?" These images have occurred in another important scene. When Clara is taken to one of the Hansens' "borrowed apartments" to see her father and mother, she looks up to see "Laura standing in a doorway, holding a glass in which ice cubes floated, looking at her. It was as though a stone had looked at her. Suddenly Laura had hurled the glass into the room." The "glass" is also a mirror that Laura is trying to smash as she sees her reflection in Clara— excluded by Laura as Laura has been excluded by Alma, her own mother. As far as theft is concerned, Laura accuses Clara of stealing her voice (the aural counterpart to her image). This kind of imitation is pandemic in the book—like the shadows of Plato's cave.[6] At one point a "sober ventriloquist" seems to have taken charge of Desmond's voice. Laura does crude imitations of the Jewishness she repudiates in her own past, and her first husband, Ed Hansen (whose "charm," like Charlie's in *Desperate Characters*, is itself a kind of mask), is said to have imitated Laura's mother wonderfully. Alma, in turn, was also a good mimic, especially good at imitating one of her sons, Eugenio, who says of his whole family what Plato says of opinion: "We have all learned by imitation. . . . In my family we could never do anything but imitate. We never *knew*."

Desperate Characters begins, in fact, with an image reminiscent of Shelley's neo-Platonic

> Life, like a dome of many-coloured glass,
> Stains the white radiance of Eternity,
> Until Death tramples it to fragments.

If light seems "everywhere at once" with Francis, and if a painter friend can describe his life with "the calm zealotry of one who has received truths from the sun," the Bentwoods' experience of life is somewhat different. The "strong light" at the beginning is "softened by the stained glass of a Tiffany shade." In their "living" room, moreover, is a standing lamp, "always lit," with a "shade like half a white sphere." These elements of transcendent unity and immanent dispersion occur throughout the book. Over the windows of the "houses on the slum street" are rags or sheets of "transparent plastic." Later on, Otto, who wants to be "left out," has the cream from a "plastic container" spill all over himself, and Sophie nurses her memories of Francis "like an old crone with a bit of rag for a baby." Francis tells Sophie how a "glass worm" can be sectioned, and the sections will survive. When someone shatters the window of the house that seems so perfect with all its original things that a sale seems in progress, Sophie and her psychiatrist friend find "a few shards of broken glass." Charlie, who wants to identify with the poor and be part of the solution, says, "Do you know that when people change slowly and irrevocably and everything goes dead, the only way to cure them is a bomb through the window. I can't live that way, as though things were just the same." When Sophie visits her friend Claire,[7] she notes that the whole surface of the building is covered with "dollops of some substance" that looks like "solidified guano," and only a trickle of light seeps through "filthy stained-glass windows." In Claire's apartment, where the light coming through the window is so murky it seems "to have texture," Leon complains that his privacy has been violated in the "age of baby shit." The book is, in fact, so full of garbage and dreck that Fox's characters often feel as if they are drowning in a tide of refuse, which also includes debased language. If an artist can, as one critic claims, "make a treasure out of trash," and "see out from inside it, the world as it's faceted by colored jewelglass,"[8] no one in Fox's novels is making treasures out of dreck. The closest we come to this kind of transformation is cooking. Leon, having looked back nostalgically on the days when he and Claire had nothing but when, handing out leaflets on Sixth Avenue, he felt that he knew the answers to everything, now shares an interest with Claire in cooking: "It's all that's left . . . . It's what is left of civilization. You take raw material and you transform it. That *is* civilization."

In *The Widow's Children* Peter recalls his first cooking lesson, which his uncle gave him on the day of his mother's death. Their pie, we learn, "tipped over . . . and then simply exploded." This sense of futility reminds us that the artist alone concocts foods "so purely spiritual and momentary they leave scarcely any stools," creates works that "insist more than most on their own reality."[9] As Peter shambles "toward disintegration" in an elemental state of fear, he sees a model ship, a "work of skill and patience, an imitation of reality that was itself a realization." A more ironical moment of transcendence occurs in *Desperate Characters* when Sophie finds Otto standing at the window (the curtains of which are "gritty" in the "monochromatic dullness" of the morning) and staring at a Negro who, as he reels silently along the sidewalk, holds a "green plastic airplane" and collapses "in violent genuflection."

In *The Widow's Children* the "foreignness" of the Maldonadas provides an unfamiliar view of the familiar. Carlos and Laura use "comic strip words," and when Eugenio says that his family could never do anything but imitate, he could be talking of the culture at large where imitation and rivalry are what we mean by individuality. Also revealing is the contrast between Laura's "thrilling displays of temperament" and Madame de Bargeton's "ambition and poignant ineptitudes" in the novel by Balzac that Sophie is reading in *Desperate Characters*. Whatever their ineptitudes, the ambition of Balzac's characters implies the "conversation, work, solutions" that Sophie finds in the hospital (where an old woman, soaking her hand as Sophie has soaked hers, parodies her sense of futility and puns ironically on "solution"). Laura, on the other hand, whose eyes are described as "drowned," relates stories with "a strange shallowness" which is part of her fascinating appearance. That others feed on this fascination is suggested, in *Desperate Characters*, by the story Francis tells of a larva that insinuates itself into the brain of a songbird in order to complete its metamorphosis.

In *The Widow's Children* we learn that Peter's friendships with both Laura and Violet, a neighbor of his, have really been a "mindless feeding on someone else's personality."[10] Violet herself, however, is "nebulous" and "indescribable" to herself, and the "increasing materiality" of her life makes her feel more and more abstract. Similarly, Sophie, who is described as "abstracted" at one point, thinks of her preoccupations as "nebulous" and experiences the materiality of her life as the "shadowy, totemic menace" of the things around her. Despite the "profound spiritual indolence of the Maldonadas," which includes Laura's own "inertia," the self-doubts of Clara and Peter mean that the former believes "no one but Laura" and the latter betrays other people as "his gift to her." The vicarious nature of Peter's and Clara's experiences is conveyed by the fact that when Peter marries, he feels that he is "marrying the Hansens, too"; his wife is important only insofar as she allows him to imitate these models. As for Clara, when Peter asks her what she is getting out of an affair, she replies, "I feel his pleasure." Peter recalls his father, a man "unadorned by temperament," as a "shelter," a "silent place," but he and Clara cannot "see things in a plain way." Peter knows that Laura arouses men "to empty purpose," and Clara knows that the "self-betraying part of her nature" awakens "in her mother's presence, compelling her to submit to a profound intent in Laura to destroy certainty," but the only "shelter" they find at the end (as they try to break Laura's spell) is in a "family sepulcher." Laura is not "a point in a continuing line of human descent but the apex of a triangle," and an "iron triangle" is the shape of Clara's fate.

The irony, however, is that Laura's difference from everyone derives from the same sense of exclusion from which the others suffer. Laura treats Clara as she feels she has been treated by Alma, her mother, and she uses her mother's death to exclude Clara further. If Alma becomes "the old child of her own daughter," Laura views *her* daughter as a rivalrous sibling: "But she didn't leave Clara. . . . She never left Clara," she says of her mother. When Peter and Clara drive to the funeral, hoping to break the grip of the past, they see a group of Hasidim whom they take to be an omen. Earlier, Eugenio, who is described like Atropos as he draws thread through a fabric and then bites it off, says, "When one forgets the past, there is nothing, is there?" Like Charlie in *Desperate Characters*, however, Eugenio can only parody true ideas since the past for him (as it is for Clara) is only something he continually trips over. Clara thinks to herself at one point, "Perhaps something had really happened, at last," while Sophie thinks, as she contemplates Otto's insistence on vindicating the law, "There was no end to it." As Baudelaire's notion of "spleen" reveals, "The man who loses his capacity for experiencing feels as though he is dropped from the calendar." If Baudelaire "holds in his hands the scattered fragments of genuine historical experience," our modern sense of *durée* "has the miserable endlessness of a scroll. Tradition is excluded from it."[11] Where "degree is shaked" and "truth" is denuded of the consistency of tradition, illusions of authority flourish. For example, people fear Laura because of her basic deficiency: "She's dead cold inside, half born. She doesn't really know that anyone else is alive. The world—it's only an expanded bubble of herself—what she hates is part of herself. . . . She never gets *outside* anything." Although this imperialism is only a variation of their own sense of exclusion—of living hypothetically—it is the source of her authority over people like Peter and Clara.

One recalls the loathing that Otto feels in *Desperate Characters* for Tanya, a woman who, with her long succession of love affairs, remains "grossly virginal." These inconsequential affairs caricature Sophie's own affair with Francis: "She had chosen him at a late moment in her life when choices were almost hypothetical. It was a choice out of time." Tanya, when staying once with Otto and Sophie, used "every drawer in an immense bureau for the few articles she'd brought with her that weekend," as though personal resources were in an inverse relation to abstract possibilities. Tanya is also related to Sophie's mother, who used to wake Sophie each morning with "derisive applause": "Early risers are the winners." Sophie has never discovered "the prize her mother's words had once led her to believe existed." During the Depression her mother drove with her through the streets where "poor people" lived in order to vindicate their middle-class existence. When Sophie repudiates Tanya over the phone, she says, "You think because somebody's husband sticks it in you, that you've *won*. You poor dumb old collapsed bag! *Who are you kidding!*" As opposed to the "prize" the man across the way exposes to Sophie, and which eventually includes his baby, winning in these instances seems an abstract assertion of superiority. In one of many uses of cold in her novels, Fox has Tanya "recovering from a cold" when she calls Sophie, and when Desmond asserts his superiority in a restaurant, we read: "His tone was cold with the tyranny people display in an environment shaped by their ability to pay." This "ability to pay," however, is only an abstract, Archimedic value.

Both *Desperate Characters* and *The Widow's Children* are also replete with animal images. At one point Laura, who has kept the news of the mother's death from everyone as her own possession and who has left the restaurant in a rage at Clara's "theft" of her voice, bemoans "the old beasts of her life"—her mysterious impulses. Longing for the "utter quietness of animal being," she remembers how she once undid a knotted string in front of a lion, whose rapt attention she maintained. If we recall that Laura has stolen Clara's inheritance after she has been deprived of her own, we can see that this knotted string resembles the more Gordian knots of R. D. Laing:

> I'm not entitled to it
> therefore ↕ because
> I've stolen it.[12]

When we recall Laing's animadversions against a society that destroys experiences inconsistent with its clichés, we can see that this sense of dispossession is also a more general problem of culture. Philip Rieff writes,

> So long as a culture maintains its vitality, whatever must be renounced disappears and is given back bettered; Freud called this process sublimation. But, as that sage among psychiatrists Harry Stack Sullivan once said,

"if you tell people how they can sublimate, they can't sublimate," The dynamics of culture are in "the unwitting part of it." Now our renunciations have failed us; less and less is given back bettered. For this reason, chiefly, I think, this culture, which once imagined itself inside a church, feels trapped in something like a zoo of separate cages.[13]

This is why characters in Fox's novels can be described as "performing bear[s]" or "sluggish beasts." To complicate matters, the bars are constantly moving so that one can never be sure whether he is inside or outside, observer or observed. The failure of Western culture is expressed in various ways in *The Widow's Children*. If our systems of symbols organize both moral demands and the expressive release from those moral demands, those two functions have fallen apart in a more remissive culture. At one point we read that Peter and Laura "understood each other; she was ruled by impulse, he, by constraint. And each pitied the other for their subjugation to opposing tyrannies." The erotic, which, as Plato reveals in the *Symposium*, is supposed to reconcile love of oneself (or of one's own) with love of the other, is parodied in this book by the pornographic. Clara, using obscene jokes to awaken a response in her relatives, wonders what these jokes take the place of, "with their abject mangling of the ways of carnal life, their special language more stumps than words." These "stumps" occur earlier in Laura's description of beggers in Madrid, who shake their stumps at her and laugh. Peter, in turn, describes the characters in the book as "beggers, pinching each other." Hours are "mutilated, debauched"; all things are "pinched, poor, broken, worn ragged"; and Peter's possessions are "shadowed clumps." The obscene joke Clara tries to recall has to do with a woman and a doorknob, and later Desmond, who is "always suspecting crooks" (and whose own narrowness he experiences as a lie) checks the doorknob of the room several times. Like the porn queen, Randy Cunny, who appears in one sequence, Laura also arouses men "to empty purpose" and conveys a false promise of intimacy. If Laura cannot get outside herself, Clara cannot get *inside* herself to experience her own pleasure. We are told, moreover, that Clara's "not wanting" is an "effort to fend off a huge collapse" against Laura's indifference—as if she is playing possum in order to avoid death. Later on, in fact, she imitates a possum, but Laura—at first amused by her squeaky rendition of a possum's birth— then accuses her of stealing her voice, of usurping her place.

While in *Desperate Characters* the problem of exchange between inner and outer is conveyed by the theme of excretion, in *The Widow's Children* it is conveyed by the theme of incorporation. As Freud teaches us, the aim of incorporation is derived from the biological aim of feeding and can occur in other systems besides the digestive one. The eyes, for example, can be involved in such a derived aim. At one point Clara has "the startling impression" that her mother's eye sockets are empty—

"like mouths, opening to scream." The sexual relations in the book reveal relations of autonomy and heteronomy. Laura, for example, swings away from intimate contact with Clara "like an accomplished old adulterer." Carlos, Laura tells us, becomes a homosexual "to avoid supporting a woman." Clara, who has hoped futilely for "rescue" by Carlos, thinks about her visits to him and her father: "They had barely acknowledged her presence, as though she'd been one of Carlos's young men whom she sometimes found there with them." As Peter and Laura talk about Peter's sisters, who excluded him as a child, Laura refers to them as "sister dykes"; and Peter, whose existence has become more and more exiguous, is described an "an old nanny." At one point Clara searches for a cartoon that Alma, who uses them to communicate with all the family, has sent to Laura. Not finding it, she thinks: "Had Laura chewed it up and swallowed it?" Among other images suggesting cannibalism, Carlos alludes to the sow that eats its farrow, "I'm becoming an old sow."

The "widow" whose children these are was once brought as a young girl to a Cuban plantation to be the bride of the master. There she was taught to betray her own experience: "La Señora had warned her that she must not notice such things [the treatment of slaves]. She did not discover what they were for until months later." She was also taught to exclude her children, whom she later comes to dominate "through the tyranny of her pathos." As the epigraph to the book suggests, Alma has pleased the "terror" of convention that has become divorced from reality: "Deprived of their first leaves her barren children stand, and seem, for all the world, to have been born because she pleased some terror." Eugenio, the child who has suffered most from his family's "fall" from privilege, has a poster on his wall of a castle in Spain: "It was a twelfth-century fortress; the mist enveloping it did not conceal its brutality." This interface between the self and the world recurs throughout the book. With drunken sentimentality, a "kind of mist" settling over his mind, Desmond thinks of the "style" that separates Laura from the middle class. Clara talks of Alma as a fog that surrounds her. Laura and Desmond, like the fortress, are both referred to as "brutes," and Laura's face, when she expresses loathing for the "self-regarding sentimentality" of the Jews, looks "brutish and empty." Laura is like the person in Desperate Characters who says, "I started out with you and ended up with myself" since the "Jew" against whom she fulminates is herself. When Violet (the other woman on whom Peter depends for her temperament) tries to reassure Peter about what she assumes to be his homosexuality, her "conventional language" is "inane, brutal and mawkish." The sentimentalist, as Stephen Daedalus points out, "is he who would enjoy without incurring the immense debtorship for a thing done."[14]

At the end of the book, moreover, Laura denies the effectiveness of what Peter and Clara have done to liberate themselves from her. In response to Clara's "questioning glance," Peter wants to cry out, "Wait! It's not nothing. . . . I've almost got hold of it!" The name "Maldonadas," however, which suggests a kind of nihilistic disease, implies that Peter has got hold of nothing. In *Desperate Characters* the hippie son of the Bentwoods' friend wears an army fatigue jacket "on which were pinned buttons shaped and painted like eyeballs, staring from nothing, at nothing," and in *The Widow's Children* Carlos, whose inertia is extreme, wears someone else's spectacles. Laura is thought to be able to "see through people," as if a dia-gnosis were possible among these optical distortions, but all Laura can see through are the "manners" she induces people to assume. What Laura *is* really good at, as she says herself, is "makeup." We learn at the very end that Peter's revelation is only a reversal of what is the case: "It" (his mother's manipulation of appearances into "some tangled thing," and Laura's own knotted strings) holds *him*. One recalls the girl in *Desperate Characters* who says of the anklet she wears: "It hurts me to wear it. . . . Every time I move, it hurts." When Peter says of his mother: "No intelligence at work, and no feeling except vindictiveness toward me because I was *hers*," he could almost be describing Laura as well. Denied by both of them at the end, Peter is bound as victim to a kind of psychological vendetta. He recalls a morning in childhood when, hearing his mother and sisters in the kitchen and seeing the paw marks of animals "braiding the snow" (an image associated with the "thick plaited design in gilt" [or "guilt"] that frames a mirror in Laura's hotel) all Peter wants is "to be good." If, as Peter [k]notes, "Families hold each other in an iron grip of definition," that happens because families can no longer reinforce the purpose of a traditional community or resist the manipulations of its contemporary counterpart.

Fox's characters seem to suffer from a Midas touch. Violet, we recall, feels "nebulous, indescribable," and the "increasing materiality" of her life seems to deprive her of any real security. Eugenio says of himself, "Beggars can't be choosers" and laughs a "grinding, metallic chuckle." Having lost his patrimony as a child and having actually been "thrown out of people's homes," Eugenio "still waits to be thrown out" as if that alone validated the worth of what is inside. What Eugenio seeks is the "blissful oblivion of wealth," which corresponds to the mindless imitation he sees as characteristic of his family. Laura's voice, similarly, is "metallic, serrated" as she contemplates the "futility" of her mother's absurd wisdom. Her own presence, however, her "elaborate killer's manners," causes only betrayal in others.[15] Her compliment to Clara, for example, is unjust because wounding. That this Midas touch has a cultural dimension is revealed in Peter's remark: "Culture makes one bitter." When Alma comes from Spain to Cuba in order to marry an older man whom she has never met, she experiences a "strange, bitter, piercing smell everywhere—it seemed green to her, like the new bitter green leaves of spring." This bitterness suggests the betrayal implicit in the promise. La Señora, as we have seen, warns Alma that she must not notice certain things, and this gesture of suppression is repeated twice in the book. When Clara visits Laura in one of the "Hansens' borrowed apartments," her father puts his finger to his lips, "warning her to be silent as though someone were sleeping"; and in the restaurant Laura makes a similar gesture when Clara claims that she is "really full."

One of the rules by which we often abide is the denial that we live by rules. Laura, for example, is thought to be lawless. But the principal rule suggested by these gestures is: "Thou shalt not implicate thy mother in matters of fullness or emptiness." The same sense of promise is conveyed in Peter's first meeting with Laura and Ed Hansen: "It had been a spring day, the room smelled of the unthawed earth and the first fresh greenness outside . . . the light had been so sweet, so clear!" "Sweetness" is associated with hope and rescue. Carlos, who is "sweet" but ineffectual, cannot "do much for anyone" although Clara has looked to him for rescue. The old man who bakes a cake with Peter after the death of Peter's mother is also described as "sweet." He is reminiscent of the character in *Bleak House*, Jarndyce, whom Charlie has always wanted to be like. When Jarndyce's offer of pastry is rejected by Dickens' pathetic little heroine, he says, "Floored again!" and flings the pastries out the window. The pie Peter makes with his uncle tips over and then explodes—like the empty form of self-realization associated with Laura: "She realizes herself only when the bomb she throws explodes. It's a self-realization I don't understand."

In the restaurant Clara has "a bittersweet recall of the outside natural world, the coarse shifting earth upon which squatted these hotel and restaurant strongholds, so close, muffled, airless." For these city people, whose longing resembles that of Socrates' pastoral prayer, the "natural world" is the name given to their disappointment with "culture." The word "coarse" is crucial in both books because it refers to the material dimensions of culture. Charlie, who wants to be an ideal benefactor like Jarndyce, bristles when Sophie calls him "coarse." In *The Widow's Children*, on the other hand, Desmond takes "visible pleasure in his coarseness" as if to defend himself against his own disappointments. In a culture which trivializes ideals by the sheer weight of its material means and which also turns ideals into fads by means of its tolerance, one can either take "visible pleasure" in one's coarseness or make capital out of one's disappointments. Although Francis Early "coarsens" a bit in *Desperate Characters*, his "limpidity of expression" derives from his ability to turn everything, even bitterness, to personal profit. Similarly, Clara has experienced a sense of "bitter triumph" in being deprived of her inheritance, and a sense of "inherent promise" in being broke, although the reversal implied by this promise never comes. The disappointment of success, however, is irreversible. In the "rainy days" of March, Desmond recalls, he had dreams in college which he cannot now recall. In their rainy country Paula Fox's characters feel deprived of their sovereignty—the inevitable result, perhaps, of each man having become his own king.

CHAPTER 6

On the Threshold:
The Fiction of Marguerite Duras

If "catching everyone out" is the American form of wisdom, "lived
anxiety" is the form of wisdom that one finds in the work of Marguerite
Duras.[1] In *Moderato Cantabile*, for example, Anne Desbaresdes, attend-
ing the piano lesson of her somewhat recalcitrant son, hears a terrible
scream from a nearby café. On going there shortly afterward, she sees a
young man clinging to the body of the lover he has killed. Compulsively
returning to the café with her son, she imaginatively reenacts the murder
and the events leading to it with a stranger named Chauvin. Becoming
habitually intoxicated during these visits, she finally creates a scandal at
a dinner party given by her and her husband, and throws up in her
child's room with her husband as witness. The "hidden desire" Anne
discovers in herself is a desire to transcend the stifling limits of her life. It
is for a passion so absolute that it seems to create around itself a world of
its own: "Toute expression en avait disparu," we read about the murderer, "exceptée celle, foudroyée, indélébile, inversée du monde, de son
désir."[2] This, as we shall see, is also the "ravissement" of Lol Stein,
another of Duras's heroines; and it leads to the absolute expense advocated in *Détruire, dit-elle.*

Perhaps the best place to begin examining this absolutism is Duras's
Hiroshima Mon Amour. In that film a French actress making a film about
the bombing of Hiroshima and a Japanese engineer have an affair. During
the opening sequences, where she tries to evoke the horror of Hiroshima
and he denies that possibility, the lovers' bodies seem drenched with a
dew or a perspiration left behind by the atomic "mushroom": "Il devrait
en résulter un sentiment très violent, très contradictoire, de fraîcheur et
de désir." Like Anne and Chauvin, this couple wants to know what it is
like to experience something absolutely—whether horror, grief, or love.
That experience they call "Hiroshima" (despite the "universal banality"
of the modernized city): "Partout ailleurs qu'à HIROSHIMA, l'artifice est
de mise. A HIROSHIMA, il ne peut pas exister sous peine, encore, d'être
nié." But nothing in time or history is absolute. The actress, who is later

described as wiping the perspiration from her forehead, says to her lover: "Comme toi, j'ai oublié. Comme toi, j'ai desiré avoir une inconsolable mémoire, une mémoire d'ombres et de pierre." To preserve such a moment against time, one would have to die, but the actress has survived a comparable moment in her personal history: the loss of her German lover at Nevers. When her current lover tells her that she should have died at Nevers, she concurs but indicates that her failure to do so cannot be helped. Similarly, to complete their "mortuary ritual," Chauvin says to Anne: "Je voudrais que vous soyez morte"; and she replies, "C'est fait." All convention seems stifling in Duras's work, but particularly troublesome is the sense that all experience has become secondhand. Unlike the so-called "literature of exhaustion," which attempts to capitalize on this exasperated sense of imitation, Duras tends toward more and more terroristic means in order to break through this secondhandedness:

> Tu me tues.
> Tu me fais du bien.
> Tu me tues.
> Tu me fais du bien.
> J'ai le temps.
> Je t'en prie.
> Dévore moi.
> Déforme-moi jusqu'à la laideur.
> (Hiroshima Mon Amour)

The oracular heroine of Détruire, dit-elle puts this command in more absolute terms. But this breakthrough is never achieved: "Ou bien elle est très fardée," we read about the actress, "elle a les lèvres si sombres qu'elles en paraissent noires, la elle est à peine tardée, presque décolorée sous le soleil."[3] In a world where, by and large, conventions no longer help us to become ourselves and no other, Duras's characters find it difficult to distinguish between experiencing something and playing a comedy in which they are experiencing something. Hiroshima and Nevers represent utopias of immediate and uncompromised experience.

A similar utopia, the Town Beach ball, occurs in Le Ravissement de Lol V. Stein. The book's heroine is described by her close friend, Tatiana, as being bored, passive, and aimless. Much to her friend's surprise, Lol's "attention" is captured by a young man named Michael Richardson, to whom she becomes engaged. At a subsequent ball, however, he is smitten by another woman, and Lol becomes temporarily mad (like the actress in Hiroshima Mon Amour, who, her German lover dead and her head shaven for collaborating with the "enemy," is placed in a cellar). Her madness, however, seems to resume her previous condition of accidie, which is why Tatiana claims that Lol has always experienced the same crisis. What the couple has provided for Lol is an "unknown" to which she can aspire because she is excluded from it—an unknown described in religious language: "Il [the word that would name the unknown] vous attend au tournant du langage, il vous défie . . . de le soulever, de le faire surgir hors de son royaume percé de toutes parts à travers lequel s'écoulent la mer, le sable, l'éternité du bal dans le cinéma de Lol V. Stein." What Lol wants is to eternalize the moment just before the dawn (just as Maria, in *Dix heures et demie du soir en été*), wants to prolong the moment before her husband and her friend culminate their passion), for in that moment she can still feel part of the "ship of light" that is about to sail. But only God could prolong this moment, and Lol, whose exacerbated pride demands that she be God (both herself *and* the others) or no one, finds that she is no one. To be God means to be a magnetic "hole": "Immense, sans fin, un gong vide, il aurait retenu ceux qui voulaient partir, il les aurait convaincus de l'impossible, il les aurait assourdis à tout autre vocable que lui-même."[4] This "word"—original and originating—would make all others look secondhand.

As is true of all romantic desire, however, the illusion of mastery can be maintained only on the verge of success (or failure). The essential difference we aspire to is always incarnated in another, whose apparent mastery is the model for our own: "Elle a posé le mot sur moi," the narrator says of Lol, and then adds: "A sa convenance j'inventerais Dieu s'il le fallait." As Lol reveals long after the ball, the other woman displaces her fiancé in her affections: "Je n'ai plus aimé mon fiancé dès que la femme est entrée." Like a magnet, this woman attracts Lol's interest, and Tatiana's as well: "Qu'avait-elle connu, elle, que les autres avaient ignoré? Par quelle voie mystérieuse était-elle parvenue à ce qui se présentait comme un pessimisme gai, éclatant, une souriante indolence de la légèreté d'une nuance, d'une cendre? Une audace pénétrée d'elle-même, semblait-il, seule, la faisait tenir debout. . . . Rien ne pouvait plus arriver à cette femme, pensa Tatiana, plus rien, rien. Que sa fin, pensait-elle." If the ashes remind us of the fallout in *Hiroshima Mon Amour*, Anne-Marie Stretter reminds us of the city. Hiroshima has come as close as we can imagine to ultimate holocaust, and Anne-Marie Stretter gives off her own kind of fallout, her own impression of the penultimate: "Michael Richardson se passa la main sur le front, chercha dans la salle quelque signe d'éternité."[5] Later in the novel, as the narrator aspires to Lol, she is described three times as being covered with the same kind of allure—a patina of perspiration. The other woman's effect of "une obscure négation de la nature" (which includes ordinary people) is amplified by the couple she forms with Michael Richardson. What Tatiana refers to as Lol's masochism is her obsession with the moment in which she must be separated, forever, from them.

Lol's recurrent fantasy, the removal of Anne-Marie Stretter's dress, is an "anéantissement de velours de sa propre personne" that she can never quite bring to its conclusion. Since it is Lol's own desire, her own obsessive regard that generates this fascinating repudiation of herself, her eyes are later described as like velvet also. The man who undresses Anne-Marie Stretter is a god grown weary of this eternal task: "Et Lol attend vainement qu'il la reprenne, de son corps infirme de l'autre elle crie, elle attend en vain, elle crie en vain." The grammar of this passage is ambiguous: does "elle" refer to Lol or to Anne-Marie Stretter? And who is "l'autre"? This ambiguity suggests the blurred boundaries brought about by mimetic identification. Lol's infirmity, to take one reading, would be her passive fascination with the couple. The god's weariness suggests the wearying experience of mastery, which finds that its privileged object has become banal. It also suggests the declining energy of the fantasy itself, which must be stimulated anew by another couple: Tatiana and Jacques Hold (the story's metamorphic narrator). "Un jour," we read, "ce corps infirme remue dans le ventre de Dieu," and Lol encounters the couple that will replace the first one in her fantasy. She "invents" and "broods on" the lovers that she watches: "Lol V. Stein guette, les couve, les fabrique, ces amants." She sleeps while watching them from a field outside their hotel room, as if she dreams or imagines this illuminated scene: "Le seigle crisse sous ses reins. Jeune seigle du début d'été. Les yeux rivés à la fenêtre éclairée, une femme entend le vide— se nourrir, dévorer ce spectacle inexistant, invisible, la lumière d'une chambre où d'autres sont."[6] The god in whose womb Lol's infirm body stirs is a god to whom she herself has given birth, just as the wings (ailes) attributed to the casino are generated by Lol (l'aile).

A similar situation occurs in Duras's *Dix heures et demie du soir en été*. The heroine, Maria, becomes obsessed with Rodrigo Paestra, who has murdered his wife and her lover and is now awaiting the dawn when he will be captured. At the same time Maria's husband, Pierre, and another woman, Claire, are drawing closer and closer together in their passion. Maria helps Rodrigo to escape but later discovers him dead in the fields, an apparent victim of his own despair; and she later sleeps through (or fantasizes perhaps) the culmination of the others' relationship (and her own betrayal). As in *Lol Stein*, where Lol's fascination with the other woman outweighs her interest in the man, Maria is constantly aware of Claire's beauty: "Maria retrouve Claire, la beauté de Claire qui en ce moment pourrait la porter jusqu'aux larmes. . . . Peut-on déjà les voir, dans ce lit blanc, à Madrid, ce soir, cachés? On le peut, excepté la nudité de Claire qu'elle ignore. —Je t'aimerai toujours, Claire, dit Maria." Later, Maria thinks, "Elle voudrait voir se faire les choses entre eux afin d'être éclairée [note the pun on Claire's name] à son tour d'une même lumière qu'eux et entrer dans cette communauté qu'elle leur lègue, en somme depuis le jour où, elle, elle l'inventa, à Vérone, une certaine nuit." In Verona Maria and Pierre once knew a night of great passion, and that night—or the memory of it—becomes the hope she has of escaping her accidie. The merging couple rekindles that memory and that hope, but Maria, like Lol Stein, does not have the power to postpone the moment of separation and betrayal. Again, hope can be maintained only at the threshold: the continued postponement of passion, of which Claire is still unaware: "Elle se tient là, souriante, prête pour une nuit qui n'aura pas lieu."[7]

Betrayal is conspicuous in the other action of the book as well: the search for Rodrigo Paestra. Rodrigo himself has been betrayed by his wife, who has slept with many other people since they have been married. He is also being betrayed by those who are searching for him: "Le grand désordre dans la salle à manger atteint son comble. Tous les garçons sont de ce village et connaissent Rodrigo Paestra. Les agents aussi sont du village. Il s'interpellent. Le service s'arrête. La directrice intervient. Attention si on dit ici du mal de Perez [the murdered man]. Les garçons continuent entre eux. La directrice hurle des ordres que personne n'entend." In Duras's work the police (and the managers—all the representatives of law and order) always betray freedom and spontaneity. One of the waiters says to Claire, who wants to make Rodrigo Paestra into a thoughtful and temperate man. "Pourquoi voulez-vous que Rodrigo Paestra le comprenne?" What people ask about him is, "A l'instar de Rodrigo Paestra, qui dans sa vie n'aurait pas l'occasion de tuer avec cette simplicité?" The police appear again at the culminating moment of Lol Stein: "La crise est là. Notre situation en ce moment, dans cette chambre où nous sommes seuls, elle et moi, l'a declenchée." At this moment Lol claims, "La police est en bas," the police she has imagined intervening the night of the ball. Finally, Maria is betrayed in a sense by Rodrigo Paestra, who has not believed in her enough to stay alive: "Je m'étais promis de jouer une grande partie avec Rodrigo Paestra. Et puis voilà, voilà qu'elle a échoué aussitôt entreprise."[8]

Obstacles and limits are everywhere in Duras's work. Détruire, dit-elle begins with these stage directions: "Temps couvert. Les baies sont fermées." Later, at dusk, the windows are open after the continuing heat of the day, and one of the characters opens her clenched fist at the window and cries: "Séparés encore." In Lol Stein the heroine is accustomed to leaving her bay windows open, but tonight—when she will establish her triangular relationship with Tatiana and Jacques Hold—she first closes them, as if to allow pressure to build up, and then opens them, in order to involve Jacques Hold (who is lingering outside) in her confidences with Tatiana. "Elle n'a pas oublié ma présence mais elle est véritablement partagée entre nous deux."[9] In Moderato Cantabile Anne shuts her windows against the profusion of flowers that make her sick (by making her dream), but the price she pays is in not being able to sleep because of the heat. Since *Moderato Cantabile* is particularly full of Duras's images of separation and enclosure, perhaps we can continue surveying that work.

The book begins, "—Veux-tu lire ce qu'il y a d'écrit au-dessus de ta partition? demanda la dame." The word for musical score, "partition," suggests division, and the form of the score suggests the railings that surround Anne's house: "Vous allez aux grilles, puis vous les quittez, puis vous faîtes le tour de votre maison, puis vous revenez encore aux grilles. L'enfant, là-haut dort. Jamais vous n'avez crié. Jamais." To scream would be a kind of deliverance: "Une fois, il me semble bien, oui, une fois j'ai dû crier un peu de cette façon, peut-être, oui, quand j'ai eu cet enfant." Anne's smile is also a "douloureux sourire d'un enfantement sans fin," a "sourire de délivrance." Her own child sits at one point clenching his hands (like the "inward look" of the murderer's desire) and facing the score. Framed in the open window is a motorboat that "passes through" (*passer dans*) the boy's blood—a verb that joins others like *arriver* and *traverser* in the lexis of transcendence. When Chauvin, for example, evokes Anne looking from her window onto the boulevard, he says, "Endormie ou réveillée, dans une tenue décente ou non, on passait outre à votre existence." "Anne Desbaresdes," we read, "traversa ce temps, ce vent" in her quest of Chauvin. When Anne wonders whether she can enact her desire with Chauvin, he remarks, "Une minute . . . et nous y arriverons."[10]

Another variation of this theme occurs in the child's silent repudiation of his music teacher: "Le bruit de la mer s'éleva, sans bornes, dans le silence de l'enfant." The sea, in turn, is associated with the voices of approaching men—workers whose memory returns to Anne at night when, as Chauvin reminds her, "rien ne s'y passe" (nothing happens). These two living, as they are conjured up by Chauvin's incantatory recollection, live, he thinks, in an isolated house by the sea, and Anne and her husband will vacation in such a place. While the hallway in Anne's house is such that the inhabitants are "ensemble et séparés à la fois," one variation of the hallway, the boulevard, is supposed to be extended beyond the limits of the dunes, beyond the limits also imposed upon Anne in her marriage: "de ce périmètre qui lui fut il y a dix ans autorisé." Part of these limits, a beech tree, overshadows Anne's room and obstructs her view of the sea. The black ink associated with the tree's shadow, moreover, evokes for us the blood shed by the murderer. When there's a wind, the hedges enclosing Anne's house grate harshly: "D'y être habituée, tenez, c'est comme si on entendait son coeur"; and the trees scream "comme des égorgés." Many women, Chauvin tells us, have died in the room behind the beech tree, which has stopped growing. The wind, which has been known to smash windows, is part of the unusual period of good weather the town has known during the eight days of encounters: "Le vent frais qui soufflait sur la ville tenait le ciel en haleine"—like the force of Anne's desire. As Anne's dinner party progresses and the wine confirms her hidden desire, she experiences the following transformation: "Le feu nourrit son ventre de sorcière contrairement aux autres. Ses seins si lourds de chaque côté de cette fleur si lourde se ressentent de sa maigreur nouvelle et lui font mal. Le vin coule dans sa bouche pleine d'un nom qu'elle ne prononce pas. Cet événement silencieux lui brise les reins."[11] This passage is compacted by the repetition of "lourd" and by the consonance of "seins," "pleine," and "reins"—an intense containment broken by a "silent event" (as later Anne will attempt to escape the "stifling simplicity" of her confession).

These kinds of images appear in all of Duras's work, where characters experience fear and trembling at the anarchic power of their own desire. In *Détruire, dit-elle* Elisabeth is recuperating from a "difficult pregnancy," in which the baby was born dead. Although she is presented as a very submissive, insecure woman who can only defer to others, she has a kind of latent power that makes her attractive to the other characters. As a result of her difficult pregnancy, she now sleeps all the time, but that sleep becomes a new period of gestation: the sleep of Alissa, the book's pythoness, which is the sleep of everyone: "Elle dort bien. . . . Oui, de notre sommeil." During this inchoate period the sky is described as a kind of grey lake—like the sky in *10:30*, which is shaken up by the storm. Out of this moment, in which the earth seems to tremble (as Elisabeth has often trembled during the story), the growing music of the scene comes from the forest: "Quelle peine. Quelle énorme peine. Que c'est difficile."[12] The forest is a place of danger—a future beyond the grounds (*parc*) of the hotel—and Elisabeth (who has been afraid to leave these grounds) finally seeks a way into the forest in order to throw up her life, just as Anne (trapped within "le parc correctement clos") throws up in *Moderato Cantabile*."Détruire" is what Alissa says earlier and is judged insane. Of this madness Duras remarks in an interview accompanying the English translation, "A madman is a person whose essential prejudice has been destroyed: the limits of the self." A period of destruction, Duras indicates, of "police," of "memory," and of "judgment," must prepare the way for a new and revolutionary society.[13] Not only screams, shouts, sirens, whistles, and vomiting, which punctuate Duras's works, suggest these violations of the given, but also laughter: "Dans son sommeil, Alissa tend sa bouche d'enfant dans une rire absolu. Ils rient de la voir rire."[14] As *Lol Stein* also shows, laughter is very close to trembling, but it is even more contagious. Its initial effect is to expel the threat to one's security, but its continuous action tends to shatter the social and personal forms that constitute that security. "C'est la musique sur le nom de Stein," Alissa says after her laughter, the mode of which is undoubtedly Dorian.[15]

What is interesting about this destruction, however, is that it is carried out in Duras's work as a kind of stately ritual. The whole of *Moderato Cantabile* is such a ritual—complete with chorus, the knitting up of fate, and ceremonial references to time. Throughout Anne's encounters with Chauvin, the *patronne* knits her red sweater, and Anne keeps arranging her disheveled hair. Disapproving at first of their meetings (like the prudential community typically represented by the chorus), the *patronne* seems solicitous and almost tender in the final sequence, when "un choeur de conversations diverses" also occurs. The dinner party itself is carried on like a ritual, at the center of which is a "victim"—a duck in its "linceul d'oranges." The "osmose à cette espèce" eating the victim (Duras's language sounds almost like that of a textbook) is another phase of the victim's own absorption of available violence. Just as the duck continues "sa marche inéluctable vers sa totale disparition," Anne's champagne has "la saveur anéantissante des lèvres inconnues d'un homme de la rue." While Anne keeps "torturing" the dying flower at her breast, the consummation (*achevé*) of the magnolias' flowering repeats that of the murder: "En bas, quelques cris, des appels maintenant raisonnables, indiquèrent la consommation d'un événement inconnu."[16] This closeness between sacrifice and the act of love, as Georges Bataille points out, has a long history: in antiquity "the feminine partner of eroticism appeared like the victim, the masculine like the sacrificer, one and the other, in the course of consummation, losing themselves in the continuity established by a first act of destruction." Dissolved in the erotic are the constituted forms of social life which found the "discontinuous order of defined individualities, but this search for continuity can be effective only if it does not succeed. That is, eroticism (like reproduction) must call being into question but not condemn it,[17] In the communal quality of Duras's work, perhaps, a tacit recognition that a deluge of violence may have no aftermath for us, and that an absolute break—in which all controls are repudiated—is impossible? In *Hiroshima Mon Amour*, Duras points to the narrowmindedness which punishes the heroine for falling in love with "an enemy": "L'Amour y est impardonnable. La faute, à Nevers, est d'amour. Le crime, à Nevers, est le bonheur. L'ennui y est une vertu tolérée." When she says of Nevers, "Dire du mal de Nevers serait également une erreur de l'esprit et du coeur,"[18] it is unclear whether she means this statement as an ironical exposure of the citizens' smugness or as a plea for understanding and tolerance.

As *Hiroshima Mon Amour* indicates, forgetting seems inevitable. Since the past does not live for us as it does for tradtional societies, Duras seems to think that we should make a virtue out of necessity: "J'ai oublié toute connaissance," says Max Thor, who now teaches "l'histoire . . . De l'avenir": "Il n'y a plus rien. . . . Alors je me tais. Mes élèves dorment."

Lol Stein, by forgetting the past, seems to control the present: "Sa présence fait la ville pure, méconnaissable. Elle commence à marcher dans le palais fastueux de l'oubli de S. Tahla." That this regality, however, is that of a rainy kingdom is shown by the "facilité royale qu'a Maria à boire et à mourir" in 10:30. The past that the narrator causes to be forgotten in Lol Stein is the immediate past of sterile fixations, but the present he asserts is no different: "Elle revoit sa mémoire-ci pour la dernière fois de sa vie, elle l'enterre. Dans l'avenir ce sera de cette vision aujourd'hui, de cette compagnie-ci à ses côtés qu'elle se souviendra. Il en sera comme pour S. Tahla maintenant, ruinée sous ses pas du présent." Since time in Duras's work lacks the resistance of tradition, it is an endless durée punctuated by periodic crises: the whistles and footsteps of the police in 10:30, for example, or the "voix vive, presque brutale" in Détruire, dit-elle. Forgetfulness is not so much a revolutionary break in the calendar as a periodic (and illusory) break with one's own impotence: "Tatiana est là, comme une autre, Tatiana par exemple, enlisée en nous, celle d'hier et celle de demain, quelle qu'elle soit. Son corps chaud et bâillonné je m'y enfonce, heure creuse pour Lol, heure éblouissante de son oubli, je me greffe, je pompe le sang de Tatiana. Tatiana est là, pour que j'y oublie Lol V. Stein. Sous moi, elle devient lentement exsangue." Similarly, those doors leading to freedom, to the great unknown, are false: "Ils commencèrent à bouger, à marcher vers les murs, cherchant des portes imaginaires." The rhetoric of liberation often disguises the paltriness of its everyday accomplishments: "Lol V. Stein se repose, dirait-on, un petit peu, lassée d'une victoire qui aurait été trop aisée. Ce que je sais d'une façon certaine c'est l'enjeu de cette victoire: le recul de la clarté."[19]

The mastery associated with wiping the slate clean has one of its most interesting instances in Duras's film Une Aussi Longue Absence. In a surburb of Paris, a woman named Thérèse, who runs a café, becomes obsessed with a tramp who reminds her of her husband—taken away many years before by the Nazis. She convinces herself (despite evidence to the contrary) that the tramp, who has lost his memory, is her dead husband, and tries to make him remember who he is. At the end, harried by people calling after him the name of Thérèse's husband, he raises his hands like someone awaiting execution and then narrowly avoids being killed by a bus while running away. Thérèse is left with the hope that he will come back during the winter, when his freedom will be more restricted. The tramp's amnesia has the same function as Alissa's insanity in Détruire, dit-elle: to disabuse him of his identity. As a result, others suspect him in the only thing that matters to them—his identity. When Thérèse faints, having convinced herself that he is her husband, we read, "Son évanouissement si long, si simple a été une correspondance de la perte de mémoire de 'Robert Landais' [the name of her husband] . . . Elle en sort [as the actress in *Hiroshima Mon Amour* wants to do from her love affair] 'défigurée', transformée pour toujours." Following the tramp during his rounds of collecting papers, Thérèse becomes temporarily "clochardisée" or "trampified." The tramp, like the director of the film, itself, does "cutting"—using a whole repertoire of scissors in order to cut pictures and advertisements out of the newspaper: "Ce que nous voulons rendre ainsi c'est l'activité absolument inventée, gratuite mais absorbante, passionante et méthodique de cet homme." He refuses to compromise this freedom in any way: "crushing" Thérèse with a look of implacable and incommunicable knowledge when she suggests cutting the various knots that hold his papers instead of undoing and redoing them; and refusing to join Thérèse in a scene of compromising domesticity. The tramp, like the "assassin de l'orage" (storm murderer) Rodrigo Paestra, is described as a "treasure," his special value consisting of his equanimity ("Il est, où qu'il se trouve, ègal a lui-même") and his innocence: "On n'entend qu'un seul 'son': celui du 'nourrissement' de cet homme par sa femme, de son nourrissement innocent par sa femme 'coupable' de mémoire." But this exemplary freedom is achieved at a price. In the mirror Thérèse sees a scar on the man's head: "Il est un homme qui a la tête trouée. Pareil à une maison bombardée, debout, mais détruite irrémédiablement. Et pourtant, il donne la parfaite illusion d'exister. Sait-il même que cette cicatrice existe?"[20]

Not only does the tramp give a perfect illusion of existing, but also he seems to monopolize the possibilities of existence for Thérèse. It is probably for this reason that Duras constantly emphasizes the enormous size of this figure: "Un dos d'homme, énorme, qui occupe l'écran du cinémascope et de chaque côté duquel, sur une toute petite marge, on voit défiler dans les lueurs éblouissantes de l'aurore un paysage des bords de la Seine." The epigraph accompanying this opening sequence reveals why Thérèse will continue to aspire to the tramp: "Loin du temps, de l'espace, un homme est égaré. Mince comme un cheveu, ample comme l'aurore." However "mince" the tramp's innocence is (it is, after all, the result of massive damage to him), its effect on Thérèse is "ample."

The "illusion of existing" is at stake in that dimension of desire that we call, in the appendix on *Women in Love*, "metaphysical" since objects are coveted only as talismans of some divine autonomy. To repeat the parable that we cite in that appendix, a man is told that he can find a great treasure underneath a stone. He spends years turning over stones without finding the treasure. At the end of that time, he can either give up the search, which means that his life is now meaningless, or he can seek out a stone so big that he cannot lift it. It is only when he encounters such a stone that he can maintain the illusion that the great treasure might still be underneath it. Both the tramp in *Une Aussi Longue Absence* and the murderer in *Dix heures et demie du soir en été* are, as we have seen, referred to as "treasures." Rodrigo Paestra, moreover, is also associated with a stone: "Il est là. Au-dessus de lui, le blé se recoupe avec naïveté. Sur une pierre, le blé se fut recourbé de la sorte, pareillement." This passage is preceded by Maria's sense of anticipation: "Comment nommer ce temps qui s'ouvre devant Maria? Cette exactitude dans l'espérance? Ce renouveau de l'air respiré? Cette incandescence, cet éclatement d'un amour enfin sans objet?" "Without object" because the fascination with the model-obstacle is what motivates desire, and the model who can best maintain this "hope" is the most inhuman. Rodrigo Paestra is ideal in this respect because not only does he transgress the norms of prudence, but his despair makes him completely unsusceptible to Maria (just as the tramp's 'innocence" makes him unsusceptible to Thérèse): "Maria se trouve privée du regard parfaitement vide de Rodrigo Paestra lorsqu'il dort." Also in *10:30* Claire's eyes are described as "blue stones" which Pierre (whose name also means "stone") wants to eat. Claire's gaze is "hagard, paralysé par l'insatisfaction, par l'accomplissement de l'insatisfaction même," but the fulfillment of fulfillment is even worse: "Les mains de Pierre sont ballantes le long de ses jambes. Huit ans qu'elles lui caressent le corps. C'est Claire qui entre maintenant dans le malheur qui coule, de source, de ces mains-là." In *Lol Stein* the fascinated narrator talks of "la raréfaction de l'air autour de ces petites planètes bleues [Lol's eyes] auxquelles le regard pèse, s'accroche, en perdition." The "stage" on which the scenario of Lol's voyeurism is played out is "bornée comme une pierre": "Et peut-être Lol a-t-elle peur, mais si peu, de l'éventualité d'une séparation encore plus grande d'avec les autres." In *Détruire, dit-elle* Duras uses the name "Stein" (which also means "stone") to explore the "illusion of existing." After Elisabeth asks who Stein is, Alissa explains her rather aggressive refusal to answer: "C'est la pensée de Stein. . . . Ce n'était pas autre chose que la pensée de l'existence de Stein" [=*sein*]. Duras uses Stein to convey both the illusion and the reality of desire. Stein desires Alissa, but that desire is an imitation of Max Thor's: "Comme je te désire," says Max, and Stein partially echoes him, "Comme il vous désire . . . comme il vous aime." But soon the "he" elides into "I": "Je ne vous connais pas, Alissa. . . . Tu fais partie de moi, Alissa. Ton corps fragile fait partie de mon corps. Et je t'ignore." Max Thor, in turn, validates his own desire by exposing Alissa to the desire of Stein:

> —Nous faisons l'amour, dit Alissa, toutes les nuits nous faisons l'amour.
> —Je sais, dit Stein. Vous laissez la fenêtre ouverte et je vous vois.
> —Il la laisse ouverte pour toi. Nous voir.
> —Oui.
> Sur la bouche dure de Stein, Alissa a posé sa bouche d'enfant. Il parle ainsi.
> —Tu nous vois? dit Alissa.

—Oui. Vous ne vous parlez pas. Chaque nuit j'attends. Le silence vous
cloue sur le lit. La lumière ne s'eteint plus. Un matin on vous retrouvera,
informes, ensemble, une masse de goudron, on ne comprendra pas. Sauf
moi.[21]

And yet Stein also represents the illusion of impermeability—of existence turned in on itself, like the "inward look" of desire in *Moderato
Cantabile.*

To see more about this illusion, let us return to *Le Ravissement de Lol
Stein.* After the ball is over, Lol begins spying again—on the man, Jean
Bedford, who is to become her husband. At first, as they walk together,
he takes the lead: "S'il s'arrêtait, elle s'arrêtait aussi. Il s'amusa à le faire.
Mais elle ne s'aperçut pas de ce jeu." He then allows the game to be
reversed: "Il la laissa faire à sa guise. Tout en ayant l'air de la mener, il la
suivit." This is the basic scenario of mimetic desire: one person following the lead of another while either ignorant of it or seeming to lead
himself. Since no real "degree" separates the two, moreover, the roles
can be quickly reversed, or the two people may follow each other's lead
simultaneously. When they marry, Jean Bedford deceives himself into
believing that he has rescued Lol from her despair. Since Lol cannot
accept her husband as an adequate replacement for the man (or couple)
she *cannot* have, she deludes herself into thinking that she has not
chosen him at all. She attempts to be superior to what she is, to be
uncommitted to the conventional existence she has chosen—in fact, to
parody that existence by taking it to extremes. With her ready-made taste
and her obsessive orderliness Lol "imitait, mais qui? les autres, tous les
autres, le plus grand nombre possible d'autres personnes." To repeat the
promise of the Town Beach ball, Lol must arrange for another threshold
on which to linger. She will "invent" another couple whose union
excludes all "preference"—all ordinary sentiment. Investing that couple
with a kind of sexual impersonality, she sets about attracting both
members of it to herself. Her own allure is the prestige of her past
insanity—and the possibility of its recurrence. In addition, she induces
Jacques Hold to spy on her conversational intimacy with Tatiana (as Lol
will spy on his sexual intimacy with her) and exasperates his interest in
herself by saying to her friend, "Le meilleur de tous les hommes est mort
pour moi. Je n'ai pas d'avis" about Jacques Hold.[22]

As we shall see, the attractions of Rodrigo Paestra and Lol Stein are
those described by Freud in his essay on narcissism: the attractions of
criminality and childishness. Before we get to that point, however, it
should be noted that Duras is ambiguous about youthfulness in her
work:

—Quel âge a Alissa? demande Stein.
—Dix-huit ans.

—Et lorsque vous l'avez connue?
—Dix-huit ans.

After May 1968, in France, this youthfulness became, for people like
Duras, an always beckoning promise of change. Duras dedicated the
filmed version of *Détruire, dit-elle* to the "youth of the world" because
she felt that they were the vanguard of the revolution. To convey this
potential she has the repressed Elisabeth, sleeping at the table with her
eyes open (as if in a hypnotic trance), make "un mouvement de tête
enfantin, appelant la silence sur sa vie." Max Thor, pointing to Stein and
Alissa, says to Elisabeth's conventional husband, "Regardez les, eux, ce
sont déjà des enfants," to which the other replies, "Tout est possible."[23]
The possibilities represented by youth are conveyed also by Elisabeth's
maiden name, "Villenueve," which suggests a new world, and Elisabeth
is still "Villenueve à dix-huit ans." She is born, moreover, on June 20,
the day of the historic tennis court oath, by which the Third Estate
declared themselves the National Assembly.

The youth of these characters, however, is also a strange and fascinating incompleteness—like those statues of Michelangelo that, incomplete, seem to emerge eternally from their marble. Rodrigo Paestra,
whose shape on the roof is "indefinite," hardly distinguishable from the
chimney, is a "monument de douleur," "drapée dans son imbécillité,"
and "là pour l'éternité." Maria thinks, "La seule supposition qu'il puisse
répondre, bouger, sortir de cette pose inhumaine fait déborder l'imagination de joie." (The shape formed by the couple in both this book and in
Détruire, dit-elle, where it is a "shapeless lump," conveys the same
sense of promise.) Lol Stein, who has a "morbidly" young look about her,
wears a perfume and a dress that convey the impression of a schoolgirl.
At the Town Beach ball the triangle of lovers is described as aging
dramatically: "des centaines d'années, de cet âge, dans les fous, en-
dormi." During an extended passage of juxtaposed conversations, Stein
says of Alissa, "Dans la chambre . . . Alissa n'a plus d'âge," which is
followed immediately by the question, "Vous vouliez beaucoup cet
enfant?"[24] Although the question is by Alissa about Elisabeth's aborted
child, its splicing conveys the attraction of Alissa's own narcissism: "For
it seems very evident that another person's narcissism has a great attraction for those who have renounced part of their own narcissism and are
in search of object-love. The charm of a child lies to a great extent in his
narcissism, his self-containment and inaccessibility, just as the charm of
certain animals which seem not to concern themselves about us, such as
cats and the large beasts of prey. Indeed, even great criminals and
humorists, as they are represented in literature, compel our interest by
the narcissistic consistency with which they manage to keep away from
their ego anything that could diminish it. It is as if we envied them for
maintaining a blissful state of mind—an unassailable libidinal position

which we ourselves have since abandoned."[25] The tennis court, then, signifies not only revolution but also the alternating patterns of mimetic rivalry. To attract and capitalize on the desires of others, one must give the kind of *appearance* that Freud describes, improperly, as an objective reality.

The repetitions and reversals of this process are like those of tennis, the sounds of which punctuate the book and suggest the alternating current of Duras's writing:

> Silence sur l'hôtel. Le tennis cesse-t-il?
> —Tu cherche à comprendre, dit-elle, toi aussi.
> —Oui. Il y aurait une lettre peut-être?
> —Oui, une lettre, peut-être.
> —"Il y a dix jours que je vous regarde," dit Max Thor.
> —Oui. Sans adresse, jetée. Je la trouverais, moi.
> Non, les tennis de nouveau. Les balles giclent dans une crépuscule liquide, un lac gris.

The letter quoted in this passage is one that Max has written to Elisabeth, "Madame, il y a dix jours que je vous regarde. Il y a en vous quelque chose qui me fascine et qui me bouleverse dont je n'arrive pas, dont je n'arrive pas, à connaître la nature." The fact, however, that it is now equally addressed to Alissa (and equally written by Stein, as we find out later) means that this letter, like Poe's, is only a form letter. As Alissa reveals, the real function of the letter is separation: "Il faudrait se séparer tous les étés ... s'oublier, comme si c'était possible?" The only real difference between Elisabeth and Alissa, from this standpoint, is that Elisabeth is separated from Max (and irremediably so) whereas Alissa is not: "Peut-être que nous nous aimons trop?" she asks. Since the letter's message is that desire demands separation, Alissa repudiates first words and first glances. The positions of lover and beloved, moreover, are subsequently reversed: "Il y avait en moi quelque chose qui vous fascinait et qui vous bouleversait," says Max to Elisabeth, "un intérêt ... dont vous n'arriviez pas à connaître la nature."

In *Lol Stein*, similarly, Lol amuses herself by thinking that she is separated from the people of South Tahla by a wide river but then wants to approach the other bank—that "rive lointaine où ils habitent, les autres. Vers quoi? Quelle est cette rive?" Her temporary seat is outside the Forest Hotel, where she watches the window behind which Tatiana and Jacques Hold make love: "ce miroir qui ne reflétait rien et devant lequel elle devait délicieusement ressentir l'éviction souhaitée de sa personne." That false window or mirror reflects nothing because Lol cannot recognize herself in the others. In the same way, the tramp in *Une Aussi Longue Absence* is "comme un miroir"—mirroring back the infinite longing of Thérèse. The doors at the Town Beach ball are also "imaginary," but one of them becomes real for Lol because it resists her efforts to get through. Later, it is Lol who becomes a door for the narrator, who is infected by her lingering sense of anticipation: "Je m'arrête: elle veut voir venir avec moi, s'avancer sur nous, nous engloutir, l'obscurité de demain que sera celle de la nuit de T. Beach." Then the "door will open" and he will go through, like the man who sits before the law in Kafka's parable. When the narrator says, "Tatiana, ma soeur, Tatiana," he is play-acting, but he is play-acting the truth he cannot experience. He says of Lol later, "Elle a été à côté de moi séparée de moi, gouffre et soeur." Despite the sororal reality, she is still the difference he aspires to: "Enlacées elles [Tatiana and Lol] montent les marches du peron. Tatiana présente à Lol Pierre Beugner, son mari, et Jacques Hold, un de leurs amis, la distance est couverte, moi."[26] By overcoming the distance between himself and Lol, he will, so he thinks, coincide with himself. But Lol, of course, imagines the same thing—her goal being the couple. The same ambition is evoked in *Moderato Cantabile*, where Anne tries not to let herself be discouraged by "une aussi longue distance"; and in *Une Aussi Longue Absence*, where time, absence, takes the place of distance. That Lol is separated from others by a river is suggestive, since the word "rival" derives from a Latin word meaning "brook." The rivalry underlying the narrator's fascination with Lol, moreover, is manifested by his occasional and inadvertent hurting of her—squeezing her too hard, as is appropriate to his name.

As we have seen, those who are most infected by this sickness of mimetic desire are often most lucid about its effects in others though blind to the same effects in themselves. Stein, for example, makes exception of himself and Max Thor when he observes how tired the convalescents are at the hotel: "Je suis comme vous, je ne suis pas malade." Alissa, having denied that she is ill and having claimed that she and Max are in this hotel by mistake, laughs in order to ward off the threat to her self-esteem. Although Alissa, ideally, represents the destruction of the old that the young people of the world will bring about (according to Duras), she also reveals Duras's intuition that revolution may have little effect on the kinds of mimesis to which we have given our attention, since mimetic desire is not dependent on real, concrete differences. Although Alissa suggests that Elisabeth should be killed, she stands with her before a mirror and comments on how much alike they are: "Nous aimerions Stein s'il était possible d'aimer," she says. Although Alissa comments on how "fascinating and terrible" Elisabeth's life is, she cuts her own hair to look more like her and also confesses, "Je vous aime et je vous désire." At one point in the book, their names are associated more closely, as Elisabeth is referred to as "Elisa." Immediately after Stein claims that he has, in his sleep, called out Alissa's name, Alissa says that Max has done the same with "Elisa." Those names begin to sound like *alias* and *alliés*—an impression reinforced by "Alione,"

Elisabeth's last name. The rhetoric of desire begins to sound tired and false, as does the (inadvertent) strategy of indifference:

—"Je ne dormais pas"? "Je faisais semblant de dormir . . . "? "Vous en étiez-vous apercu?"?
—"Il y a des jours que je fais semblant de dormir"? "Il y a des jours que je dors"? "Il y a dix jours"?

These characters, as Duras herself points out in an accompanying interview, are interchangeable although she doesn't explain why. Despite the various *pas de deux* (and occasional ensembles) that take place in the book, the only thing that seems to constitute them as a group is the presence of Elisabeth's conventional husband. When Elisabeth plays cards with the other three, she is uneasy because they do not seem to be playing by any rules. This anarchy, plus their mocking small talk, causes Elisabeth to laugh until her underlying fear comes out. In Bernard Alione's presence, however, Elisabeth becomes part of them. "Nous sommes tous dans cet état," Stein says to him, "tous les quatre."[27]

Before we return to Bernard Alione, whose treatment is crucial in this novel, perhaps we should consider the hypnotic aspect of Duras's work. Many of her characters seem to be influenced by one another in hypnotic fashion. In *10:30*, for example, Pierre's voice becomes precise to the point of being "oratorical." In *Détruire, dit-elle* Alissa's distraction seems almost like that of a medium; she is sometimes described as being like someone asleep; her voice is almost inaudible; and when she begins to speak she is "deaf." Like Alissa, Elisabeth Alione relapses into slumber. Finally, Stein says everything in the same monotonous voice, and Max stands "rigid" at one point, his eyes half-closed. In *Moderato Cantabile* this dimension is most insistent, for Chauvin's influence over Anne is hypnotic (or even possessive). At one point Anne keeps staring at his mouth, which is lit by the dying rays of the sun. At another point the sun is reflected in his eyes "avec la précision du hasard"—a phrase that compresses the process by which chance, in divination, is used to control chance. Chauvin, in fact, seems clairvoyant: "Vous êtes Madame Desbaresdes. La femme du directeur d'Import Export et des Fonderies de la Côte. Vous habitez boulevard de la Mer." He also describes the spatial disposition of the furniture in the music teacher's room, a room he has presumably never entered. He has returned to the café, he tells Anne, for the same reason she has, and he recounts at various times the daily rhythm of desire and suppression in her life. During the dinner party, where a process of "osmosis" takes place, the two of them seem to merge. Chauvin's role becomes more and more trance-like until, overwhelmed, "il ne la connut plus." He describes the relationship between the other couple "comme d' un souvenir," and at one point uses "une voix neutre, inconnue jusque là de cette femme." Anne's voice, in turn, is sometimes reasonable and alert but is also "une voix de sourd." Her emphasis on "les yeux de cet homme" suggests a certain hypnotic power, as do his incantatory suggestions about her daily life.[28]

Connected with this theme is the theme of authorship. In *Détruire, dit-elle* books are associated with pills: "Il y a six jours quand il est arrivé elle était déjà là, le livre devant elle et les pilules." People only pretend to read, the books seem to circulate only as a matter of protocol: "Ce livre, il n'est pas à moi, il faut que je le rende. Vous le voulez peut-être?" Although Max is in the process of becoming a writer, his "book" seems to resemble the interminable analysis of Freud: 'Où en est ce livre?" he is asked. "Est-ce que tu penses à ce livre?" To which he replies, "Non. Je te parle." After Max tells Alissa how strongly he feels that the book should never be written, Alissa transfers authorship to Stein, "Stein écrira. . . . Alors nous n'avons pas besoin d'écrire," and "Stein regarde pour moi. Je décrirais ce que Stein regarde."[29] This transference is arbitrary, however, since Stein is distinguishable in no way from the others. Interminable analysis and arbitrary transference are signs, as we have seen, of crisis— the prolonged crisis of our culture. Hypnotism, in turn, is a caricature of mimetic desire. Everything is done in order to fix the subject's attention on a model, whose desire will become the template of his own. And even the forgetting advocated by Duras plays a crucial role in this process.

The book that will be written through Stein, consequently, is about "les tennis qui sont regardés" by a woman preoccupied with "le néant."[30] The infinite exchanges of desire suggested by those courts are the void although Duras seems to mistake it for some new difference between the old and the new: "I am speaking, if you will, of man's passage through a void: the fact is, he forgets everything. So as to be able to start over." [31] What is this void, however, this much ado, but everyday fashion—the rapid turnover of idols? And who authors fashion? During one scene Alissa, dazzled by light, discovers Elisabeth. Behind a dining room window Max watches her watch Elisabeth, and Stein watches Max. "Alissa sait," Max says, "Mais que sait-elle?" Stein's silence indicates that this too is a matter of infinite regress. In *Lol Stein*, similarly, the narrator, Jacques Hold, "invents" a good deal of what he "sees," but he, in turn, is invented by Lol: "Lol V. Stein guette, les couve, les fabrique, ces amants." In this narrative, then, Jack is inventing Lol inventing him. . . . This Moebius-like arrangement is common in contemporary fiction, which reveals the delirious possibilities of mimesis.

What kind of choice can we make? Stein announces in *Détruire, dit-elle*,"La femme que je cherchais ici depuis si longtemps . . . c'est Alissa," but we know that he is imitating another. Lol Stein, having avoided the "grotesque incongruity" of a choice in getting married, tells Tatiana that she never had a chance to choose her life. When she cannot explain to Jacques Hold why she has "picked" him, he feels that he is "dans la nuit de T. Beach—that their relation is only a repetition of the earlier trauma (Lol, moreover, keeps insisting that he love Tatiana). Maria realizes, in *Dix heures et demie du soir en été*, that she has not chosen Rodrigo Paestra: "Je n'ai pas eu le temps de le choisir. . . . Il est tombé sur moi." In the fields where Rodrigo lies down for the last time, a harvest is taking place, but this image of fecundity disappears: "La blé disparaît. Il n'y a plus que des pierres, des amas de pierres complètement décolorées par le soleil." Madrid later appears as "une montagne de pierre tout d'abord," which is pierced with "trous noirs que le soleil creuse"; its "masses rectangulaires" are spread out geometrically at various levels, "départagées par des espaces vides où la lumière s'engouffre." Stone, as we have seen, is the talisman of desire in Duras's work, which is why names like "pierre" and "stein" recur so frequently. Infinite longing, which nothing can satisfy, finally seeks its own divine essence in this hard but porous landscape. The sun that bores these black holes is the energy of desire. Chauvin, for example, whose name suggests the mutual exclusion of mimetic desire, reflects the dying rays of that sun. When Maria, the "heat in her hair," sets out to rescue Rodrigo Paestra, she recalls a sunny day in which the depths of a lake are suddenly revealed: "L'eau était pure. Des formes apparurent. Habituelles, certes, mais violées par le soleil"—distorted by desire.[32] In Thérèse's eyes appears "le soleil de la folie." The mountain of stone, like the geometrical landscapes of Robbe-Grillet and Poe, is the promised land of desire. "All trains finish there. They don't go on anywhere," says Jake Barnes of this same Madrid in *The Sun Also Rises*.[33]

In the self-defeating game that desire becomes, "l'enjeu de . . . victoire" is "le recul de clarté." Toward the end of *10:30*, in which clarity is mocked by the figure of "Claire," Pierre finds himself perversely intrigued by the devastation he has brought about in Maria. "Il avait à Pierre le goût pressant d'amours défuntes. Quand il entre dans la chambre de Maria, il est dans cet endeuillement de son amour pour Maria. Ce qu'il ignorait c'ètait l'enchantement poignant de la solitude de Maria par lui provoquée, de ce deuil de lui-même porté par elle ce soir-là." Maria looks at him, "horrified." In *Moderato Cantabile* Anne, thinking back to the young man's "inward look" of desire and to his embrace of his dead lover, asks whether anything but despair could have driven him to the point of no longer caring whether she was dead or alive. Chauvin conjures up an image of the man driving the woman over and over again from their house. When Anne questions the futility of it, Chauvin remarks, "Ça doit être difficile d'éviter ces sortes de pensées, on doit en avoir l'habitude, comme de vivre. Mais l'habitude seulement." Just as this futility culminates in murder (desired by her as well), Anne's own habitual walks and intoxication culminate in scandal: "Quand le retard devient tellement important . . . qu'il atteint le degré où il en est main-

tenant pour moi, je crois que ça ne doit plus changer rien à ses consé-
quences que de l'aggraver encore davantage ou pas."[34] In fact, to "aggravate further" is the only cure she can find for her continuing malaise.

The rhythm of Anne's desire, "Anne Desbaresdes se rétracta et,
comme à son habitude parfois, s'alanguit," pervades the novel in sequences like "resta fixé . . . fléchit vers." At the threshold of desire, then,
stands the young man who represents hope for his lover—hope in her
obedience and in his repudiation: "De lui obéir à ce point, c'était sa façon
à elle d'espérer. Et même, lorsqu'elle arrivait sur le pas de la porte, elle
attendait encore qu'il lui dise d'entrer." But the threshold exists for her
and for Anne only because he keeps her outside: "Il lui a poussé, au bout
des bras, un destin." As the reality of Anne's desire becomes confirmed,
Chauvin becomes more and more a kind of automaton. It is death alone,
as supreme otherness and repudiation, that will satisfy her. As she and
Chauvin accomplish their "mortuary ritual," we are told that the murdered woman "n'était pas seule à avoir découvert ce qu'elle désirait de
lui."[35]

As we have seen repeatedly, sacrifice is the ether in which the imagination, smothered by mimetic rivalry, tends to breathe. Duras, in the
interview accompanying the English translation of Détruire, dit-elle,
says that Max Thor is in a state of catharsis;[36] but since all of the
characters are interchangeable, it is toward a general purification that
the book tends. Since sacrifice, however, is a deception, so is the difficult
birth referred to by Elisabeth: "Voici venir le mensonge," Max says,
having overheard her reference to it. And Stein adds, "Il est encore
lointain." Does Duras understand that scapegoating the "bourgeoisie"
and the past will not bring about a new and better world? Perhaps
Bernard Alione is the key. A businessman, an ideal scapegoat for revolutionary manicheism, he is ultimately treated with some tenderness:
"'Vous savez,' dit Alissa avec une incomparable douceur, 'vous savez,
nous pourrions, vous aussi, vous aimer'." And Stein confirms that possibility: "D'amour."[37]

CHAPTER 7

Getting Even, With William Gass

Storm murderers, stones, and other obstacles appear also in the work of William Gass. In "The Pedersen Kid," the first story in his collection *In the Heart of the Heart of the Country*,[1] the handyman of the Segren household discovers, after a snowstorm, the body of a neighbor's son in the barn, brings him inside, and revives him with rubbing and whiskey. Upon regaining consciousness, the young man tells the handyman, Big Hans, a terrible story of a stranger dressed in black cap, green mackinaw, and yellow gloves who has murdered the young man's family. Big Hans, Jorgen (the young narrator), and Jorgen's alcoholic father start out for the Pedersen place, where Jorgen's father is shot, Big Hans runs away, and Jorgen survives to contemplate his independence. Complicating this plot, however, which could be the summary of a story by Hemingway, are the embedded elements of one of Freud's case studies, the so-called "Little Hans case," which concerns a little boy who, after seeing a horse fall down in the street, develops a fear of horses and their heavily loaded carts. The horse, we discover, represents the boy's father, and the fear of the horse's falling is a repressed wish for the father's death. Since Little Hans also anticipates his father's punishment of him for this wish, he becomes afraid of the horse's biting him and later has dreams expressing a fear of castration. The elements of horse and cart, however, are over-determined for the little boy in that they also symbolize both moving one's bowels and giving birth—confused in the mind of Little Hans, who has both resented and been curious about the birth of a sibling. Finally, Little Hans does not only perceive his father as a rival, but he also identifies with him—playing horse himself and even biting his father.

In "The Pedersen Kid" a "Little Hans," who apparently belongs to the Pedersen household but who never appears in the story, remains an absent counterpart to both Big Hans and Jorgen. At one point Jorgen's father accuses his son of discovering his whiskey. After Jorgen denies that he is the "nosy bastard" his father says he is, the name "Little Hans" is suddenly introduced for the first time: "Little Hans ain't no fool, Big

Hans said," to which the father replies, "He ain't no kin to you. . . . Little Hans is half your size and worth twice. You—you got a small dick." In Freud's case study Little Hans suffers from the anxiety attendant upon masturbation—or upon his parents' supervision of it. He also experiences a revulsion from his curiosity about feces—even experiencing disgust at his mother's black colored and yellow colored panties (which suggest feces and urine respectively to him). In "The Pedersen Kid" Gass situates Big Hans as a kind of formidable figure of phallic exclusion: "The bottle and the glass were posts around which Big Hans had his hands." In another scene Jorgen is instructed to search for his father's phallic bottle in the snow, which also comes to suggest feces: "Hey, get your hands in it, your *hands*. It's clean. You was always that way about manure." In this scene, moreover, broken traces seem to realize the idea of "kicking over the traces," which is what the Oedipal conflict is all about.

Other crucial elements of Little Hans's complex occur in "The Pedersen Kid." The Segrens' horse, Horse Simon, is associated with one of the fathers in the story by the latter's name—"Pedersen" or "Holy Pete"—and by images of stones: a horse's head, for example, is described as being "uncovered like a rock." Much is made of the fact that Pedersen's own horse is black, like the horse whose fall disturbs Freud's patient because it is associated both with his ambivalent feelings toward his father and with his curiosity about the act of giving birth (confused with the act of excretion). Gass reproduces this sense of overdetermination in many ways. Jorgen describes his father as looking "like dung covered with snow"; he imagines the Pedersen kid, who has been found in a "crib," as being uncovered "like a black stone . . . in a field"; and he expects to see a "bump of black" where the killer disappeared. The motif of birth continues when Pa's bottle and the killer are said to have "hatched," and when Jorgen, setting out with Big Hans and his father on the adventure that is to liberate him from them, tries to hold a feeling that is as "warm as new bathwater." As for the elements of boxes and falling in the Little Hans case—the former associated with full bowels and pregnancy and the latter associated with the father's death and the mother's delivery—while Jorgen finds boxes to contain the snow used to thaw the Pedersen kid, Big Hans rejects a pail containing some tell-tale coal dust; and the Pedersen kid is described as falling from the sky or coming out of the ground. Just as Little Hans recalls particularly the wiggling legs of the fallen horse in Freud's case, Jorgen himself falls and discovers the legs of a dead horse.

Toward the end of the story, Gass writes a kind of coda to recapitulate the disseminated motifs we have examined: "The wagon had a great big wheel. Papa had a paper sack. Mama held my hand. High horse waved his tail. Papa had a paper sack. We both ran to hide." These elements are repeated over and over like a children's chant. Papa's sack hides his phallic bottle: "I'm not going to grieve," says Jorgen. "You're no man now. Your bottle's broken in the snow." The wagon recapitulates the earlier motif of boxes. Its "great big wheel" is the colloquial "big wheel" (vied for by father and son), just as the "high horse" is the colloquial "high horse" Jorgen is on now that his father is dead. "Mama held my hand" and "We both ran to hide" recall the wish expressed by Freud's Little Hans to hide with the mother away from the father—the wish to supplant the father. Perhaps the killer, then, in his mysterious transparency—"Why did he stand there so pale I could see through?"—represents the neurosis that Freud describes as something set up "against the ego as an element foreign to it."[2] One interesting point in this respect is that Freud points out how Little Hans confuses the words "shooting" and "shitting" ("*schiessen*" and "*scheissen*").[3]

This Oedipal scenario is compounded by religious imagery. Big Hans and the Pedersen kid, for example, are associated with Christ. Hans's last name, "Esbyorn," is a vaudevillization of "He's born," and "Big Hands" sounds like a good epithet for God: "The bottle and the glass were posts around which Big Hans had his hands." The narrator, moreover, accuses Hans of feeling "like a savior." The disguised "Peter" in "Pedersen" is elicited by Jorgen's father's characterization of him as "Holy Pete" and, as we shall continue to see, by the imagery of stones that qualifies both the kid and others. After the Pedersen kid is found in a crib, his resurrection is described in terms that evoke communion: the kitchen table on which he is revived being covered with dough, "pasty with whiskey and water, like spring had come all at once to our kitchen." "We were getting him ready to bake," the narrator thinks. When Hans revives the kid (who is never, by the way, present to us alive), Jorgen says, "Well I felt him   cold   christ! Ain't you proud? He was dead, right here, dead. And there weren't no yellow gloves. Now, though, there is. That's what comes of rubbing. . . . You can't believe the kid was lying good enough to fool you. So he was dead, But now he ain't. Not for you. He ain't for you." Big Hans replies, "He's alive for you too. You're crazy. He's alive for everybody." But Jorgen denies this evangel and claims that one consequence of Big Hans's faith in the kid's revival is a belief in "yellow gloves"—the storm murderer.

The narrator's father also becomes part of this scheme. He "looks like a judge," which suggests the Old Testament ruler in this context. His name is "Magnus," and the "Mag" used once of him in the story suggests the Magi. At one point the narrator says of him, "I hated him. Jesus, how I did. But no more like a father. Like the burning space." The father, in turn, accuses Pedersen of having brought on one of the Biblical plagues: "Pedersen *asked* for hoppers. He *begged* for hoppers." As we have seen, during times of cultural crisis, the efforts people make to thwart the "illegitimate" violence of others only increases that violence: "It's his own fault for putting out all them snow fences, Pa said. You'd think, being here the time he has, he'd know the forces better." "Pa" himself seems like a seasonal god at times. His hair is "fuzzed, like a dandelion gone to seed," and later Jorgen recalls going into a meadow "with an old broom like a gun, where the dandelions had begun to seed and the low ground was cracked"—like the "crack" or "slit" one finds in Pa's face, Jorgen's eyes, and Mrs. Pedersen's crotch. Pa is also "another snowman" who will melt.

The killer also is associated with Biblical imagery. The narrator imagines him falling when the horse runs into a barberry, rearing "as the barbs go in." Being "worn like a stone in the stream," he is also identified with Horse Simon, "He was in the wind now and in the cold now and sleepy now like me. His head was bent down low like the horse's head must be"—the rhyming of "he," "me," and "be" making these identifications quite emphatic. Since the "he" that occurs at the end of the previous paragraph, moreover, refers to Big Hans, "Even if his cock was thicker . . . I was here and he was in the snow," the killer is identified with him also. If we recall that the horse Jorgen uncovers is "white where frozen snow clung to his hide," the killer's paleness becomes reminiscent of *Revelation* 6, where the pale horse signifies death. His circling round and round in the snow, like the snake Jorgen thinks of and the snake Hans is said, figuratively, to kill, suggests the cycle over which he presides (Blake's rebellious Orc also appears as an snake). Finally, he is talked about in a passage reminiscent of the paradigm of the decisive step in the New Testament—whether it is the crossing of a lake to visit the country of the Gerasenes or the passage from one level of meaning to another in parable: "He must be gone, I thought. It's such a little way. He must be gone. He never came. It isn't far but who will go across?"

If plot has to do with the change in situation between the beginning of a story and the end, the plot of this story concerns two kinds of relations: the relation between Jorgen and his family (particularly his father) and between Jorgen and Pedersen kid. At the beginning Jorgen is resentful toward his family and contemptuous of the father who intimidates him; and he is disdainful toward the Pedersen kid, whom he does not want to acknowledge as a rival: "Pedersen's kid was just a kid. He didn't carry any weight. Not like I did." At the end he feels free of his family and fraternal toward the Pedersen kid: "The kid and me, we'd done brave things well worth remembering." Bringing about this change is a knightly quest somewhat more reluctant than Jorgen's name would lead one to expect: "It was like I was setting out to do something special and big—like a knight setting out—worth remembering."

The most salient aspect of the killer (like the green knight confronted by Sir Gawain) is the colors in which he is figured: "Green, black, and yellow: you don't make up them colors neither," and these color support the motif of a quest. Of the knight as a symbol of spiritual apprentice-ship, Cirlot notes, in his *Dictionary of Symbols*, "The Green Knight is the preknight, the squire, the apprentice sworn to knighthood; the Black Knight stands for him who undergoes the tribulations of sin, expiation and obscurity in order to attain to immortality by way of earthly glory and heavenly beatitude; the White Knight . . . is the natural conqueror, the 'chosen one' of the evangelists, or the 'illuminated one' reemerging from a period of *nigredo*."[4] The Red Knight, bloodied from sacrifice, finally achieves the gold of glorification, the yellow of which appears in an ironically debased form when the "sour yellow sick insides" of Jorgen's father are described and when Jorgen accuses both Hans and his father of being "yellow." But the yellow is present also in the "golden tail" of Jorgen's fantasized horse, in his memories of summer and child-hood; in the sun that dominates the story; and in the yellow gloves that Hans seems to create by rubbing (à la Aladdin's lamp). As the action begins, the colors on the towels used to warm up the Pedersen kid begin to run—anticipating the thawing of spring. Jorgen, however, wants to convince everyone that he wouldn't run before the storm murderer. Later, having called Jorgen a little "smart-talking snot," Jorgen's father says "wisely," "Cold makes the snot run." And omnipresent, vacant, and cold is the heavenly color of blue: "Sometimes the snow seemed as blue as the sky. I don't know which seemed colder."

These colors, associated with various aspects of the knight's quest, associated also with the changing seasons (and with the lives and deaths of the gods thereof) are generated by the sun. With the sun withdrawn the world is "black and white and everything the same," the killer's horse circling aimlessly in the snow. The snow is sometimes used to convey Jorgen's sense of constriction by his father. "You were always after killing me, yourself, pa . . . I was the one wrapped in the snow. Even in the summer I'd shiver sometimes in the shade of a tree." The first two sentences of the story suggest the conflict between this cold and the energy of the sun (or son): "Big Hans yelled, so I came out. The barn was dark, but the sun burned on the snow." Despite the two subjects in the first sentence, the verbs suggest birth, and Jorgen's emerging from the darkness is paralleled by the sun's burning on the snow. He will later imagine his father's eyes blinking at him—"as if I were the sun off the snow and burning to blind him." In Blake's Preludium to "America A Prophecy," the "shadowy daughter of Urthona" says to the terrible and serpentine Orc, rebel against the father's power: "Thy fire and my frost / Mingle in howling pains" (11. 35-36). Jorgen says of his father, "Everything about Pa was frozen. The white hair that stuck out from his hat looked hard and sharp and seemed to shine like snow." He resembles the Urizen of "America," whose head and limbs are "leprous" in their whiteness and who pours forth snow. Jorgen, on the other hand, sometimes looks like the fiery Orc: "I beat the logs with the poker so that sparks flew in my hair."

The whiteness of the snow also conveys the indefiniteness associated with whiteness in *Moby Dick*: "Is it that by its indefiniteness it shadows forth the heartless voids and immensities of the universe, and thus stabs us from behind with the thought of annihilation, when beholding the white depths of the milky way? Or is it, that as in essence whiteness is not so much a color as the visible absence of color, and at the same time the concrete of all colors; is it for these reasons that there is such a dumb blankness, full of meaning in a wide landscape of snows—a colorless, all-color of atheism from which we shrink?"[5] It is a "new blank land" to which Jorgen feels he has been given by the storm murderer: "Well, he [the storm murderer] was sudden. The Pedersen kid—maybe he'd been a message of some sort. No, I liked better the idea that we'd been prisoners exchanged. I was back in my own country. No, it was more like I'd been given a country. A new blank land." Early in the book Jorgen imagines himself "losing at the drift game" as he steps through a drift of snow and finds the body of the Pedersen kid. Later, he imagines himself sledding off a steep drift into space—the "stair" to which he clings in fact becoming the "star" around which he floats in fancy. The broken traces that Big Hans temporarily mends are also tracks—visible marks of passage which tend to be obliterated by the blankness of snow: "There wasn't any road to go. There wasn't any track." After the killer leaves, "nothing now" shows any signs of his passage.

Gass's play on words like "something" and "nothing," which pervade the story, reinforces the ambiguities surrounding both the storm murderer and the "kid." When Pa is shot, Jorgen says, "My god . . . he's real," but he can imagine the storm murderer only "back where I wasn't any more"—standing in Jorgen's own kitchen and threatening his own family. Elsewhere, as we have seen, the killer is transparent. If the killer comes "mysteriously through the snow" to do Jorgen and the kid "such a glorious turn," he may also be the part of Jorgen that has been "slipping out" of himself, "pushed out by the cold maybe." When Jorgen imagines himself "tilting dangerously" off the barn and then discovering the Pedersen kid "floating chest down," he says: "They were all drowned in the snow now, weren't they? Well more or less, weren't they? The kid for killing his family. But what about me? Must freeze." Who is the murderer and who is the victim? Does the tmesis created by "But what about me" establish Jorgen's responsibility or his innocence? One thing that is certain, however, is that the alliterating *k*'s give "kid" and "killing" a common semantic charge, just as the alliterating *f*'s do "family" and "freeze."

The kid, then, is alternately victim and killer, and this cycle is represented by the storm murderer, who circles round in the snow like some figure of nemesis: "And pa—I didn't touch you, remember—there's no point in haunting me. *He* did. He's even come round maybe. Oh no jesus please. Round." The traces of this cycle, however, are constantly being obscured. Of the kid's coming we read, "All I could see was a set of half-filled prints jiggling crazily away into the snow until they sank under a drift. There wasn't anything around. There wasn't anything: a tree or a stick or a rock whipped bare or a bush hugged by snow sticking up to mark the place where those prints came up out of the drift like somebody had come up from underground." Of the killer's going we read,

> He'd gone off this way yet there was nothing now to show he'd gone; nothing like a bump of black in a trough or an arm or leg sticking out of the side of a bank like a branch had blown down or a horse's head uncovered like a rock; nowhere Pedersen's fences had kept bare he might be lying huddled with the horse on its haunches by him; nothing even in the shadows shrinking while I watched to take for something hard and not of snow and once alive.

As Pa pointed out, his own vindictiveness miming the sanctimoniousness of his neighbor, those fences have not kept anything bare but have become part of the snow they were supposed to obstruct. Similarly, the rock in both passages is again the model-obstacle: the "stone in the stream" to which the storm murderer is compared, or the stone Hans finds and seems fascinated by: "When he saw the stone he stopped. On his knees in the snow he simply stared at it." Brought to himself by hearing his name, Hans says, "The bastard. I'd have killed him."

Perhaps the killer, then, is the whole complex of traits that we associate with mimetic desire. As an apotheosis of the father, he is the model-obstacle whose violence against the son is imitated by him: "The way that fellow had come so mysteriously through the snow and done us such a glorious turn—well it made me think how I was told to feel in church." As a function of the son, he is that violence turned against the obtrusive father: "You were always after killing me, yourself, pa, oh yes you were." Violence alternates like the interminable "coming round" of the killer, which is why Jorgen and the Pedersen kid are said to be "prisoners" exchanged for one another. The kid as victim is exchanged for the kid as killer, but both remain prisoners of the same mimetic process. Early in the story Jorgen is not sure what has come through the storm although it has something to do with Hans's rubbing the kid in the colloquial wrong way: "Something besides the kid came through the storm . . . I ain't saying yellow gloves did neither. He didn't. He couldn't. But something else did. While you were rubbing you didn't think of that." The coming in this passage is really a becoming—Jorgen's becoming. Hating his father "like the burning space," Jorgen comes to incorporate that antagonist in a passage that recalls Freud's use of mourning to explore the formation of the ego: "I stood as still as I could in the tubes of my clothes, the snow shifting strangely in my eyes, alone, frightened by the space that was howling up inside me, a white blank of glittering waste like the waste outside, coldly burning, roughed with waves, and I wanted to curl up, face to my thighs, but I knew my tears would freeze my lashes together. My stomach began to growl." Just as the "burning space" that is the father becomes his, the snow that has constricted him becomes his snow: "The light was going. The snow was coming. It was coming almost even with the ground, my snow." His triumph over the model-obstacle, which allows Jorgen to discard the huddled being he had been in his father's house, accounts for his momentary sense of transcendence: "I was on the edge of something wonderful, I felt it trembling in me strangely, in the part of me that flew high and calmly looked down on my stiff heap of clothing." It is a gnostic universe that this resurrected Jesus occupies.

The lamb of innocence, we are told, is destroyed by Jorgen's father:

> Down a long green hill there was a line of sheep. It had been my favorite picture in a book I'd had when I was eight. There were no people in it.
> I'd been mad and pa had laughed. I'd had it since my birthday in the spring. Then he'd hid it. It was when we had the privy in the back. God, it was cold in there, dark beneath. I found it in the privy torn apart and on the freezing, soggy floor in leaves.

That malevolence generates the "tyger" of wrath: "The winter time had finally got them all, and I really did hope that the kid was as warm as I was now, warm inside and out, burning up, inside and out, with joy." The energy for this joy comes from the sun, the power of which contrasts with the ordinary world of objects: "We were safe from the sun and it felt good to use the eyes on quiet tools and leather. . . . Only the line of the sun that snuck under him and lay along the floor and came up white and dangerous to the pail seemed a living thing." At the moment when Jorgen is trying to avoid the implications of "the kid for killing his family," he becomes himself one of those things: "I was something to run my hands over, feeling for its hurts, like those worn places in leather. . . ." But at the end he is a point of extreme incandescence. The old god, whose energy has waned, has tried to renew it with whiskey: "Pa liked the summer. He wished it was summer all year long. He said once whiskey made it summer for him." But his "burning inside himself"—a wrathful burning—has ignited the triumphant Jorgen at the end—in fearful symmetry.

Jorgen says at one point, "There was no way of getting even," but getting even seems to motivate the writing of William Gass: "I suspect," Gass says in an interview in *The Paris Review*:

> that in order for me to produce my best work I have to be angry. At least I find that easy. I am angry all the time. . . . Getting even is one great reason for writing. . . . I write because I hate. A lot. Hard. And if someone asks me the inevitable next dumb question, "Why do you write the way you do?" I must answer that I wish to make my hatred acceptable because my hatred is much of me, if not the best part.[6]

This strategy is not unlike the phenomenon described in *Monsieur Teste*, a book much admired by Gass: "Each one founds his existence on the non-existence of others, but from them he must extort their consent not to exist." Unlike the violence of the Hegelian struggle, the resentment of teste-iness described by Gass must *induce* others to accept its worth. As Valèry puts it, the mechanism indicating our self-respect "flickers with a terrible nimbleness between the zero of a beast and the maximum of a god,"[7] and Gass insists often enough in his critical writings on the godlike role of the writer.

In "Order of Insects" this godlike role is aspired to by the narrator, a housewife who begins studying the insects she finds dead around the house: "Strange. Absurd. I am the wife of the house. This point of view I tremble in is the point of view of a god, and I feel certain, somehow, that could I give myself entirely to it, were I not continuing a woman, I could disarm my life, find peace and order everywhere." In Gass's other stories the "wife" of a house is clearly the effeminated will—powerless in practice but sometimes murderous in intent. As we shall see, in "Icicles" the narrator, beleaguered by his sense of repudiation by others, attempts to retire and to transform the signs of his humiliation into some kind of "radiant order." In "Mrs. Mean" the narrator's "idleness"—his indifference to others masks his "idolness"—his desire to be recognized by them. His frustration, however, leads to malediction and to voyeurism. In the title story the narrator excoriates a Mrs. Desmond for his own frustration: "I wanted to be famous, but you bring me age—my emptiness. Was it *that* which I thought would balloon me above the rest?" That Mrs. Desmond's daughter lives in "Delphi" may indicate the inevitability with which accusations fall back on the head of the accuser. "Her talk's a fence," we read about Mrs. Desmond, and that seems true of the speaker also. Similarly, the narrator of "Order of Insects" claims to be "innocent and improperly armed" when she looks at the bugs, but she realizes that her innocence is just a ploy and that the disease she attributes to them is really her own "murderous disease."

The point of view of a god turns out to be "infected"—by the violence that passes back and forth between men when religion has decomposed. Violence is the sign of another's transcendence and the means for appropriating it. That the insects are "fierce, ugly, armored things" reveals the hardness of denial that stimulates the narrator's fascination: "Am I grateful now my terror has another object? From time to time I think so, but I feel as though I'd been entangled with a kind of eastern mystery, sacred to a dreadful god, and I am full of the sense of my unworthiness and the clay of my vessel." That these insects, however, use "their shadows to seem large" reveals the reality: that the others who fascinate us are only people like ourselves. The "dreadful god" and the narrator's "dreadful eyes" are connected in a circuit in which desire and denial create and reinforce each other.

The narrator's idea that the insects are "manufactured by the action of some mysterious spoor" is one version of the fact, mentioned in "Mrs. Mean," that we tend to blame others for the meanness that's our own: "This shit's not mine." The insects are really the stuff of her own life—transformed by fear and anger: "looking when I first saw them like rolls of dark wool or pieces of mud from the children's shoes, or sometimes, if the drapes were pulled, so like ink stains or deep burns they terrified me." She discovers through them—through "the consequences of finally coming near to something"—the murderous resentment that underlies her dutiful habits: "Two prongs extend like daggers from the rear." Possessed by her possessions ("Property owns people," we read in "Icicles"), she feels dispossessed of her life and longs to move on: "I could go away like the wise cicada who abandons its shell to move to other mischief. I could leave and let my bones play cards and spank the children."

To be free is to become a kind of curator of one's life: "I suspect if we were as familiar with our bones as with our skin, we'd never bury dead but shrine them in their rooms, arranged as we would like to find them on a visit; and our enemies, if we could steal their bodies from the battle sites, would be museumed as they died"—the parts of enemy and friend "still repetitious, still defiant, angel light, still worthy of memorial and affection." But curator she is not: the "worst of angers" continues to hold her through the day, "vague, searching, guilty and ashamed." She confesses that she no longer owns her own imagination. As we have seen, mimetic desire—uncontrolled by religion—begins with an overweening hope of life, which is, however, embodied in Others. Because the hope can be kept alive, ultimately, only by the Other's inaccessibility, it may become associated (as it does in *Women in Love*) with inhuman images: of insects, organic decay, and death. This inversion of desire, which seeks its own divine essence is what repudiates it, is the mysterious "passage" that the narrator never witnesses: "Never alive, they came with punctures . . . and they were dead and upside down when they materialized." The narrator identifies with the cat who pounces on this species: "It was in that moment that our cat, herself darkly invisible, leaped and brought her paws together on the true soul of the roach." Just as the narrator feels that her "jaw has broken open," a cat in the title story walks around with "death in . . . [his] jaws," and the narrator of that story gathers himself together "for a bound." Our housewife also identifies, however, with the insects, whose soul is "so static and intense, so immortally arranged, I felt, while I lay shell-like on our bed, turned inside out, driving my mind away, it was the same as the dark soul of the world itself." The "dark soul of the world itself" is mimetic rivalry, which is so fascinated by appearance that body and soul seem to change places. The "secret" of the insects turns out to be their bones, which remain inaccessible when the cat has squeezed out the pulp of life. The narrator is also inside out since one's soul comes to lie in the appearances that are acknowledged by others.

The mobility contemplated by the narrator, which is the closest she can come to the omnipresence of a god, takes pathetic form in "Icicles." The protagonist, a real estate salesman named Fender, is described as a "log in the stream," a man without a past: "There's no one to help you, Fender, you have no history, remember?" In musing over the word "prospects," Fender considers his own. The word is a "sour betrayer" since it suggests "gold," "clear air," and "great and lovely distances"; since it suggests "the fire of the mountain . . . the glittering air, distance sloping brilliantly away" to an "immense snowfield" that blinds Fender "pleasantly"; since it suggests that moment of incandescences (and all its accompanying images) that we witnessed in "The Pedersen Kid." The reality, however, seems somewhat less pleasant since "prospects" remind him of dirt: "They made him think rage, snakes, picks, and the murder of companions." They also suggest the "caves" or houses that Fender's imagination is supposed to redeem: "So he'd hear Pearson [his boss] preach the power of imagination." P(e)arson's name seems to compress "power" and "preach" in order to stand for some power of transformation that Fender will try to assume. The image of the cave, however, which recurs several times in this story, suggests Plato's cave, where the phantasmagoria of common opinion prevail, while the dazzling sun suggests the truth outside.

As "The Pedersen Kid," using the Freudian scenario of the family, revealed, the "murder of companions" is the ultimate resort of mimetic desire. In this story Fender, like the frustrated clerk of Dostoevsky's *Notes from the Underground*, is doing insidious battle with those around him and is suffering from a sense of his own insignificance. After denying that he is, like his colleague Glick, "countably discreet" like the peas in a pot pie, he concludes that he lives, after all, "in his pie like the peas." If Glick is associated with dried flowers, "cut when young, bound in loose bunches hung upside down, cold dry place, where a breeze would be helpful," Fender is associated with icicles that hang in similar fashion from his windows and door. Glick is "Glick, the wiseman, Glick, the joker—green all winter like a pine," but his greenness is also that of a pickle—preserved by brine. Similarly, Fender is a wiseman (or a joker) who no longer believes in the clichés of selling, who no longer believes in Pearson's "beautiful belief"—that everything is property—but who cannot find a way to renew his life: "You got a place and nobody wants to live in it," Fender says as he compares his body to a house. He feels oppressed by Pearson, who seems to pass judgment on him as he often does on a street. When he contemplates his icicles, which are, as he says, "a sign of the beauty of their possessor," he feels as conspicuous as a "fish in a bowl" and closes the curtain to escape the dreaded surveillance. He also, however, feels insecure when Pearson is not around: "The office, for some reason, wasn't safe this morning, it didn't feel right. He didn't feel himself. He was, for one thing, a good deal smaller than his skin." This sense of *esse est percipi* conflicts with Fender's desire to become the kind of master—"magician," "prophet," "god"—Pearson is, although he knows at the same time that Pearson does not sell anything. When Fender talks about the needs of his clients, he is talking also about himself: "Clients are thin with the worms of worry, skinny from the scares inside them. Fatten them on certainty. They want to believe." Fender also wants to believe—to the extent that he even becomes property to validate the belief of the master: "Arms in arms of the chair. Armchair."

When Fender and his clients enter a house, he thinks, "We are diseases entering it. We are three diseases. We differ among ourselves: which of us shall be the reigning sickness?" The reigning sickness is Fender's paranoia, which causes him to chase after a child who has made off with some icicles that "come with the house"; but, like the primitive scapegoat, he seems to absorb the more everyday sickness of the others: "She's got the flu or something, and I'll catch it." His treatment of the child derives from the vindictive treatment he has experienced from others—particularly Glick and another colleague, Isabelle, with whom he is apparently in love. As he endures their derision of the absent Pearson and of himself, he anticipates the culmination of the crisis: "What was epilepsy, Fender thought, but a struggle with the powers of the air"—those mysterious powers from whom one wrests the prize of *kudos* or supremacy. When Glick contemplates Pearson's defeat, he imagines him fallen "on the impertinent pick of an icicle" so that everyone will wonder, when the icicle has melted from the wound, "as much at how he let the air out of his life as they ever had before at how he'd pumped it in her." Such are the vicissitudes of inspiration.

The wound in Gass's work is a frequent sign of inadequacy or impotency. Fender, for example, worries a good deal about the kind of damage to his integrity that Freudians associate with the threat of castration. The icicles are overdetermined in that respect. First, they are compared to teeth, and Fender worries about being "mashed against the teeth." He experiences, at first, the same fear of icicles that he has of sharpened pencils—"that one might pierce his eye." Second, however, they are associated with a kind of phallic authority, which is why Fender takes pride in measuring his icicles against those of his neighbors. Fear *for* his icicles, moreover, is such that he wishes they could grow within— "where he might measure them in private, examine them in any way he liked. But if one broke off. . . . The thought was dismaying." This growing within is associated, in "In the Heart of the Heart of the Country," with the artist: "All poets have their inside lovers. Wee penis does not belong to me, or any of this foggery. It is *his* property which he's thrust through what's womanly of me to set this down." We also find in the title story the inversion characteristic of the dead insects in "Order of Insects" and the icicles and dried flowers of "Icicles": "My every word's inverted, or reversed—or I am." He says of his relation to the world, "We meet on this window, the world and I, inelegantly, swimmers of the glass; and swung wrong way round to each other, the world seems in." The implication is that the artist incorporates life, transforms it in such a way that he can compensate for his weakness by the power of his imaginative vision and by the vitality of his language: "It was a look [the sexual blush of a woman's body] I'd like to give this page. For that is poetry: to bring within about, to change." In "Icicles," similarly, Fender is said to be "melting down": "But those icicles gather the snow as it softens, oppose their coldness to the sun, and turn their very going into . . . Isabelles"—the beloved who, in life, does not reciprocate Fender's affection. One is reminded of the story of Pygmalion and Galatea, in which the artist not only wants his statue to live but also wants to be loved and recognized by it. He wants to recuperate the energy that he has spent in his work.

Fender wants to experience the same kind of renewal that occurs in "The Pedersen Kid": "Fender was weary—weary of winter." His waning energy is reflected in his description of the icicles, which is also accompanied by *w*'s: "Drops of water were wavering at the points of the icicles and he decided there must be a breeze," although it does not seem to be the creative breeze of the romantic imagination. Later, however, having lost his job, he seems more daring: "They [the icicles] could capture his eyes, for all he cared, and grind them like lenses." What the Freudians call assuming the risks of castration is relinquishing the false claims of the self—the "dreadful eyes" claimed by the frustrated housewife of "Order of Insects." At this moment in "Icicles," the icicles seem more incandescent: "He would frequently rest to watch his icicles, the whole line, firing up, holding the sun like a maiden in her sleep or a princess in her tower—so real, so false, so magical." But the beleaguered end of the story indicates that Fender has not been entirely successful in assuming the risk. Some children gather together on a hill in front of his house: "At last they stood fixed for an instant, brightly, in a red knot. . . . Then it was as though, suddenly, a fist had opened, and they came down the hill like a snowfall of rocks." Rhyming with this ending is the ending of "Order of Insects": "How can I think of such ludicrous things— beauty and peace, and dark soul of the world—for I am the wife of the house, concerned for the rug, tidy and punctual, surrounded by blocks." Art in these stories seems to substitute for experience or compensate for it: the "image" of the insect being tossed into the air by the cat's paw "takes the place of jumping." Because the artist is as beleaguered as the two endings suggest, the "radiant order" that he seeks is marked by the conflict out of which it emerges: "But this bug that I hold in my hand and know to be dead is beautiful, and there is a fierce joy in its composition that beggers every other, for its joy is the joy of stone, and it lives in its tomb like a lion"—or like a tyger.

Freud, we recall, distrusted the work of art for its narcissistic gratifications, and the imaginative power of Pearson shows how this problem relates to society in general. Pearson, like Big Hans in "The Pedersen Kid," is a kind of magician. He is described as twisting his ring, and, by the "power of imagination," he turns everything into a commodity whereas Hans revived a thing into a living person. Fender, like the narrator of "The Pedersen Kid," refuses this wizardry, "I'm no magician," but later gives vent to his own. What is puzzling in this story is the quality of this imagination. What are we to make of it? We read about Pearson's muse-ings over the newspaper, "Because he read on slowly, cautiously, and artfully, because of his devotion, his passion, his love, because—it was really impossible, Fender thought, to be absolutely certain why, the effect so dwarfed the causes—still, whatever the reason, he remembered everything." This disparity between effect and cause is like the "stylization of desire" that is the subject of one of Gass's essays. Once our immediate needs (for food, shelter, and so on) are satisfied, Gass notes, we can transform their fulfillment into art by imposing more and more difficult and precise means: "The amalgamation of means and ends, because it makes for a new aim, clearly shifts the original desire still further from its natural base. The fact that the straight expression of desire is hindered, not by want of objects but by increasing scrupulosity concerning means, makes contemplation possible, and this contemplation discovers what the object is, beyond its mere utility."[8] The lines and stars that decorate Pearson's newspaper eventually obscure the text of the newspaper itself, and the fortunes he tells for the streets that are his "person," the body of his "beloved"—a kind of parody of the eucharist— go beyond the utility of selling. Pearson becomes, in this story, a kind of pop artist—with all the ambiguities that figure entails. However satirical his portrait may be, the "beautiful belief" that Fender admires in him reminds us of how difficult it often is in modern art to distinguish between criticism and promotion of the thing itself. As one critic observes, "The point seems to have been reached at which artistic intransigence is indistinguishable from celebration of the dynamisms of mass society. It is impossible to say whether the artistic 'vanguard' is actually leading society or struggling to keep up with it."[9]

We shall return to the ambiguities of art when we come to "In the Heart of the Heart of the Country," but first let us follow the "snowfall of rocks" that ends "Icicles" into the world of "Mrs. Mean," where they become the rock with which David smites Goliath: "The boy Toll raced in front of Mr. Wallace like a bolting cat [like a "catapult"] and swung around a sapling like a rock at the end of a string, deadly as little David." The narrator of that story, a somewhat reclusive man whose occupation remains unknown, tries to achieve a superiority over his neighbors by an appearance of detachment. He becomes obsessed, however, with a neighbor whom he calls "Mrs. Mean" and speculates on her life both within and outside her house. Having lost the struggle for supremacy, he ends up prowling the lanes behind the houses and planning his entry into the Means' house.

At the beginning he thinks of himself as "idle in the supremely idle way of nature." To be idle for him, however, is also to be an idol:

> When I communicated nothing to them [his neighbors]; when I had nothing, in confidence, to say to anyone; then they began to treat my eyes like marbles and to parade their lives indifferently before me, as if I were, upon my porch, a motionless, graven idol, not of their religion, in my niche; yet I somehow retained my mystery, my potency, so that indifference was finally superficial and I fancy they felt a compulsion to be observed—*watched* in all they did. I should say they dread me as they dread the supernatural.

As his relation to both Mrs. Mean and another neighbor, Mr. Wallace, reveals, however, these claims are pretty dubious. Although he claims that Mrs. Mean wants his attention, he also says that her indifference to him is such that he does not exist. The truth is that Mrs. Mean represents for him the kind of imperviousness that he wants for himself: "However, I try, I cannot, like the earth, throw out invisible lines to trap her instincts. . . . And so she burns and burns before me [as his stomach "turns and turns" later on in synchrony]. She revolves her backside against a tree." The image is that of Apollo and Daphne combined in one person—an image of completeness that excludes the observer. The narrator, in imagining the inside of the Means' house, says that while his wife is subject to "failures of the imagination," he can "cut surgically by all outward growths, all manifestations, merely, of disease and reach the ill within." Although he admits that his wife's description of Mrs. Mean's house as cool and airy is superficially right, he claims that his own description of it as a kind of dank cave is "emotionally right, metaphysically appropriate." Any real relationship with the Means, he says, would destroy his "transcendence," would entangle him "mortally in illusion." One recalls again Plato's myth of the cave, where only the exceptional view can transcend the world of common illusions. One recalls also the role of the physician that Oedipus assumes in trying to cure Thebes of its plague, and the ensuing role of patient who must be cured by surgery. Whatever malaise the narrator in "Mrs. Mean" finds in the mean-ing of his neighbors, the "disease" within is also (if not only) his own. His speculations about their "cave" recall a childhood memory in which he places his hand accidently on a "cold wet pipe" that rises out of the ground, and then sees, near his nose, "four fat white slugs": "I think of that when I think of the Means' house and of pale fat Mr. Mean, and the urge to scream as I did then rises strongly in me." This revulsion or fear—clearly sexual in nature—is, as we shall see, a further stimulus to his desire.

Both Mrs. Mean and Mr. Wallace are associated with things Oedipal. Mrs. Mean is seen "executing" the stems of flowers, leaving them "be-headed and shattered." She is seen "hobbling" on her lawn, "stick in her hands to beat her scattered children." Her arm "points accusingly" at her son's "eyeless back. She curses him." Mr. Wallace has a cane that "comes out of his belly," that can "gouge cement." Although the cane "rises with difficulty," its tip "waves above the tree tops" and he "hurls the cane like a spear." His feet "are sore, the ankles swollen." That this imagery has less to do, however, with the traditional complex of psycho-analysis and more to do with the paradoxes of mimetic desire is shown by the whole network of themes in which it occurs. When the narrator observes Mrs. Mean close the distance between herself and the children whom she caused to flee, he also observes something about his own desire. Having withdrawn, it seems, from any purposeful activity in life, he measures time by playing Achilles to the Other's tortoise. Mrs. Mean, we read, is "worse for witnesses. She grows peculiar"—more and more the essence of mean-ness. Her "reality" is not only mechanical, it is geological: "Following her gyrations in the grass . . . I forgot her geo-logical depth, the vein of meanness deep within her earth." The increas-ing density of this abstraction corresponds to the narrator's increasing compulsion to penetrate it. Part of Mrs. Mean's fascination for him is the double bind posed by her anger: "Her anger is too great to stand obedi-ence. The offense must be fed, fattened to fit the feeling, otherwise it might snap at nothing and be foolish"—as Mrs. Mean snaps at the dandelions that defy her tyranny. In his Paris Review interview, we re-call, Gass himself seems to feed the offenses he attributes to others in order to write.

The other focus for this conflict is Mr. Wallace. When, having dropped his cane, he cries out, "Cane, cane, cane," Gass seems to be playing on the Latin word for "prophesy." And later in the story the narrator calls on "prophecy" to help him penetrate the "mystery" of that figure. The narrator's first words in this story, "I call her Mrs. Mean," remind one of the first words of *Moby Dick*: "Call me Ishmael." They suggest how dependent the narrator's identity will be on the mysterious quality of mean-ness. Like Ishmael the narrator describes himself as a "castaway," and like Jonah his prophecy leads him to be swallowed by a whale. As with Mrs. Mean, his "transcendence" is threatened by Mr. Wallace: "More and more I knew my budding world was ruined if he were free in it. As a specimen Mr. Wallace might be my pride." His "budding world" becomes the "bud in the blood of her back" that he becomes when he curses Mrs. Mean and desires to strike her down. Similarly, he imagines entering Mr. Wallace's belly like a harpoon:

> Mr. Wallace was before at large, as I have said; gigantic in the landscape, swallowing life ["Wallace" and "swallow" become almost anagrams of each other]. There was, in him, no respect for my mysteries, only for his own: signs, omens, portents, signatures and symbolings whose meaning he alone was privy to. Mr. Wallace [like Pearson in "Icicles"] was the paramour of prophecy, yet it came to me when the boy Toll catted across his path that day that it was a stone symbolic more than real that struck the light from Goliath's eyes. It was for prophecy that Jonah fled the Lord. For Jonah's flight the tempest rose, and for the tempest was Jonah flung between the whale's jaws. To be properly swallowed, then, was the secret; to cause, in going down, the oils to flow that would convulse the membranes of the stomach. What must that whale have felt, his moist cavernous maw reverberating prayers and pledges! Would Mr. Wallace be a dog and eat his vomit? I judged that I should soon be cast on dry land. Thenceforth the mystery would be mine, as it was Jonah's. To be the bait, to carry the harpoon down and in that round and previously unshaken belly stick it, then escape—that would be the trick. And prophecy would do it.

The Lord, we are told in *Omensetter's Luck*, frustrates "the omens of liars";[10] but, in a world where religion has lost its power, omens proliferate. Functions of pride and resentment, of the obsessive scrutiny that generates the Other's prestige, omens are part of the struggle between the narrator of "Mrs. Mean" and Mr. Wallace. For a while the narrator plays on Mr. Wallace's belief in omens while maintaining what appears to be a skeptical detachment, but despite his understanding that "all omens are imaginings," he comes to believe in them himself. When Mr. Wallace, clinging "tenaciously to his secrets," escapes the narrator's designs, he is described as a "monster" (from the Latin *mōnstrum*: prodigy, portent; from *monēre*: to warn). In "Icicles," we recall, the detested Glick is associated with the botanical term "*monstrosum*," which seems to summarize his fraudulence: "Lord. The show-off. The fake." Similarly, the minister in "The Purloined Letter" is a "*monstrum horrendum*." Only love can transform these monsters back into men, but Gass's world is particularly loveless. As the devil in *Omensetter's Luck* says of his victim, "After my lies, he spelled love: luck."

The symbolic stone with which the light is struck from Goliath's eyes is the obstacle of mimetic rivalry, which is found everywhere in Gass's work.[11] In *Omensetter's Luck*, the protagonist is associated with stones. In one scene Furber, a frustrated preacher who longs to be a kind of St. Jerome—particularly for the latter's prestige among women—watches Omensetter skip stones on the water. While imagining himself throwing down the Mosaic tablets in rage, he watches Omensetter make *his* stones fly: "How differently we give the semblance of life to the stone, he thought. And it did seem a stone until it skipped from the water . . . effortlessly lifting . . . then skipped again, and skipped, and skipped . . . a marvel of transcending." Both Furber and Henry Pimber, another anemic soul, take Omensetter for an exemplary being: "Omensetter lived by *not* observing—by joining himself to what he knew." "More than a model" to them, he is a "dream" to be entered. Henry's despair of achieving this dream leads his to suicide: "I shall be my own stone" in death, he thinks; but he also says longingly that he would have made a worthier Omensetter. Furber, having struggled with Omensetter as he does with God ("You and I—you, master builder, spinner of threads, you and I, like Jacob and angel, we—fight"), destroys him with calumny. In "Mrs. Mean" the victimized Goliath is also Polyphemus, who threatens the narrator with being Noman. As we have seen, it is the boy "Toll" who leads the attack on this monster, who makes him bellow "like a burnt blind Polyphemus." Through him and the other children, the narrator can take a vicarious "toll" on the giant. Since mimetic rivalry, however, derives from illusory differences, it is the narrator who has the cyclops' "singleness of sight." Imagining his confrontation with the giant, he says, "It is amazing how the feelings of the universal fables sometimes focus in a single burning vision. Of course that singleness of sight has always been my special genius." It has always been the special genius of myth, which recapitulates, from the point of view of the community, the act of violence that allowed harmony to be restored. "I sensed the wet and dry together," says the narrator at the moment of crisis, but since violence has lost its reconciling power, the savior who "to save us from death first kills" is seen to be evil.

The image of Mr. Wallace as a dog recurs when the narrator recalls the medieval tale about a stream of spring-fresh water that made men eloquent: "Yet when men followed its turnings to its source they found it sprang from the decaying jaws of a dead dog." Although this story is taken to imply a kind of millennial hope—the world transformed into a better place—it also suggests the fact that all civilization can be traced back to founding acts of violence. Consistent with this idea is the story of Jonah, who is made a scapegoat for the violence that threatens a reprobate community. While the ship (a counterpart of Nineveh) flounders at sea, each man calls on his own god; after the crisis is resolved (by lot) they acknowledge the new god of Jonah. In "Mrs. Mean," however, the secret of existence rests with the whale, whose gigantism makes the secret meaningful. To have penetrated the whale and stimulated his responses—and to escape with the secret—is the "trick" of prophecy: the art of overcoming distances.[12]

At the end the narrator describes himself as a "necromancer carrying a lantern," but the lantern gives no light: "I have fallen into the circle of my own spell." A victim of self-defeating desire, he has learned from experience that the object he can have always turns out to be worthless. He therefore seeks out the object he cannot have—however much it offends what is best in him:

> Oh I know the thought is awful, yet I do not care. To have her anger bite and burn inside me, to have his brute lust rise in me at the sight of her sagging, tumbling breasts, to meet her flesh and his in mine or have the sores of Mr. Wallace break my skin or the raw hoot of his wife crawl out my throat . . . I do not care . . . I do not care. The desire is as strong as any I have ever had: to see, to feel, to know, and to possess!

His suffering remains a sign of hope—that this time his life will be complete if only he can overcome the obstacles that fate places in his path. The lantern illuminates the obstacle clearly, but it darkens the situation as a whole since the only escape he can find from his frustration is to aggravate it. He can see the obstacle, but he cannot renounce the desire that makes the obstacle necessary.

As he prowls through the alleys at the end, he experiences again the fascination of the cave: "I am at the entrance and frightened by it as a child is frightened by the cold air that drifts from a cave to damn the excitement of its discovery." Having consigned the Means to a cave in order to preserve his own Platonic transcendence, he is now fascinated by the cave of his own imagining. The "darkness of the Means" is charged with sexual imagery: the alleys pass by "the backsides of the houses," which recall the "backside" that Mrs. Mean revolves against a tree; trash "spills over the cinders and oil flavors the earth" in an orgy of emissions; and an "oiled ash" urges him "strangely." As he breaches the preliminary fortress of the Means' garage, he senses how success would devalue his goal: "I realize that I have breached the fortress, yet in doing so I lost all feeling for the Means and sense only myself, fearful, hiding from a child." But his stomach "burns" and "turns" as he longs for the power within. Signs of his non-existence are everywhere as he slips over the "rim of reality" into a fairy tale. Lying "like a fog" between the garages, he sees everything in terms of his failure to be. Mrs. Cramm, a kindly and motherly figure, becomes "utterly gray and unshaped . . . a thin gray mist by a tree trunk." She is also "gray and grotesque as primitive stone"—the stumbling block that recalls the altars of the past.

This failure to be is recapitulated in the title story, which purports to be the reflections of a poet and teacher on his situation in Middle America and on his failure in love. The first words, "So I have sailed the seas and come . . . to B . . . a small town fastened to a field in Indiana," echo the beginning of Yeats's "Sailing to Byzantium," but the implication of "Be" is reinforced later by the town of Bemidji (emphasis mine). The poem by Yeats helps Gass articulate the relation between *eros* and *poiēsis*—between the vagaries of desire and rivalry and poetic creation. To be gathered "into the artifice of eternity" might help the poet forget (or even capitalize on) his futility in the world of begetting and dying. "No one notices," he says, "when they walk by, that I am brimming in the doorways. My house, this place and body, I've come in mourning to be born in." His failure in love becomes a kind of poetic gain since his mourning allows him to absorb the beloved into the persona who is coming to Be(B). "You are bread in my mouth," he says to the beloved; but the frustration of making a virtue out of a necessity causes the narrator to vent his spleen: "For I am now in B, in Indiana: out of job and out of patience, out of love and time and money, out of breath and out of body, in a temper." That "Indiana" also contains "die" becomes clear when the narrator completes this diatribe with an imaginary outburst against Mrs. Desmond, one of his interlocutors: "So shut your fist up, bitch, you bag of death; go bang another door; go die, my dearie. Die, life-deaf old lady. Spill your breath." As we shall see, his anger against Mrs. Desmond is also anger against himself since he too is a kind of woman (Mrs. Desmond brings him a cucumber for that reason, he thinks); since he too may be deaf to life; and since he too will spill his breath.

The narrator feels cut off from life, deprived of his potency: "There's a row of headless maples behind my house, cut to free the passage of electric wires. High stumps, ten feet tall, remain, and I climb these like a boy to watch the country sail away from me." Since wires, as we shall see, are associated with poetry, this passage suggests that the cost of *poiēsis* is castration. When, at dusk, "starlings darken the single tree—a larch—which stands in the middle," this tree reminds one of another poem by Yeats, "Vacillation," in which the poet is like the priest of Attis, himself castrated in honor of the god. The poet, sacrificing his life for art, knows the ecstasy of transcending the contradictions of life:

> And he that Attis' image hangs between
> That staring fury and the blind lush leaf
> May know not what he knows, but knows not grief.

The fact, however, that the country (or "cunt-ry," perhaps) is sailing away from him—in contradiction of "Sailing to Byzantium"—indicates that this sacrifice may only appear to be voluntary. The first section on wires reads:

> These wires offend me. Three trees were maimed on their account, and now these wires deface the sky. They cross like a fence in front of me, enclosing the crows with the clouds. I can't reach in, but like a stick, I throw my feelings over. What is it that offends me? I am on my stump, I've built a platform there and the wires prevent my going out. Their cut trees, the black wires, all the beyond birds therefore anger me. When I've wormed through a fence to reach a meadow, do I ever feel the same about the field?

The poet, maimed like these trees, feels excluded from the world. The stick with which he compares his feelings has many associations in Gass's stories. The protagonist in "Icicles," for example, compares his futile life to a "stick on the river." The staff associated with the crossroads of *Oedipus the King* occurs in both "Mrs. Mean" and the title story. Aunt Pet, in the latter, has broken the back of a dog and, to illustrate her "vigor," will raise "the knob of her stick to the level of your eyes." In the former, Mr. Wallace's cane, which presides over the conflict between himself and the narrator, becomes "a staff of self-deceiving hope." Finally, in *Willie Masters' Lonesome Wife* Willie Masters ("Will he master?") has "twin canes, leg sticks, rubber nosed and handles wrapped" and beats his wife, who is also the written page: "We can't make love like that anymore—make love or manuscript. Yet I have put my hand upon this body, here, as no man ever has, and I have even felt my pencil stir, grow great with blood. But never has it swollen up in love. It moves in anger, always, against its paper."[13]

The narrator of the title story confesses that he is a "cripple." The wires that "change perspective, rise, and twist" [like the "twisted" tune at the end] are "voices in thin strips. They are words wound in cables. Bars of connection." Playing on the homographs of "wind" and "wound," as well as on "window," the narrator intimates that *poiēsis* is a violent response to the wounds inflicted by others—wounds of exclusion:

> My window is a grave, and all that lies within it's dead. . . . Downwound, the whore at wagtag clicks and clacks . . . rest the world beyond my window, me in front of my reflection, above this page, my shade. Death is not so still, so silent, since silence implies a falling quiet, stillness a stopping, containing, holding in; for death is time in a clock, like Mr. Tick [the cat], electric . . . like wind through a windup poet. And my blear floats out to visible against the glass, befog its country and bespill myself. The mist lifts slowly from the fields in the morning.

The "wind through a windup poet" is a parody of poetic inspiration and an indication that the narrator is driven by a fear of death. Mrs. Desmond, one of the poet's personae, has a "thin white mist of hair" that manifests the "climate of her mind." In memory she is all of her ages at once, and her talk is a "fence—a shade drawn, window fastened, door that's locked" against death. The narrator also is all his ages as he listens to her and recalls the "winds" that he endured politely from his grandfather. Not only does the past speak of failure—both the town's and the narrator's—but the images of the present are dead ("stones," "memorials"), and no "monuments of unaging intellect" console the poet. The window—the page—is a trap as well as a protection since it reflects the poet's frustration. Having bespilled himself on the glass, he cannot distinguish between his own mist and the mist lifting from the world outside. In the act of mo(u)rning, he confuses himself with both the world outside and his beloved: "A steeple stands up in your head. You speak of loving; then give me a kiss. The pane is cold. On icy mornings the fog rises to greet me (as you always did)." As the world "tips" magically, one is reminded of the steeple in *Omensetter's Luck*, a sign of transcendence that becomes the stake for men's pride: "Hell's the tip of an inverted steeple." The theme of the fall pervades that novel, which begins almost with an anecdote about a man falling from a Methodist steeple. Similarly, when the narrator of "In the Heart of the Heart of the Country" fell in love, he says, he fell to his death, and he envies his cat because it does not have to "rise to" its own nature. To rise, for the narrator, is to "hat" one's head with a steeple; "turn church; devour people." To rise to one's own nature is to incorporate and to overcome others.

Another figure for the poet is "Billy Holsclaw," who "lives alone—how alone it is impossible to fathom. In the post office he talks greedily to me about the weather. His head bobs on a wild flood of words, and I take this violence to be a measure of his eagerness for speech." Dressed in "tatters," wobbling into the wind with a paper sack in the fold of his arm, he resembles the discarded mortality of "Sailing to Byzantium":

> An aged man is but a paltry thing,
> A tattered coat upon a stick, unless
> Soul clap its hands and sing, and louder sing
> For every tatter in its mortal dress.

But for the narrator there is "no answer" in poetry, which does not seem to give back more than it receives. Billy, perhaps, is "a surgeon cleansing a wound or an ardent and tactile lover," but the seed spilled by the narrator is the kind forbidden by *Leviticus*: "It's true there are moments—foolish moments, ecstasy in a tree stump—when I'm all but gone, scattered I like to think like seed, for I'm the sort now in the fool's position of having love left over which I'd like to lose; what good is it now to me, candy ungiven after Halloween?" Since the church's steeple is like the "hat of a witch," we can infer that the narrator's turning in on himself in pride and frustration has prevented him from spending the love that would renew him. He has not been able to go to seed, as the Gospel recommends: "Unless a grain of wheat falls into the earth and dies, it remains alone; but if it dies, it bears much fruit." How to adhere to the world properly becomes the concern of one who is "in retirement from love." The "claw" in "Holsclaw" is taken up later when the narrator sinks his "claws" into the fur of his cat, who becomes, in turn, a figure of poetry: "Mr. Tick . . . has a tail he can twitch, he need not fly his Fancy. Claws, not metrical schema, poetry his paws." Those paws suggest poetry's desire for adherence to the world, just as the alliteration embodies its desire for coherence. If the wires led to his beloved, that narrator says, he would know what they are: "But they do not lead to you. . . . They fasten me"—like the poet fastened to a "dying animal" in "Sailing to Byzantium."

"For all those not in love," we read, "there's law: to rule . . . to regulate . . . to rectify." Although the narrator claims that he does not write "the poetry of politics," he also says, "I chant, I beg, I orate, I command, I sing." If one aspect of the poet is Uncle Halley—a lying figure of Mnemosyne whose memorabilia "flowed like jewels from his palms"—another aspect is Miss Jakes, the local teacher, who, like the killer in "The Pedersen Kid," is "worn fine and smooth" and who, like Mrs. Mean, encourages the children to circumvent her (to put lines around her in their drawings) in order to stimulate her resentment. If the poet is, as he says at one time, nothing but mouth, he is also the organ associated with "jakes"—an organ of constriction and release, of refusal and trust. At one point he gave that he wants to "rise so high" that when he shits he "won't miss anybody." The play in Gass's language is such, moreover, that we begin to hear the word "own" in "wound," as the conflict between inner and outer, one's self and others continues. When the Russians launch their first satellite—an image appropriate to the narrator's isolation—people begin to speculate about the dog inside:

> I wouldn't want to take that mutt from *out* that metal flying thing if he's still living when he lands, *our own* dog catcher said; anybody knows you shut a dog up by himself to toss around the first thing he'll be setting *on* to do you let him *out* is bite somebody.
> This Midwest. A dissonance of parts and people, we are a *consonance* of *Towns*. Like a man grown fat in everything but heart, we overlabor; our outlook never really urban, never rural either, we enlarge and linger at the same time [in this] section of the *country*" (emphasis mine).

The cold war is never sufficiently cold to explode like the trees in Bemidji: "It is snow without any [cathartic] laughter in it . . . we are never sufficiently cold here." Or it is never sufficiently hot in summer for these parts to become "beautiful Death Valleys." The narrator him-self remains a kind of sputnik. Looking at a rickety stair, he imagines that if he went carefully up and turned the corner of the landing, he would find himself "out of the world"—like the boy in "The Pedersen Kid," who, clinging to a stair, imagines himself "fallen into space" and floating around "a dark star." The alternatives for one "in retirement from love," then, seem to be: to live "in" oneself or to live "out of the world." At moments the narrator seems to long for something else, for the kind of unmediated knowing he associates with the small North Dakota town of his childhood: "as I dreamed I'd know your body, as I've known noth-ing, before or since; knew as the flies knew, in the honest, unchaste sense." His childhood, he says, in this unchaste language, "came in the country" ("cunt-ry"). "Childhood," however, "is a lie of poetry"—he has never known anything in this unmediated way. Implicit in that childhood are the anger and separation associated with windows and other obstacles: when he swatted flies, "they might have thought they'd flown headlong into a summered window." In the present his knowing is of a different sort: "The pane is cold. Honesty is cold, my inside lover. . . . We meet on this window, the world and I, inelegantly, swim-mers of the glass; and swung wrong way round to one another, the world seems in." What the narrator longs to do is "to bring within about, to change" (emphasis mine)—to create works of arf that will affect others the way his gaze once affected the blooming of his beloved's body. But poetry seems more like the "worming" through a fence he mentions earlier, which is taken up when he describes himself as a poet: "I declare that though my inner organs were devoured long ago, the worm which swallowed down my parts still throbs and glows like a crystal palace"—the work of art. His poems are poems of experience—pervaded by the dark secret love of mimetic desire: "Even as the apples reddened, lit their tree, they were being swallowed." The "worm had them all," we read, in a phrase that recalls the tyger's wrath of "The Pedersen Kid": "The winter had finally got them all."

At the end of the story, in a high school gym, a whole community joins in "to form a single pulsing ululation . . . and the same shudder runs through all of them and runs toward the same *release*. Only the ball moves serenely through this dazzling din. Obedient to law it scarcely speaks but caroms quietly and lives at *peace*" (emphasis of the rhyming words is mine). Is this the old catharsis by violence or is it a kind of *agape*? What of the peace the narrator invokes in one of his sections on politics? "O all ye isolate and separate powers, Sing! Sing, and sing in such a way that from a distance it will seem a harmony, a Strindberg play, a friendship ring." He himself remains alone at the end and love-less, unable to decide whether the "twisted" strains he hears are "Joy to the World" or something else.

Conclusion: An Angel Can Come Too Late

One day, while still a boy, the Yiddish poet H. Leivick was beaten on the street by a drunken Pole. Later, in his *kheder* or Hebrew school, he heard the verses about the sacrifice of Isaac:

> Isaac accompanies his father Abraham to Mount Moriah, and now Isaac lies bound upon the altar waiting to be slaughtered. Within me my heart weeps even harder. It weeps out of great pity for Isaac. And now Abraham raises the knife. My heart is nearly frozen with fear. Suddenly—the angel's voice: Abraham, do not raise your hand against your son; do not slay him. You have only been tested by God. And now I burst into tears. "Why are you crying now?" the teacher asked. "As you see, Isaac was not slaughttered." In my tears I replied,"But what would have happened had the angel come one moment *too late?*" The teacher tried to console me with the reassurance that an angel cannot be late.[1]

But, as the history of our century alone shows us, the angel can indeed come too late. Only the victims seem to arrive consistently on time. As I pointed out in this introduction, much in modern and contemporary literature seems to be working through the nature and effectiveness of our sacrificial resources. Less dramatic than the lessons of the holocaust but just as revealing is the intuition expressed in different ways by both great literature and current manuals of psychology that blame is the root of our most serious problems. We blame ourselves because we cannot come up to the standards of freedom and autonomy that have become our philosophical commonplaces. We blame others because their *appearance* of such autonomy seems insolent and demeaning to ourselves, but we blame them even more when their weakness and susceptibility reveal them to be no *different* from ourselves. To free ourselves from the fascination of appearances, we attempt to debunk those appearances. Catching people out, as one of Paula Fox's characters puts it, is the American form of wisdom. But catching people *out* leaves us trapped *within* the dingy, many-coloured dome that is our ordinary world; and so appearances begin to exert their fascination again. Even art, as William Gass discusses it, is a constant attempt to get even with a world that can never be adequate to our desires.

The central question of this book, then, was raised movingly by Camus in *The Plague*: Can one be modest without God? In that book Tarrou wants to be "a saint without God"—someone who, by dint of unremitting attention, will remain surgically sterile—free of the microbes of violence. In every predicament, Tarrou says, he will take the victim's part in order to reduce the damage that can be done. Dr. Rieux, who is less self-justifying, replies that he does not want to be a saint but only a man.[2]

Mimetic Desire in *Women in Love*

In "A Propos of *Lady Chatterley's Lover*" D. H. Lawrence discusses the breakdown of vital relationships between man and "the living universe," between man and man, and between man and woman. Although his notion that "we have abstracted men and women into matter and force" and that "we have abstracted men and women into separate personalities" is consistent with a Marxist analysis of the dehumanizing effects of a market economy, Lawrence does not, like Marx, see class consciousness and struggle as means of restoring human values and a sense of community: "Class hate and class-consciousness are only a sign that the old togetherness, the old blood-warmth has collapsed, and every man is really aware of himself in apartness. Then we have these hostile groupings of men for the sake of opposition, strife. Civil strife becomes a necessary condition of self-assertion."[1] Although individualism is responsible for most of the ills that Lawrence discusses in modern society, it is to the individual that he looks in this essay and in *Women in Love* for solutions to the problems of alienation: "We must get back into relation, vivid and nourishing relation to the cosmos and the universe. The way is through daily ritual, and the reawakening. We must once more practise the ritual of dawn and noon and sunset, the ritual of the first breath, and the last. This is an affair of the individual and the household, a ritual of day."[2] The "we" in this quotation is not a coherent group or class, nor is Lawrence concerned with changing the economic structure of society. His notion of alienation, his observation that "the more mental and ideal men are, the more they seem to feel the bodily pressure of any other men as a menace, a menace, as it were, to their very being," is what we, following René Girard, call "mimetic desire."

An enormous burden is placed on the individual in the modern age. Whereas in feudal society the individual's model for conduct was either Christ or someone (like the king) invested with surpassing authority, modern man prides himself on his own autonomy, on the absolute spontaneity of his desire. This Romantic deification of man, this turning in on oneself is accompanied by an impulse of panic toward the other, since man's need for transcendence is not eliminated but simply diverted toward his neighbor. That is, instead of imitating Christ, man, crushed by the burden of his individualism, unable to realize the divine autonomy which he has been led to anticipate, imitates his neighbor. Since his isolation induces the illusion that he alone is too deficient, too weak to sustain the burden of his freedom, he imitates certain external characteristics of his neighbor (who becomes the mediator of his desire) in the hope that he will thereby gain the latter's apparent self-assurance. This triangle of subject, object, and mediator is similar to Thorstein Veblen's model of "conspicuous consumption," where "keeping up with the Joneses" means desiring to possess what they possess regardless of the real use value of the object. Because the real goal of this desire is the strength and autonomy of the mediator rather than the concrete qualities of the object, this desire can also be called "metaphysical."

As soon as the subject begins to emulate the mediator, he perceives him as a rival for the desired object. As Birkin notes of the worker's desire for a pianoforte in *Women in Love*: "It makes him so much higher in his neighboring collier's eyes. He sees himself reflected in the neighboring opinion, like a Brocken mist, several feet taller on the strength of the pianoforte, and he is satisfied. He lives for the sake of that Brocken spectre, the reflection of himself in the human opinion."[3] Gerald Crich's father is attracted toward his miners, who, like all mediators of mimetic desire, have already in the eyes of their beholder inherited the earth: "He had always the unacknowledged belief that it was his workmen, the miners, who held in their hands the means of salvation. To move nearer to God, he must move towards his miners, his life must gravitate towards theirs. They were, unconsciously, his idol, his God made manifest. In them he worshipped the highest, the great, sympathetic, mindless Godhead of humanity." Mr. Crich's charity is a means of gaining recognition from this "idol," which is elevated precisely in order that it may be overcome.

This rivalry extends into erotic relationships, where the beloved's withholding himself from the lover is interpreted by the latter as a sign of his prestige. As Flaubert notes about love in the modern world, "Two beings never love each other at the same time." If the Hegelian struggle of master and slave involved the use of violence to attain the recognition of the other, the modern struggle for recognition involves deceit, the suppression of one's own desire to gain the desire of the other. The master (or mediator) becomes the person who can withhold his desire, for this withholding is interpreted by the slave (or subject) as the mediator's desire for himself. Imitating that hypothetical desire by his own desire, the subject actually stimulates the pride (the desire of self) of the mediator, which in turn stimulates again the subject's desire, and so on.

Although it is the same contagious desire passing back and forth in this circuit, the subject suffers from the illusion that some kind of absolute difference separates him from the mediator, whose divine autonomy is signified by the contempt he shows for the subject. Just as Mr. Crich abstracts from the material interests that separate him from his workers some notion of spiritual difference, he abstracts from the sexual difference between himself and his wife a radical discontinuity that enables him to continually aspire toward her. Frustrated by his parasitic philanthropy, repelled by the "world of creeping democracy," Mrs. Crich loses her connection with the world—becoming absorbed, unconsciously, in the master-slave struggle to withhold recognition. Although Mr. Crich triumphs over her outwardly, although she is made demented by his unassailable self-delusion, she is ultimately his victor: "Only death itself would show the perfect completeness of the lie. Till death, she was his white snowflower. He had subdued her, and her subjection was to him an infinite chastity in her, a virginity which he could never break, and which dominated him as by a spell." She is ultimately and against her will the cancer which erodes her husband from within, having been forced into the "fierce tension of opposition, like the negative pole of a magnet." Fascinating him by "the terrible white destructive light that burned in her eyes" (which he has kindled there), her superiority lies in her ability to remain "unbroken and unimpaired within" while letting go of "the outer world."

As Lawrence's depiction of "the industrial magnate" shows, there is no discontinuity between the social area and the erotic one, the latter being in fact the most intense example of "deviated transcendency." In the cancelled Prologue to *Women in Love*, Lawrence expatiates on the ambivalent relationship between Birkin and Hermione much more fully than he does in the published edition. He describes Hermione's predicament in the first chapter of the published edition as follows: "She always felt vulnerable, vulnerable, there was always a secret chink in her armour. She did not know herself what it was. It was a lack of robust self, she had no natural sufficiency, there was a terrible void, a lack, a deficiency in her. And she wanted someone to close up this deficiency, to close it up for ever." Lawrence notes in the cancelled Prologue,

> She believed in herself as a priestess, and that was all. Though there were no God to serve, still she was a priestess. Yet having no altar to kindle, no sacrifice to burn, she would be barren and useless. So she adhered to her God in him, which she claimed almost violently, whilst her soul turned in bitter cynicism from the prostitute man in him. She did not believe in him, she only believed in that which she could gather from him, as one gathers silk from the corrupt worm. She was the maker of Gods.[4]

Birkin, both attracted and repelled by Hermione's "spiritual" abstraction, made restless by the sterility of his godhood, "turned round upon his priestess, and became the common vulgar man who turned her to scorn." Attracted by Gerald as the "traveller in unknown countries," Birken "felt a passion of desire for Gerald Crich, for the clumsier, cruder intelligence and the limited soul, and for the starving, unenlightened body of his friend." As Hermione, with the perspicacity of someone at an advanced stage of this ontological illness, notes, Birkin's attraction to a "coarse, unsusceptible being" like Gerald means that "nothing was anything." Or rather, at the last stage of this illness, nothing becomes everything. Birkin also is under no illusions about his relation to Hermione, which is based entirely on "ecstasy and on pain and ultimate death." He describes the wilful nature of his desire as follows, "Never to be able to love spontaneously, never to be moved by a power greater than oneself, but always to be within one's own control, deliberate, having the choice, this was horrifying, more deadly than death." Hermione's "tremulous" seeking of death at Birken's hands indicates the real truth (*entelecheia*) of this desire, which is that the ultimate and most unequivocal confirmation of the other's divine autonomy is the last and most extreme repudiation.

This advanced stage of desire is sado-masochistic, where the subject desires precisely the obstacles which the mediator can place in his path. Since he has learned from many experiences that the object which he can possess is valueless, he will be interested in the future in only those objects which are forbidden to him by an implacable mediator. René Girard illustrates this stage by a parable. A man is told that he can find a great treasure underneath a stone. He spends years turning over stones without finding the treasure. At the end of that time, he can either give up the search, which means that his life is now meaningless, or he can seek out a stone so big that he cannot lift it. It is only when he encounters such a stone that he can maintain the illusion that the great treasure might still be underneath it. In the case of the master-slave struggle, as soon as the master has triumphed, as soon as he obtains the other's recognition, that other becomes part of "the kingdom of the banal" from which the master is trying to escape. It is only in being defeated, repudiated, that man feels that he is at least close to the divine autonomy of which the other partakes. Man's desire becomes ultimately a desire for death since the most extreme repudiation (which he interprets as a sign of the most extreme autonomy) comes from those beings who are the most inhuman, who are the least responsive to the subject's human appeal. If spiders and snakes haunt the dreams of Svidrigailov and Stavrogin, if the mediator in *Notes from the Underground*, Zverkov, bears a symbolic name meaning "animal," "beast," eros in *Women in Love* is associated with insects, organic decay, and machinery.

Having been attracted in the Prologue to the "rat-like" eyes and the "rabbit-like" manner of eating which he observes in the "strange Cornish men," Birkin later describes Aphrodite in terms of this organic decay: "When the stream of synthetic creation lapses, we find ourselves part of the inverse process, the blood of destructive creation. Aphrodite is born in the first spasm of universal dissolution—then the snakes and swans and lotus—marsh flowers—and Gudrun and Gerald—born in the process of destructive creation." Even more striking, Gudrun and Minette, like Halliday's African statue, are associated with both rats and insects. That this destructive process has all the characteristics of mimetic desire can be seen in the mutual alienation that characterizes all the relations in the book at one time or another. Gudrun, for example, feels that she is an outcast from life. Suffering from a sense of her own negation, from her knowledge that she depends for her being on the recognition of others, she envies both Ursula's ability to partake of life and her self-sufficiency. This paradoxical sense of Ursula's partaking of life "at the center of her own universe" is exaggerated in Gudrun's later relations with Gerald and Loerke—the partaker of life being increasingly the one who most repudiates it. In the "Moony" chapter, Ursula is torn between her hard repudiation of others (associated with the "moon-brilliant hardness" of the night) and her desire for love, as is Birkin, who stones the forbidding image of the moon and yet denies that the intimacy of love is what he wants. Ursula is both attracted and repelled by Birkin's detachment, "He was the enemy, fine as a diamond, and as hard and jewel-like, the quintessence of all that was inimical." As both rival and lover in this competitive relationship, Birkin is the object of a "transfiguring" hatred. Though himself a victim of this same desire, Birkin perceives its dynamic, noting that what most people call love is really hate.

The most fatal examples of this desire are, of course, Gudrun and Gerald. Their struggle for mastery has its first crisis in the "Rabbit" chapter, where, at the moment when Gudrun seems most slave-like and Gerald senses his greatest power over her, he is also afraid of her as his ultimate victor. The rabbit (whose mysterious brutality fascinates Winifred) engraves the knowledge of their desire on Gudrun's arm, where "the long, shallow red rip" implies "obscene" or "abhorrent" mysteries that remind one of the "unspeakable rites" offered up to Kurtz in *Heart of Darkness*. Some kind of human sacrifice seems to be implied in both contexts, as Gerald glimpses "the forever unconscious, unthinkable red ether of the beyond, the obscene beyond." Gerald's dependence on Gudrun for recognition means that when he compels such recognition, it is only the recognition of a slave (like Minette); and when Gudrun is worthy of giving such recognition, she withholds it as master. As Flaubert's statement revealed, love in the modern world has been deprived of the communion that we still associate with it, the struggle for desire meaning that the two lovers are never really together. The possibility of communion is intimated in "Water Party," where Gerald and Gudrun "lapse out" toward each other and seem to fulfill, "balanced in separation, in the boat," Birkin's normative relationship. This moment of "melting," however, is immediately dispelled by disaster (murder, as Gerald describes it), and their sexual union occurs quite differently, with Gudrun lying awake all night ("destroyed into perfect consciousness") while Gerald sleeps soundly on top of her.

If the struggle between Gerald and Gudrun is in one phase a struggle to overcome desire for the sake of desire, their ultimate ambition is for a spontaneous state of non-desire that Gerald associates with the fixity of a stone. Just as Gudrun admires Ursula's self-sufficiency, in the penultimate chapter Gerald desires what he considers Gudrun's self-complete, desireless condition. Observing that only an extreme effort of the will is necessary to achieve this same self-completeness, Gerald also recognizes that he cannot really face the consequences of this immunity, "But then to have no claim upon her, he must stand by himself, in sheer nothingness." Ultimately unable ("too serious") to make precisely this nothingness the meaning of life (the final stage of ontological illness), Gerald seeks absolute repudiation from Gudrun as a paradoxical confirmation of his being:

> She was the determining influence of his very being, *though* she treated him with contempt, repeated rebuffs and denials, *still* he would never be gone, since in being near her, even, he felt the quickening, the going forth in him, the release, the knowledge of his own limitation and the magic of the promise, as well as the mystery of his own destruction and annihilation (emphasis mine).

Noting the "deep structure" of his expressed desire, one perceives that "though" and "still" are really preconscious transformations of "because" and "so." Although Gudrun has successfully suppressed her desire for Gerald, moreover, she has not attained the kind of autonomy that he attributes to her. This autonomy is always an illusion except in the last stages of ontological illness, when the mediator becomes insect-like, merely organic, and finally inorganic or mechanical.

After contemplating Gerald's "instrumentality" (in much the same way Gerald has contemplated the instrumentality of his workers), Gudrun considers ironically the kind of life she would lead with him. Snobbism occurs when real, concrete differences have disappeared and when individuals or classes posit arbitrary differences between themselves and others. The height of snobbism is to desire something that one knows to be spurious, as when the remnants of the French nobility tried to reinstate privileges that the revolution had shown to be arbitrary. Gudrun understands that "the whole coinage of valuation [is] spurious," but she also accepts the fact that "in a world where spurious coin was current, a bad sovereign was better than a bad farthing." Despite her contempt for Gerald's social standing and for his position as captain of industry, she cannot help caring for these false values: "Yet, of course, she cared a great deal, outwardly—and outwardly was all that mattered, for inwardly was a bad joke." Gudrun eventually leaves Gerald behind in her tropism toward death (Gerald being the *ne plus ultra* of the "world of men" for her) and begins the final process of disintegration with Loerke, whose subhumanness is equivalent in this world to superhumanness. As a "pure, unconnected will, stoical and momentaneous" he attracts both sisters although Ursula eventually rejects the brutality which continues to fascinate Gudrun.

The final stage of ontological illness is, as we have seen, destructive and self-destructive. The phenomena connected with this stage, moreover, tend to be of a collective nature. Pointing up Stephan Trofimovitch's revelation at the end of *The Possessed* is the parable of the Gadarene swine, the unclean spirit of which is called "Legion." This parable seems to reverberate in the following apposition concerning Birkin's own infection by the collective disease of his civilization: ". . . he, who was so nearly dead, who was so near to being gone with the rest of his race down the slope of mechanical death." That the "will" which Birkin, Gerald, and Hermione debate about has become a "collective thing" accounts for their inability to act spontaneously or passionately. Just as "sex in the head" is the reverse side of Hermione's profession of unself-conscious spontaneity, collective hate is the reverse side of "individualism"—imitated desire passing back and forth in its circuit until it explodes.

If Lawrence contemns Marxist solutions to alienation, seeing class consciousness as a critical stage of social dissolution, he seems to maintain some faith in individual redemption. Rejecting the "plausible ethics of productivity," Birkin chastises Gerald for being an "unbeliever" and states his own belief in the true union between a man and a woman. The passage echoing the parable of the Gadarene swine, moreover, expresses Birkin's belief that his union with Ursula has been redemptive. This faith will be our final concern.

Overcoming mimetic desire means renouncing the difference posited arbitrarily between oneself and one's rival (who may also be one's lover). An image of such renunciation, an image of *vertical* transcendency, appears toward the end of *Women in Love*—but as a terrible realization of Gerald Crich's defeat, "It was a half-buried crucifix, a little Christ under a little sloping hood at the top of a pole. He sheered away. Somebody was going to murder him. He had a great dread of being murdered. But it was a dread which stood outside him like his own ghost." As Birkin pointed out early in the book, this dread is really a "lurking desire." And if God becomes a parrot for the dehumanized heroine of Flaubert's *A Simple Heart*, He becomes the murderous rival for Gerald in this scene. Gerald's final alienation from himself, his dread standing "outside him like his own ghost," is unlike the death of Julien Sorel or the illness of Proust's Marcel that bring about their conversion, their reconciliation to the human condition. But Birkin's professions of faith are also in doubt at the end. His final question (concerning an "eternal union with a man") is like the question he poses earlier regarding his ambition with Ursula: "Was it really only an idea, or was it the interpretation of a profound longing?" The rose that emerged after Birkin stoned the forbidding image of the moon does not quite emerge again, despite the fact that Birkin has to some extent renounced his "stellar" ambitions (persuasively characterized by Ursula as "the old Adam") and resigned himself to a less demanding kind of relationship.

The problem lies in Birkin's relation to Gerald. The cancelled Prologue reinforces the difficulty one feels in accepting the erotic imagery of the "Gladiatorial" chapter as expressing Whitmanian comradeship. Throughout the Prologue Gerald is presented as a rival to Hermione, Birkin swinging back and forth between the two. Between Birkin and Gerald is a subconscious interplay, "the interchange of spiritual and physical richness, the relieving of physical and spiritual poverty, without any intrinsic change in either man." It is Gerald's "coarse unsusceptibility" that attracts Birkin, as does the inaccessible sensuality of the other men whom he desires: "They divided themselves roughly into two classes: these white-skinned, keen-limbed men with eyes like blue-flashing ice and hair like crystals of winter sunshine, the northmen, inhuman as sharp-crying gulls, distinct like splinters of ice, like crystals, isolated, individual; and then the men with dark eyes one can enter and plunge into, bathe in, as in a liquid darkness, dark-skinned, supple, night-smelling men, who are the living substance of the viscous universal heavy darkness." These two types of being are like the two ways to death that Birkin describes in the "Moony" chapter, both of which are terrible and seductive. Ursula also perceives Gerald as a rival; and Birkin's most intense experience of Gerald (described in clearly sexual terms) occurs immediately after he has been rejected by Ursula. It is a *radical* difference that he posits between himself and Gerald, "as far, perhaps, apart as man from woman, yet in another direction."

Is Birkin's desire for a relationship transcending love (a desire deflated by Ursula in the "Mino" chapter) a reversal of discredited feelings or a culmination of them? Ursula seems to win most of her arguments with Birkin, and yet she sometimes parodies the "Syria Dea" that Birkin curses in "Moony." Despite his occasional deflations by Ursula, moreover, Birkin often seems to carry a good deal of narrative authority, and Ursula sounds very much like him when she tells Gudrun toward the end, "Love is too human and little. I believe in something inhuman, of which love is only a little part. I believe what we must fulfill comes out of the unknown to us, and it is something infinitely more than love. It isn't so merely *human*." Just as the "transcendent intimacy" that Birkin feels for Gerald in the Prologue is like the "strange conjunction" that he wants with Ursula, Birkin's notion that a union between a man and a woman is all important, "seeing there's no God," is like Hermione's "religious" attitude toward Birkin in the Prologue. The nature of desire seems to be consistent in all these relationships, whether they exclude or complement each other, and the exchange between Birkin and Ursula at the end does not give us a sense of mimetic desire having been transcended.

It is interesting that Lawrence repudiated homosexuality as a positive alternative to conventional love, associating it in a dream with the beetles that pervade *Women in Love*. These beetles, connected with the African statue in "Moony" and with the slave-like degeneracy of Minette and Gudrun, are symbols of the anality that so many critics have associated with the cycles of dissolution and regeneration in Lawrence's books. It is not terribly important to decide whether or not Birkin's relation to Gerald is homosexual; what *is* important is that the "structure" of desire is common to all Birkin's relationships. Gerald, in addition to the animal attraction he exerts on Birkin, represents all that Birkin detests in his civilization: the "pure instrumentality of man," the collectivization of will, the outworn ideal of a dead humanity. He is, moreover, more like the eviscerated Hermione than is any other character in the book, his "keen attentiveness, concentrated and unyielding in himself" being much like Hermione's painful self-consciousness. Underneath their surface dislike and opposition is this basic alikeness. The mediator is desired for the very qualities that the subject detests—what René Girard calls "the prestige of baseness." Birkin's final assertion, therefore, seems to bring us full circle, despite his insistence that an *additional* perfect relationship is what he wants. It leaves us with the same sense that Mark Schorer talks about in "Technique as Discovery" that Lawrence has not sufficiently allowed his technique to discover the fullest meaning of his material.

APPENDIX II

Music to the Name of Stein

Scapegoating is the subject also of Gertrude Stein's little mystery "A
Water-fall and a Piano"—written at a time when the world seemed to
be filling up with distressing fathers: "Everybody nowadays is a father,
there is father Mussolini and father Hitler and father Roosevelt and
father Stalin and father Lewis and father Blum and father Franco is just
commencing now and there are ever so many more ready to be one. . . .
The periods of the world's history that have always been most dismal
ones are the ones where fathers were looming and filling up everything."[1] The epigraph to her little tale of cultural crisis is:

> There are so many ways in which there is no crime.
> A goat comes into this story too.
> There is always coincidence in crime.

"No crime" because the crime against the scapegoat coincides ideally
with the reconciliation of those who have turned their own violence
against it.

   Helen is an orphan whose mother is "put away" and whose father goes
to war in order to escape the mother's craziness: "She played the piano
and at the same time put cement between the keys so that they would not
sound. You see how easy it is to have cement around." Playing the
piano is a cultural act, requiring a scale that articulates continuity into
meaningful discontinuity. The phrase "cement around" almost contains
"crime" or "no crime," and the missing "I" occurs at the beginning of the
next sentence: "I have often noticed how easy it is to have cement
around." When the mother fills up the keys so that music cannot sound,
she is enacting symbolically the cultural crisis to which Stein gives the
name "father" and to which Nietzsche and Kafka gave the name "Law."
The father in this story, turning his back on this "craziness"—on the
bankruptcy of the old order—goes to war, which conducts violence
outside against a common enemy. As the story goes on, however, this

134

solution is repeated *within* the society—in the form of a "crime," whose Indo-European root is *skeri*: to cut, separate, sift.[2]

The renewal brought about by this separation of "legitimate" from "illegitimate" violence is represented by the waterfall: "She [the orphan] went to stay where there was a water-fall." In contrast to the playing of the mother's piano—a refinement of an already established cultural order—is the work loved by the woman with whom she stays. That woman also has a dog who gives birth to nine puppies—symbolic of a period of gestation, transformation, or renewal. To nourish these puppies the woman seeks to buy a goat, but the deal falls through. The goat having been paid for, "no one would let the goat go. This often happens." We then read, "Do you see how the whole place was ready now for anybody to be dead." "Goat" and "dog" are almost anagrams for each other, and "dog," of course, suggests the further transformation into "god." Here at the source of nourishment—the goat—and the source of fertility—the waterfall—is the crime that separates things out. The falling through of the deal, however, suggests Stein's awareness that the scapegoat has lost its effectiveness as a means of renewal.

The "anybody" who will be dead turns out to be an "Englishwoman, this was all in France, and the rest were French." Her death seems to emerge from the matrix of certain dichotomies: country vs. city, French vs. English, and married vs. unmarried. The putting "away" of the crazy mother, moreover, is recalled by the following observation: "The more you see how the country is the more you do not wonder why they shut the door. They the women do *in a way* and yet if they did not it would be best" (emphasis mine). This sense of inside and outside is continued when the Englishwoman "went away for a month's holiday and then she came back" to be dead. Her death is surrounded by controversy since the two bullets in her head make the theory of suicide—which lets the other women off the hook—questionable. At the end her place is taken by another figure who is marginal to French culture, an American, who "has not come to be dead" yet. Reinforcing this sense of periodic failing is the fact that the puppies—symbols of gestation or rebirth—become "changed" or spayed—like the woman herself, who lives only with other women. The orphan, moreover, ends up marrying an "officer," like her father—a representative of law and order.

Like Oedipus, who discovers what lies at the origin of man's existence—chaos and night and all things mixed together—Stein uses an interval of free reflection to suggest the indeterminacy that haunts this tale: "Nobody refuses fear. Not only for themselves but for their dreams because water as if it were a precipice in the moon-light can not disturb because of there being no origin in their dreams." Stein, who tends to refer to herself in her works as "everybody" or "anybody," is playing here on the word "nobody." Later on "nobody" is told what happened to the dead woman, and the doctor says that "nobody could shoot themselves twice." Consequently, "nobody refuses fear" could mean that "everybody" accepts fear or that "everybody," whose identity is in crisis, refuses fear (Stein's earlier use of "anybody," moreover, may suggest her own identification with the scapegoat soon to be dead). In the dreams in which water—the element of indeterminacy—is evoked, it does not disturb because "no origin" is revealed. That is, dreams—like the analyses of myth made by Lévi-Strauss—transform the scandals that generate them but do not reveal their *raison d'être*. As long as this origin remains concealed, water is made, by moonlight or imagination, into the stuff of dreams. The sun does not appear in this tale of detection, nor does a detective.

Notes

Chapter 1
After the Law

1. René Girard, *Deceit, Desire, and the Novel*, trans. Yvonne Freccero (Baltimore: The Johns Hopkins Press, 1965), p. 59.
2. *Violence and the Sacred*, trans. Patrick Gregory (Baltimore: The Johns Hopkins Press, 1977); and *Des choses cachées depuis la fondation du monde* (Paris: Grasset, 1978).
3. *Denver Quarterly*, 13,2 (Summer, 1978), 38.
4. Raymond Olderman, *Beyond the Waste Land* (New Haven: Yale University Press, 1972), pp. 171, 52.
5. Norbert Wiener, *The Human Use of Human Beings* (New York: Avon, 1967), p. 50. On the Manichean side, some recent films are explicit rites of exorcism. *The Exorcist* and the spate of demon films that followed it are remakes of *The Bad Seed* and convey the terrifying fantasy of the younger generation's normal rebellion against the older generation mutating into some kind of relentless evil. Similarly, Brian De Palma's recent films are adolescent fantasies of revenge against an older generation that is pathologically repressive or cynically manipul. The telekinetic power of the films' protagonists is a sign of impatience with the ordinary processes of social and political life, which are resolved by the furious power of adolescent resentment.
6. *Denver Quarterly*, p. 38.
7. John Gardner, *Grendel* (New York: Ballantine Books, 1971).
8. Philip Rieff, *Freud: The Mind of the Moralist* (New York: Viking, 1959), p. 253.
9. Philip Rieff, *The Triumph of the Therapeutic* (New York: Harper Torchbooks, 1968), p. 55.
10. Gertrude Stein, "A Transatlantic Interview 1946," in *A Primer for the Gradual Understanding of Gertrude Stein*, ed. Robert Bartlett Haas (Santa Barbara: Black Sparrow Press, 1973), p. 15.
11. William Gass, *The World Within the Word* (New York: Knopf, 1978), p. 74.
12. Gass, p. 107.
13. René Girard, *Des choses cachées depuis la fondation du monde*, p. 242. The translation is mine.
14. Allen Mandelbaum, *Chelmaxioms* (Boston: David R. Godine, 1977), p. 70.
15. Mandelbaum, p. xvii.

16. Edmond Jabès, *The Book of Questions*, trans. Rosemarie Waldrop (Middletown: Wesleyan University Press, 1976), p. 19.
17. Jabès, pp. 37, 45, 115.
18. Mandelbaum, p. 11.
19. Jabès, p. 71.
20. Mandelbaum, pp. 37, 44.
21. Gershom G. Scholem, *On the Kabbalah and its Symbolism*, trans. Ralph Manheim (New York: Schocken, 1965), p. 50.
22. Jabès, p. 35.

Chapter 2
Robbe-Grillet's Café des Alliés

1. All references are to Alain Robbe-Grillet, *Les Gommes* (Paris: Les Éditions de Minuit, 1953). The translations provided in footnotes are taken from Richard Howard's translation, *The Erasers* (New York: Grove Press, 1964).
2. "Definitely a good victim, a sad little spider's face, perpetually reconstituting the tatters of his frayed intelligence."
3. The ideas in this book concerning mimetic desire, scapegoat mechanism, and the sacred derive from the magisterial work of René Girard: *Deceit, Desire, and the Novel*, trans. Yvonne Freccero (Baltimore: The Johns Hopkins Press, 1955); *Violence and the Sacred*, trans. Patrick Gregory (Baltimore: The Johns Hopkins Press, 1977); and *Des Choses cachées depuis la fondation du monde* (Paris: Grasset, 1978).
4. Some allusions to the myth are: Wallas remembers being in this city as a child with his mother. As it turns out, they have been searching for his father, with whom he is later identified as "une vieille relation." The streets in the book have names like "Rue de Brabant" (which recalls the images of ploughing in Sophocles' play) and "Rue de Corinthe." The name "C. Laurent" may be a disguise for "Creon." Wallas, whose feet become swollen from walking, encounters some statuary entitled "Le Char de l'État," the sculptor of which is "V. Daulis." Wallas also encounters a display representing an artist drawing "d'après nature." In this first occurrence, "nature" turns out to be "un immense tirage photographique d'un carrefour de ville"— in fact, the location of Dupont's house. The artist's drawing, however, represents the ruins of a Greek city. Just as Oedipus attempts to negate the oracle's representation of his fate, the image of the city "est la négation du dessin censé le reproduire." In the next occurrence the ruins are named as the ruins of Thebes, but here "nature" and representation switch roles: the model is the city of Thebes and the "painting" is a snapshot of the scene of Dupont's house. The point is that the very distinction between a "natural" given and its "cultural" interpretation is often dubious—as our various "needs" and psychosomatic symptoms show.
5. "a mass-produced allegorical subject: shepherds finding an abandoned child, or something of the kind."
6. "a soft, crumbly gum eraser that friction does not twist but reduces to dust." This "yellowish cube, about an inch or two long, with the corners slightly rounded—maybe by use."
7. "a kind of cube, but slightly misshapen, a shiny block of gray lava, with its faces polished as though by wear, the edges softened, compact, apparently

hard, heavy as gold, looking about as big as a fist; a paperweight? It is the only trinket in the room." This cube is described again as a "cube of vitrified stone, with its sharp edges and deadly corners."

8. "lost cities, petrified by some cataclysm for centuries—or only for a few seconds before their collapse, a wink of hesitation between life and what already bears another name: after, before, eternity." That the cube on Dupont's desk is made of gray lava portends the fantasy Wallas will have of a "Pompeian-style city" in which he is talking to "people he cannot distinguish from one another but who were at the start clearly characterized and individual. He himself has a distinct role, probably a major one, perhaps official."

9. "And suddenly, preceded by a ripple of foam, appears from under the arch of the bridge the blunt bow of the barge, which moves slowly on to the next bridge.
   "The little man in the long greenish coat who has been leaning over the parapet straightens up."

10. To give a few more examples of this pandemic doubling: "Daniel Dupont" and "Albert Dupont" are confused; various kinds of overcoats and raincoats identify characters: Wallas, for example, is identified as the man in the raincoat who puts Dupont's bell out of order for the murderer; the conspirator with whom Wallas is identified wears glasses that make him look like a doctor—like Dr. Juard, perhaps, with whom Dupont is identified. Dupont's disguise, moreover, includes medical glasses that make him look like a villain. Bona and Garinati, as well as Wallas and Fabius, are confused. All of this, like the setting of Dupont's kitchen, is indeed "en faux-semblant."

11. "One image has remained vivid to him, the dead end of a canal; against one of the quays is moored an old wreck of a boat—the hull of a sailboat? A lone stone bridge closes off the canal. Probably that wasn't exactly right: the boat could not have passed under the bridge."

12. "We don't always manage to prevent crime, sometimes the criminal even manages to escape, but there's never been a case where we haven't found his tracks, whereas this time we're left with a lot of unidentified fingerprints and some drafts that open doors. Our informers are no help here. If we're dealing, as you think, with a terrorist organization, they've been very careful to keep from being contaminated: in this sense, their hands are clean, cleaner than those of a police that maintains such close relations with the men they're watching."

13. "His footsteps are as silent as a priest's . . . footsteps so light they leave no traces on the surface of the sea."

14. Alain Robbe-Grillet, *Two Novels*, trans. Richard Howard (New York: Grove Press, 1959), p. 117. In *La Jalousie* vision is fragmented by the blind and the ballustrade of one side of the house, or restored bit by bit by a lamp. These motifs are in conflict with the "continuous" landscape and the "engulfing" darkness. In *Les Gommes* a "dim, fragmentary illumination" is "interrupted by gaps, more or less widely fringed with vague areas where the mind hesitates to venture." See Jacques Leenhardt, *Lecture Politique Du Roman* (Paris: Minuit, 1973).

15. Alain Robbe-Grillet, *For a New Novel*, trans. Richard Howard (New York: Grove Press, 1965), p. 24.

16. Ibid., p. 140.

17. Ibid., pp. 23 and 19.

18. Ibid., pp. 162–163.

19. Roland Barthes, "Objective Literature: Alain Robbe-Grillet," included in Alain Robbe-Grillet, *Two Novels*, p. 14.

20. *For a New Novel*, p. 32.

21. Ibid., pp. 53–58.

22. Ibid., pp. 58–60.

23. Ibid., p. 151.

24. Ibid., p. 155. See also Roland Barthes, *Mythologies*, trans. Annette Lavers (New York: Hill and Wang, 1972), p. 142.

25. See *For a New Novel*, p. 137 and *Mythologies*, pp. 128 and 157.

26. "An absent-minded wipe of the rag, as an excuse, over the funny spot. One way or another vague masses pass, out of reach; or else they're just holes." is raised a "gables' line of defense, where the openings instinctively grow more myopic and the ramparts thicker."

27. Franz Kafka, "The Silence of the Sirens," in *The Complete Stories*, ed. Nathum N. Glatzur (New York: Schocken, 1971), pp. 430–432.

28. "Above the sixteenth step, a small painting is hanging on the wall, at eye level. It is a romantic landscape representing a stormy night: a flash of lightning illuminates the ruins of a tower; at its feet two men are lying, asleep despite the thunder or else struck by lightning? Perhaps fallen from the top of the tower." Later, the painting appears as follows: "It is a nightmare scene. At the foot of a ruined tower, illuminated by a flash of sinister lightning, two men are lying. One is wearing royal clothes, his gold crown gleams on the grass beside him; the other is a simple peasant. The lightning has just dealt out the same death to both of them."

29. J. E. Cirlot, *A Dictionary of Symbols*, trans. Jack Sage (New York: Philosophical Library, 1962), pp. 105–106. Evidence of the scapegoat mechanism pervades *Les Gommes*: Scattered fragments of debris form "un visage grotesque de clown, une poupée de jeu de massacre" ("a grotesque clown's face, a Punch-and-Judy doll"); the raincoat that tears until "il forme à présent une immense cloche d'où s'échappe, semblable aux tentacules d'une méduse géante, le tourbillon de rubans entremêlés à quoi s'est réduit, finalement, le reste du costume" ("it now forms a tremendous bell from which escapes, like the tentacles of some giant octopus, the vortex of intertwined ribbons to which, finally, the rest of the coat has been reduced").

30. "Sometimes," Wallas thinks, "you go through hell and high water to find a murderer, and the crime hasn't even been committed."

31. Dupont "has even accepted dark glasses so that no one will recognize him; the only pair to be found in the clinic was a pair of medical glasses, one of whose lenses is very dark and the other much lighter—which gives the professor the comical look of a villain in a melodrama."

32. "A tremendous voice fills the hall. Projected by invisible loudspeakers, it bounces back and forth against the walls covered with signs and advertisements, which amplify it still more, multiply it, reflect it, baffle it with a whole series of more or less conflicting echoes and resonances, in which the original message is lost—transformed into a gigantic oracle, magnificent, indecipherable, and terrifying."

33. "*takes place* anywhere, every day, now here, now there. What actually happened in Professor Dupont's house the evening of October twenty-sixth? A replica, a copy, a simple reproduction of an event whose original and whose key are elsewhere."

34. "After a few steps he again finds himself in front of the building he has just left. He raises his hand to his ear with irritation: will that damned machine never stop?"

35. "On the other side of the barrier, it was apparent that everything was not yet over; because of a certain elasticity in the materials, the platform's descent had not stopped when the machinery did; it had continued for several seconds, moving a fraction of an inch perhaps, creating a tiny gap in the continuity of the roadway which brought the metal rim slightly above its position of equilibrium; and the oscillations—growing fainter and fainter, less and less noticeable, but whose cessation it was difficult to be certain of—consequently approximated—by a series of successive prolongations and regressions on either side of a quite illusory fixity—a phenomenon completed, nevertheless, some time before."

36. As we have mentioned, the Café des Alliés is near the Boulevard Circulaire, within which the problem of what is the shortest distance between two points arises: "Le seul chemin d'un point à un autre." The name *Loxias* suggests the "oblique" character of the oracle that consigns Oedipus to his fate in order to relieve society of its violence. This diversion of bad reciprocity, however, does not appear to those who believe in the victim as the repository of all badness. In *Les Gommes* one character observes, "Je peux très bien . . . suivre une ligne oblique par rapport au canal et marcher quand même en ligne droite" ("I could still . . . be walking obliquely to the canal and be walking a straight line anyway"). One wonders what the knights on a chessboard think. Wallas considers his own rationalizations of these detours: "Quel mauvais sort le force donc, aujourd'hui, à donner des raisons partout sur son passage? Est-ce une disposition particulière des rues de cette cité qui l'oblige à demander sans cesse son chemin, pour, à chaque réponse, se voir conduit à de nouveaux détours?" ("What kind of spell is it that is forcing him to give explanations wherever he goes today? Is it a particular arrangement of the streets in this city that obliges him to be always asking his way, so that at each reply he finds himself led into new detours?").

In another novel, *Second Skin*, by another author, John Hawkes, the kind of "farce" called into question by Dr. Juard is perpetuated. The expulsion of "bad" violence and its absorption by a god (transcended evil having become transcendent good) is suggested by the connection made by the protagonist, "Skipper," between vomiting and prayer: "Anyone who has gotten down on his knees to vomit has discovered, if only by accident, the position of prayer." In addition, the profound deception necessary for this expulsion, the deception that invests the internecine violence of the community in one person, is suggested by the self-deception noted in Skipper by almost every critic writing on this book. His self-deception has been interpreted either as an irony of narrative unreliability or as a necessary gambit in the face of almost universal evil, but the *self*-deception of the god is only the necessary and profound self-deception of the community that expels him. If Skipper is a "large and innocent Iphigenia betrayed on the beach," each person around him is "his own Antigone—the sand-scratchers, the impatient sufferers of self-inflicted death." The Skipper who says, "I won't ask why" after his daughter's suicide becomes an Atlas holding up a lighthouse on his shoulders. Although the greater willfulness of this self-deception makes this scapegoat comic through most of the book, the final passage, in which Skipper relinquishes his crucifix to the mother of new life, conveys the stillness and silence of death:

> Now I sit at my long table in the middle of my loud wandering night and by the light of a candle—one half-burned candle saved from last night's spectacle—I watch this final flourish of my own hand and

muse and blow away the ashes and listen to the breathing among the
rubbery leaves and the insects sweating out the night. Because now I
am fifty-nine years old and I knew I would be, and now there is the sun
in the evening, the moon at dawn, the still voice. That's it. The sun in
the evening. The moon at dawn. The still voice.

It also recalls Gorgias' intuition about tragic deception: "Tragedy . . . with
its myths and its emotions has created a deception such that its successful
practitioner is nearer to reality than the unsuccessful, and the man who
lets himself be deceived is wiser than he who does not." See John Hawkes,
Second Skin (New York: New Directions, 1963); and Mario Untersteiner,
The Sophists, trans. Kathleen Freeman (New York: Philosophical Library,
1954), p. 113.

Chapter 3
Dupin Meets the Sandman

1. Edgar Allan Poe, "The Murders in the Rue Morgue," in *The Short Fiction of
   Edgar Allan Poe*, ed. & annotated by Stuart and Susan Levine (Indianapolis:
   The Bobbs-Merrill Co., 1976), p. 190. All references to Poe's stories will be to
   this edition.
2. *The Complete Works of Edgar Allan Poe*, Volume XVII, ed. James A. Harrison (New York: AMS Press, 1965), p. 265.
3. Alexis de Tocqueville, *Democracy in America*, ed. Richard D. Heffner (New
   York: Mentor, 1956), p. 248.
4. D. H. Lawrence, "A Propos of *Lady Chatterley's Lover*," in *Sex, Literature,
   and Censorship* (New York: The Viking Press, 1959), p. 108.
5. Walter Benjamin points out that Baudelaire uses the word "dupe" for
   someone who is cheated and fooled, and that this person is contrasted with
   the "connoisseur of human nature": "The more uncanny a big city becomes, the more knowledge of human nature—so it was thought—it takes to
   operate in it. In actuality, the intensified struggle for survival led an individual to make an imperious proclamation of his interests. When it is a matter of
   evaluating a person's behavior, an intimate acquaintance with these interests will often be much more useful than an acquaintance with his personality. The ability of which the *flâneur* likes to boast is, therefore, more likely to
   be one of the idols Bacon already located in the marketplace." *Charles
   Baudelaire: A Lyric Poet in the Era of High Capitalism*, trans. Harry Zohn
   (London: New Left Books, 1973), pp. 39–40.
6. *The Complete Works of Edgar Allan Poe*, Volume XVI, ed. James A. Harrison
   (New York: AMS Press, 1965), p. 205.
7. Ibid., pp. 233, 208, 311.
8. Tocqueville, p. 255.
9. *The Complete Works of Edgar Allan Poe*, Volume VII, ed. James A. Harrison
   (New York: AMS Press, 1965), pp. xlii & xxxvi.
10. René Girard, *Des choses cachées depuis la fondation du monde: rech-
    erches avec J.-M. Oughourlian et Guy Lefort* (Paris: Grasset, 1978), p. 310.
    The translation is mine.
11. D. H. Lawrence, *Studies in Classic American Literature* (New York: An-
    chor, 1951), p. 85.
12. See Appendix I for an analysis of Lawrence's *Women in Love*.

13. As we have noted, Poe plays on "odd" and "even" in these detective stories. One of his paragons of intelligence is a schoolboy who is expert at the game: he can anticipate his opponent's move without any fear of reciprocity. If the word "odd," moreover, is associated with the Prefect, who calls anything "odd" that he does not understand, the word "even" is associated with Dupin, who sets about getting "even" with a world that has destroyed his "credit."

14. Having mentioned the "dupe" in Baudelaire's work, do I dare point out the "dupe" in "Dupin" or the "Dunno" in the "Rue Dunôt" (Dupin's address)? I think not.

15. *Semiotexte* I, 3, 1975, 52.

16. Jean Starobinski, "The Struggle with Legion: A Literary Analysis of Mark 5: 1–20," *New Literary History* IV, 2, 355.

17. Mehlman, p. 53.

18. Mehlman, pp. 63–65.

19. *The Complete Works of Edgar Allan Poe*, Volume XVI, p. 205.

20. *Selected Writings of E. T. A. Hoffman*, Volume I, ed. and trans. Leonard J. Kent and Elizabeth C. Knight (Chicago: The University of Chicago Press, 1969).

Chapter 4
In Search of Narcissus: *The Crying of Lot 49*

1. All references to Thomas Pynchon, *The Crying of Lot 49* will be to the Bantam paperback (New York: Bantam Books, 1967).

2. The name "Scurvhamites" can be broken down into "the scum varies," which is an implied critique of Manicheism. The name "Thurn and Taxis" seems to generate "taciturn," which links this family with its silent adversary.

3. The name is also sometimes spelled "Trystero"—the "tryst" of which suggests the uncanny collisions of rivals.

4. "Unpenetrated" contrasts with "Pierce Inverarity, whose prename is also signalled by Metzer's "radiant eyes," which "flew open, pierced her."

5. Henry James, *What Maisie Knew* (Garden City: Doubleday Anchor, 1954), p. 11.

6. W. Ehrenberg, "Maxwell's Demon," *Scientific American* (November 1967), p. 109.

7. The tyranny of binary thought in *Lot 49* reminds one of the abuse of *technè* in Plato's *Symposium*. Stanley Rosen notes of the relation between Protagoras and his disciples: "Protagoras is not a physicist; his livelihood depends on the primacy of politics . . . Pausanias, however, is a consequence of the generation of Protagoras and his professional colleagues. Pausanias is not a political teacher, but a citizen who has been trained to use nomos for his private advantage . . . Pausanias thus prepares us for the link between sophistry and physics." *Plato's SYMPOSIUM* (New Haven: Yale University Press, 1968), p. 68. Such a link exists also in *Lot 49* between communications and thermodynamics, where the "outer form" of communication seems to be divorced from the "inner form" of substantive reason. Since whatever triumphs over the interference of other systems is construed as communication, Oedipa's husband calls her "Mrs. Edna Mosh" on the radio to allow for

distortion. When the medium becomes the message, sophistry becomes truth.

8. Thomas Pynchon, "Entropy," *The Kenyon Review*, 22 (1960), 283–284.

9. See Walter Benjamin, "Some Reflections on Kafka" and "The Storyteller," in *Illuminations*, ed. Hannah Arendt (New York: Schocken, 1969), pp. 141–145 and 83–109.

10. In *John* 8, 43–44, Jesus says, "Why do you not understand what I say? It is because you cannot bear to listen to my message. You are the children of your father, the Devil, and you want to follow your father's desires. From the very beginning he was a murderer. He has never been on the side of truth, because there is no truth in him. When he tells a lie he is only doing what is natural to him, because he is a liar and the father of lies." *Good News for Modern Man* (New York: Simon and Schuster's Pocketbooks, 1969).

11. At one point Oedipa decides to embrace chance (her "lot"), to wander at random through San Francisco. This decision, made in the midst of much confusion, is not unlike the sailors' decision in *Jonah* to play dice when their ship, carrying the reprobate prophet, is assaulted by a storm. As in primitive societies, where the rites of chance are intended to force the "chance" transcendence of their reciprocal violence, Oedipa's wandering precipitates signs of Tristero.

12. Paul Ricoeur, *La Metaphor Vive* (Paris: Éditions du Seuil, 1975), p. 249. The translation is mine.

13. As his name suggests, Fallopian's own ideas are always miscarrying because their only function is opposition.

14. See my "Interview with René Girard," *The Denver Quarterly* 13, 2 (Summer, 1978), 38.

Chapter 5
Royalty in a Rainy Country: Two Novels of Paula Fox

1. Paula Fox, *Desperate Characters* (New York: Avon Books, 1971).

2. Paula Fox, *The Widow's Children* (New York: E. P. Dutton, 1976).

3. The pandemic nature of this irony is revealed by phrases like "murderous gratification," "jeering applause," "derisive applause" and "murderous patience."

4. Rudolf Arnheim, *Entropy and Art* (Berkeley and Los Angeles: University of California, 1971), p. 2.

5. In *The Widow's Children* Eugenio, who is said to never touch anyone for fear of contamination, has been heard screaming "in the middle of the night like a horse pitched onto barbed wire."

6. Laura's attempt to damage Desmond's reputation is described as the work of "The Shadow." The face of the woman who does not resemble the ideal woman of Desmond's "reverie" is "shadowed." Peter experiences "negative pleasures" and a "shady desire" to refute Laura. Sophie experiences the "shadowy totemic menace" of the things around her.

7. The names of Fox's characters are often revealing. The names "Clara," "Claire," and "Carla," for example, suggest light (as does "Carlos" by association with them). The name "Alma," which also seems part of this paradigm, means "nourishing," which is ironic in view of her failure in that respect. "Lance," the name of Carlos' lover, suggests the wounds that make it impossible for Carlos to support a woman. His original name, "Leroy," along

with the "laurels" from which Laura's name is derived, suggests the opening of Baudelaire's poem.

8. William Gass, "The Leading Edge of the Trash Phenomenon," in *Fiction and Figures of Life* (New York: Vintage, 1972), pp. 101 and 103.

9. William Gass, "The Artist and Society," in *Fiction and the Figures of Life*, pp. 285 and 282.

10. Violet resembles Charlie of *Desperate Characters* in certain respects. Charlie assumes virtuous opinions in order to vindicate himself (instead of the law). Violet undergoes "depthless, transient seizures of sociological or political fashion."

11. Walter Benjamin, *Charles Baudelaire: A Lyric Poet in the Era of High Capitalism*, trans. Harry Zohn (London: New Left Review, 1973), pp. 144-145.

12. R. D. Laing, *Knots* (New York: Vintage, 1970), p. 36.

13. Philip Rieff, *The Triumph of the Therapeutic* (New York: Harper and Row, 1968), p. 5.

14. James Joyce, *Ulysses* (New York: Vintage, 1961), p. 199.

15. In *The Widow's Children* Laura and Carlos feel as though they lie "wounded together among strangers" who cannot help them. Between Clara and Laura is "a presence, raw and bloodied." In *Desperate Characters* Sophie, rising from Francis' couch, has the impression that she is "covered with blood" and that the blood is "the outline of his body on hers." Among these "strangers" the presence of others is experienced as too much and their own presence as too little: "He saw Laura glance at each one of them, then at himself, as though she were calculating their substance," If, as Erik Erikson says, "Emptiness is the female form of perdition" ("Inner and Outer Space: Reflections on Womanhood," *Daedalus*, 93 (Spring 1964), 596), Fox's characters tend to suffer from this "feminine" malaise.

Chapter 6
On the Threshold: The Fiction of Marguerite Duras

1. "An Interview with Marguerite Duras," in *Marguerite Duras, Destroy, She Said*, trans. Barbara Bray (New York: Grove Press, 1970), p. 130.

2. Marguerite Duras, *Moderato Cantabile* (Paris: Les Édition de Minuit, 1958). The other editions being used are: *Détruire, dit-elle* (Paris: Minuit, 1969); *Dix heures et demie du soir en été* (Paris: Éditions Gallimard, 1960); *Le Ravissement de Lol V. Stein* (Paris: Gallimard, 1964); *Hiroshima Mon Amour* (Paris: Gallimard, 1960); and *Une Aussi Longue Absence* (Paris: Gallimard, 1961). English translations, which will be provided in the notes, come from the following translations: *Destroy, She Said*, trans. Barbara Bray (New York: Grove Press, 1970); *Moderato Cantabile*, trans. Richard Seaver and *Ten-thirty on a Summer Night*, trans. Anne Borchardt in *Four Novels* (New York: Grove, 1965); *The Ravishing of Lol Stein*, trans. Richard Seaver (New York: Grove, 1966); and *Hiroshima Mon Amour*, trans. Richard Seaver (New York: Grove, 1961). The translations from *Une Aussi Longue Absence* will be my own.

3. "It should produce a violent, conflicting feeling of freshness and desire."
   "Everywhere except at Hiroshima guile is an accepted convention. At Hiroshima it cannot exist, or else it will be denounced."

"Like you, I forgot. Like you, I wanted to have an inconsolable memory, a memory of shadows and stone."

"I wish you were dead . . . I am."

"You destroy me. You're so good for me. You destroy me. You're so good for me. Plenty of time. Please. Take me. Deform me, make me ugly."

"Either she is very heavily made up, in which case her lips are so dark they seem black, or else she is hardly made up at all and seems pale under the sun."

4. "It awaits you just around the corner of language, it defies you . . . to raise it, to make it arise from its kingdom, which is pierced on every side and through which flows the sea, the sand, the eternity of the ball in the cinema of Lol Stein."

"Enormous, endless, an empty gong, it would have held back anyone who had wanted to leave, it would have convinced them of the impossible, it would have made them deaf to any other word save that one."

5. "She has placed the word on me. . . . To make her happy, I would invent God if I had to."

"From the first moment that woman walked into the room, I ceased to love my fiancé."

"What had she, Anne-Marie Stretter, experienced that other women had missed? By what mysterious path had she arrived at what appeared to be a gay, a dazzling pessimism, a smiling indolence as light as a hint, as ashes? A certain self-assured boldness was all that seemed to hold her upright. . . . Nothing more could ever happen to that woman, Tatiana thought, nothing more, nothing. Except her death, she thought." Lol later seems to assume these qualities: There is a sadness about her, a grayish pallor; she is described as "in ashes"; and Tatiana remarks how dead and unexpressive Lol's body seems compared to hers. Is this an unconscious imitation of the other woman's prestigious insensibility?

"Michael Richardson wiped his forehead with his hand and scanned the room for some sign of eternity."

6. "velvet annihilation of her own person"

"And in vain Lol waits for him to take her again, with her body rendered infirm by the other she cries out, she waits in vain, she cries out in vain."

"One day this infirm body stirs in the womb of God."

"The rye rustles beneath her loins. Young, early-summer rye. Her eyes riveted on the lighted window, a woman hearkens to the void—feeding upon, devouring this non-existent, invisible spectacle, the light from a room where others are."

7. "Maria became aware of Claire again, and of Claire's beauty which nearly made her cry. . . . Could she see them already, in their white bed, in Madrid, that night, hiding? Yes, except for Claire's nakedness which she didn't know. 'I'll always love you, Claire,' Maria said."

"She wanted things to happen between them so that she too would be illuminated like them and enter the world she bequeathed them, since the day, in fact, when she herself invented it, in Verona, one night."

"She was there, smiling, ready for a night that wouldn't happen."

8. "The confusion in the dining room had reached a new peak. All the waiters came from this village and knew Rodrigo Paestra. The policemen also came from the village. They questioned one another. The waiters stopped serving. The manager intervened. Be careful not to say anything bad about Perez. The waiters went on talking. The manager shouted orders that no one heard."

"Why do you want Rodrigo Paestra to understand?"

"Who would ever have the chance to kill with such simplicity, like Rodrigo Paestra?"

"I was planning on starting a big project with Rodrigo Paestra. And now, now it has collapsed before we even started."

9. "An overcast sky. The bay windows shut."

"She has not forgotten my presence, but she is truly divided between the two of us."

10. "'Will you please read what's written above the score?' the lady asked."

"You go to the railings, then you go away and walk around the house, then you come back to the railings. The child is sleeping upstairs. You have never screamed. Never."

"I think I must have screamed something like that once, yes, when I had the child."

"painful smile of endless childbirth," a "smile of deliverance"

"Whether you were asleep or awake, dressed or naked, they passed outside the pale of your existence."

"Anne Desbaresdes braved this weather, this wind."

"Wait a minute . . . and we'll be able to."

11. "The sound of the sea rose, boundless, in the child's silence."

"together and separated at the same time"

"beyond the limits imposed upon her ten years before"

"When you get used to it, it's like . . . like listening to your own heart."

"like someone murdered"

"The brisk wind sweeping the town would keep the sky clear."

"Unlike the others, its warmth fires her witch's loins. Her breasts, heavy on either side of the heavy flower, suffer from its sudden collapse, and hurt her. Her mouth, filled with wine, encompasses a name she does not speak. All this is accomplished in painful silence."

12. "She's having a wonderful sleep. . . . Yes. Our sleep."

"What pain. What immense pain. How difficult it is."

13. "An Interview with Marguerite Duras," pp. 108–109.

14. In her sleep Alissa's childlike mouth widens in pure laughter. They laugh to see her laugh."

15. See Appendix II for more music to the name of Stein.

16. "a chorus of various conversations"

"orange shrouded coffin"

"osmosis of the species"

"its ineluctable advance towards total annihilation"

"the annihilating taste of the unknown lips of the man outside in the street"

"the magnolias will be in full bloom"

"Below, a welter of shouts and orders proved the consummation of an unknown incident."

17. Georges Bataille, L'Érotisme (Paris: Les Éditions de Minuit, 1967), pp. 25–26. The translation is mine. Anne's "sourire d'un enfantement" is pertinent to this point. Bataille also claims that the sacred and the obscene are near allied, that both trouble our sense of self-possession. In this sense, perhaps, we can appreciate Chauvin's insult (probably the word "bitch"), which makes Anne's expression slowly "dissolve" and "soften."

18. "Love is unpardonable there. At Nevers, love is the great sin. At Nevers,

happiness is the great crime. Boredom, at Nevers, is a tolerated virtue."

"To speak deprecatingly of Nevers would also be an error of the mind and heart."

19. "I've forgotten everything I know," says Max Thor, who now teaches "history of the future": "There's nothing left . . . so I don't say anything. The students go to sleep."

"Her presence renders the town pure, unrecognizable. She begins to walk in the sumptuous palace of South Tahla's oblivion."

"regal gift for drinking and dying"

"She is seeing her present memory for the last time in her life, she is burying it. In the future it will be today's vision she will recall, this companion beside her in the train. This trip, in the future, will be like the town of South Tahla is for her now, lying in ruins beneath the footsteps of the present."

"sharp, almost brutal voice"

"I plunge myself deep into her warm and muzzled body, an idle hour for Lol, the resplendent hour of her oblivion, I graft myself upon her, I pump Tatiana's blood. Tatiana is there, so that I can forget Lol Stein in her. She slowly becomes bloodless beneath me."

"They began to move, to walk toward the walls, searching for imaginary doors."

"Lol Stein is resting, it would appear, resting for a moment from the exertion of a victory which might have been too easily won. One thing of which I am certain is the price of that victory: the retreat of clarity."

20. "Her fainting spell, so long, so simple, has corresponded to the loss of memory of 'Robert Landais'. . . . She comes out of it 'disfigured,' transformed forever."

"What we wish to render in this way is the totally invented, gratuitous but absorbing, passionate and methodical activity of this man."

"Wherever he is, he is equal to himself."

"One hears only a single 'sound': that of this man being 'nourished' by his wife—an innocent nourishment by a wife 'guilty' of memory."

"He is a man whose head is damaged. Like a bombed out house, standing but irremediably destroyed. And yet he gives a perfect illusion of existing. Does he even know that his scar exists?" The casino in *Lol Stein* is munificent in its milky whiteness and in its *rodomontades*, but it is also, by implication, *rodé* from within.

21. "The back of a man, enormous, which takes up the large screen and on each side of which, narrow in margin, the stunning lights of dawn shine on a landscape along the Seine."

"Far in time, in space, a man has wandered. Thin as a hair, ample as the dawn."

"He was there. Over him, the wheat, naively, came back together. It would have done the same over a stone."

"What would Maria call the time that opened ahead of her? The certainty of her hope? This rejuvenated air she was breathing? This incandescence, this bursting of a love at last without object?"

"Maria was deprived of Rodrigo Paestra's perfectly empty glance while he was sleeping."

"haggard, paralyzed by frustration, by the very fulfillment of frustration"

"Pierre's hands were dangling beside him. For eight years they had caressed her body. Now Claire was stepping into the misfortune that flowed straight from those hands."

"the rarified air in the vicinity of these tiny planets which attract, ensnare . . . [his] gaze, until it is helpless"

"circumscribed as a stone"

"And perhaps Lol is afraid, but ever so slightly, of the possibility of an ever greater separation from the others."

"It's the thought of Stein. . . . It was just the thought of Stein's existence."

"I want you so much. . . . He wants you so much. . . . He loves you so much."

"I don't know you, Alissa. . . . You're part of me, Alissa. Your fragile body is part of mine. And I don't know you."

" 'We make love,' Alissa says. 'Every night we make love.' 'I know,' says Stein. 'You leave the window open and I see you.' 'He leaves it open for you. To see us.' 'Yes.' Alissa has put her childish lips on Stein's hard mouth. He speaks like that. 'Do you see us?' Alissa says. 'Yes. You don't say anything. Every night I wait. Silence clamps you to the bed. The light stays on and on. One morning they'll find you both melted into a shapeless lump like tar, and no one will understand. Except me'."

22. "Whenever he stopped, she stopped too. He amused himself by testing her. But she failed to notice the game he was playing."

"He let her do as she pleased. While seeming to lead the way, he followed her."

"Lol was imitating someone, but who? the others, all the others, as many people as possible."

"The best man in the world is dead for me. I have no opinion . . ."

23. " 'How old is Alissa?' asks Stein. 'Eighteen.' 'And when you met her?' 'Eighteen'."

"a childlike toss of her head, calling for silence concerning her life"

"Look at them. . . . They're children already."

"Anything's possible."

24. "monument of suffering," "wrapped in its own stupidity," and "there for eternity."

"The possibility that he might answer, move, abandon this inhuman position was enough to make her imagination leap with joy."

"that kind of age that lies lurking, within the insane"

"In the bedroom . . . Alissa isn't any age."

"Did you want the child very much?"

25. See Sigmund Freud, "On Narcissism: An Introduction," trans. Cecil Baines, in *General Psychological Theory* (New York: Collier, 1963), p. 70.

26. "Silence fills the hotel. Has the tennis playing stopped? 'You're trying to understand, too,' she says. 'Yes. Perhaps there'd be a letter?' 'Yes, perhaps.' 'I'd have been watching you for ten days,' says Max Thor. 'Yes. Just left lying about, without any address. I'd find it.' No, there goes the tennis again. The balls ping in a liquid dusk, a grey lake."

"Madame, I have been watching you for ten days. There's something about you that fascinates me, puts me in a turmoil, and I can't, simply can't, make out what it is."

"Maybe we ought to separate every summer. . . . Forget one another, if that were possible?"

"Perhaps we love each other too much?"

"There was something about me that fascinated you, put you in a turmoil . . . something interesting . . . you couldn't make out what it was."

"distant bank upon which they, the others, dwell. Toward what? What is that bank?"

"that mirror which reflected nothing and before which she must have shivered in delight to feel as excluded as she wished to be."

"I'm ceasing to be: she wants to see, and to have me witness with her, the darkness of tomorrow, which will be the darkness of the night of Town Beach, advance upon us, swallow us up."

"She was beside me and separated from me by a great distance, abyss and sister."

"Arm in arm, they ascend the terrace steps. Tatiana introduces Peter Beugner, her husband, to Lol, and Jack Hold, a friend of theirs—the distance is covered—me."

27. "I'm not an invalid any more than you are."

"We'd love Stein if it were possible to love."

"I love and desire you."

" 'I wasn't really asleep'? 'I was only pretending'? 'Did you realize?' ?" "For days I've been pretending'? 'For days I've been sleeping'? 'Ten days'?"

"We all feel the same. . . . All four of us."

28. "with all the exactitude of chance"

"You are Madame Desbaresdes. The wife of the manager of Import Export et des Fonderies de la Côte. You live on the Boulevard de la Mer."

"He was no longer aware of her"

"as if it were a memory"

"a flat, expressionless voice that she had not heard from him before"

"the eyes of this man"

29. "When we arrived six days ago she was already there, the books and the pills in front of her."

"The book doesn't belong to me. I have to give it back. But perhaps you'd like it?"

"How's the book getting on? Are you thinking about it?" "No, I'm talking to you."

"Stein will write. . . . So we don't need to."

"Stein looks for me. I'd describe what he looks at."

30. "the tennis courts being looked at" by a woman preoccupied with "the void."

31. "An Interview with Marguerite Duras," p. 110.

32. "The woman I've been looking for so long . . . is Alissa."

"I had no time to choose him. . . . He fell on me."

"The wheat fields disappeared. All that was left were stones, heaps of stones, completely discolored by the sun."

"a mountain of stone . . . black holes bored by the sun . . . rectangular shapes . . . separated by empty spaces" that swallow up the light.

"The water was clear. Shapes appeared. Normal shapes, but raped by the sun."

33. Ernest Hemingway, The Sun Also Rises (New York: Charles Scribner's Sons, 1926), pp. 239–240. This porous landscape, moreover, recalls the "word" in Lol Stein that would name the unknown: "Son royaume percé de toutes parts à travers lequel s'ecoulent la mer, le sable, l'eternite du bal dans le cinéma de Lol V. Stein."

34. "He felt an urgent taste for a dead love. When he walked into Maria's room, he felt enshrouded in his love for Maria. What he didn't know was the poignant magic of Maria's solitude, brought on by him, and of Maria's mourning for him that evening."

"It must have been difficult to keep from having such thoughts, you get into the habit, like you get into the habit of living. But it's only a habit."

"When being late becomes as serious a matter as it is now for me . . . I think that a little while longer isn't going to make it any more serious."

35. "Anne Desbaresdes stiffened and, as was sometimes her custom, went limp."

"sat rigidly . . . was falling"

"To obey him like that was her way of hoping. And even when she reached the threshold she waited for him to tell her to come in."

"There, at arm's length, a destiny was decided."

"wasn't the only one to discover what she wanted from him"

36. "An Interview with Marguerite Duras," p. 106.

37. "Here comes the lie. . . . It's still a long way off."

" 'You know,' Alissa says with incomparable gentleness, 'you know, we could love you too'."

"Really love you."

Chapter 7
Getting Even, With William Gass

1. New York: Pocket Books, 1977. In the first story Gass's variable spacing has been suppressed, as being of no interest in this analysis.

2. Sigmund Freud, *The Sexual Enlightenment of Children*, ed. Philip Rieff (New York: Collier Books, 1963), p. 142.

3. Freud, p. 136.

4. J. E. Cirlot, *A Dictionary of Symbols*, trans. Jack Sage (New York: Philosophical Library, 1962), p. 162.

5. Herman Melville, *Moby Dick* (New York: The Modern Library, 1930), p. 282.

6. "William Gass: The Art of Fiction LXV," *The Paris Review*, 18 (Summer, 1977), pp. 64–65.

7. Paul Valèry, *Monsieur Teste*, trans. Jackson Matthews (New York: Alfred A. Knopf, 1947), pp. 56–57.

8. William Gass, "The Stylization of Desire," in *Fiction and the Figures of Life* (New York: Vintage, 1971), p. 000.

9. Gerald Graff, "The Politics of Anti-Realism," *Salmagundi*, 42 (Summer Fall, 1978), p. 26.

10. William Gass, *Omensetter's Luck* (New York: New American Library, 1966).

11. René Girard has a fascinating discussion of this stone in *Des choses cachées depuis la fondation du monde* (Paris: Grasset, 1978), pp. 438–453. He points out that the *skandalon* in the New Testament is desire that is always obsessed by the obstacles it arouses—the opposite of love in the Christian sense: "He who says he is in the light and hates his brother is in the darkness still. He who loves his brother abides in the light, and in it there is no cause for stumbling. But he who hates his brother is in the darkness and walks in the darkness, and does not know where he is going, because the darkness has blinded his eyes." *The First Letter of John*, 2, 9–11.

12. That the whale is associated in this story with mimetic rivalry is brought out by a cautionary tale. A child named Harry goes fishing against his father's wishes. Having caught a number of fish, he goes home and, while reaching for a dish, is himself caught by a large meat hook. The Means, we are told, must be Calvinists—those attorneys for nemesis: "Their meanness must proceed from that great sense of guilt which so readily becomes a sense for

the sin of others, and poisons everything." But the narrator himself believes in getting even: "A tooth for a tooth would suit me fine," and he also contemplates poisoning the Means' household: "Oh if the force of ancient malediction could be mine, I'd strike him too!" Mrs. Mean, by the way, threatens to "whale" her children, whose resistance she encourages.

13. William Gass, *Willie Masters' Lonesome Wife* (New York: Alfred A. Knopf, 1971), no page numbers.

Conclusion: An Angel Can Come Too Late

1. Irving Howe and Eliezer Greenberg, eds., *A Treasury of Yiddish Poetry* (New York: Holt, Rinehart, and Winston, 1969), pp. 37–38.
2. Albert Camus, *The Plague*, trans. Stuart Gilbert (Harmondsworth: Penguin, 1960), pp. 202–209.

Appendix I
Mimetic Desire in *Women in Love*

1. D. H. Lawrence, "A Propos of *Lady Chatterley's Lover*," in *Sex, Literature, and Censorship* (New York: The Viking Press, 1959), p. 109.
2. *Ibid.*, p. 106.
3. D. H. Lawrence, *Women in Love* (New York: The Viking Press, 1960).
4. D. H. Lawrence, "Prologue to *Women in Love*," in Casebook Series on *The Rainbow* and *Women in Love*, ed. Collin Clarke (Nashville: Aurora Publishers, Inc., 1970). All quotations are from this edition.

Appendix II
Music to the Name of Stein

1. Gertrude Stein, *Everybody's Autobiography* (New York: Vintage, 1973), p. 133. "A Water-fall and a Piano" is taken from *How Writing is Written* (Santa Barbara: Black Sparrow Press, 1977), pp. 31–32.
2. When our cultural restrictions begin to fail, they manifest themselves as symptoms. Fredric Jameson, for example, says that "Reich shows how sexual repression is something like the *cement* which holds the authority fabric of society together" (emphasis mine). See "Imaginary and Symbolic in Lacan: Marxism, Psychoanalytic Criticism, and the Problem of the Subject" in *Yale French Studies* 55/56 (1977), 386. For the most cogent analysis of this failure, see Philip Rieff, *Fellow Teachers* (Harper and Row, 1972).